RICHARD J. SALVUCCI

Textiles and Capitalism in Mexico

AN ECONOMIC HISTORY
OF THE OBRAJES,
1539-1840

PRINCETON
UNIVERSITY
PRESS

Library of Congress Cataloging in Publication Data will be
found on the last printed page of this book

ISBN 0-691-07749-5

Publication of this book has been aided by the Whitney Darrow Fund
of Princeton University Press

This book has been composed in Linotron Caledonia

Clothbound editions of Princeton University Press books
are printed on acid-free paper, and binding materials are
chosen for strength and durability. Paperbacks, although satisfactory
for personal collections, are not usually suitable for library rebinding

Printed in the United States of America by Princeton University Press,
Princeton, New Jersey

For Linda
A Warren Vaché tune

CONTENTS

CONTENTS

LIST OF TABLES

LIST OF MAPS

LIST OF FIGURES

ACKNOWLEDGMENTS

WHEN I began this project nearly a decade ago, I had no idea of how important the influence of several colleagues would be. Each might have written or preferred a different book for, as scholars, they are as disparate a group as one could find. But their advice, support, disagreement, and encouragement sustained me, and I would like to tell them so here. Stanley J. Stein directed the dissertation from which this book emerged. His imaginative scholarship and incisive criticism encouraged independent thinking, a quality all too rare in American education. I have also had the privilege of working closely with Woodrow Borah, a man as learned as he is generous. My personal and professional debts to him are large, too much so to be described here. Two finer teachers no one could have.

Both David Brading and John Coatsworth read earlier versions of the manuscript and made extensive and substantive comments. Dissimilar in approach but alike in powers of mind, they made me rethink large parts of my analysis. Jan de Vries gave freely of his time and brilliance in untangling the economic fundamentals of the *obraje*. For this, and for his support as a colleague, I thank him. Herbert Klein read the dissertation and gave me much to think about. James Oakes gave the first draft of the manuscript searching criticisms. Linda K. Salvucci read, criticized, and edited the final version. I owe many improvements to both of them. Susan Deans-Smith, extraordinary critic and good friend, will see her influence throughout.

No historian spends time in the field without receiving help from colleagues. So many people have contributed that I can mention only a few. Jacques Barbier, Paul Ganster, Gabriel Haslip-Viera, Stanley Hordes, Victoria Cummins, Murdo MacLeod, Lorne McWatters, Ramón Sánchez Flores, William Taylor, Guy Thomson, Benjamin and Patricia Warren, and Eugene Wiemers all helped my research through discussions, arguments, citations, and simple exchange. Richard Greenleaf merits special appreciation. His work first turned my attention to the obrajes and remains a necessary point of departure. He welcomed and, indeed, encouraged me.

Javier Ortiz de la Tabla, historian, and Salvador Victoria Hernández, archivist, tolerated the interloper in their midst with humor, patience, and kindness. It must be tiresome dealing with the idiosyncracies, linguistic atrocities, and odd theories of foreigners bent on penetrating the history of the Spanish Empire in collections in Seville and Mexico City. But both have done so many times over; for their guidance and open friendship, I am particularly grateful.

Most of what follows is based on primary sources found in Spain and Mexico. Without the cooperation of archivists and their staffs, little could be done. The Archivo General de la Nación in Mexico City, under the successive direction of don José Ignacio Rubio Mañé and Dra. doña Alejandra Moreno Toscano, provided the core documentation. Equally important materials were drawn from the Archivo Judicial of the Tribunal Superior de Justicia del Distrito y Territorios Federales and from the Archivo de Notarías, both in Mexico City. Dr. don Efraín Castro Morales, director of the Centro Regional Puebla-Tlaxcala of the Instituto Nacíonal de Antropología e Historia (INAH), graciously gave access to judicial records preserved in Puebla. I was also permitted to work in the archive of the state of Querétaro, another source of valuable information. All students of colonial history ultimately find their way to the Archivo General de Indias in Seville. Doña Rosario Parra Cala and her efficient staff make work there a fringe benefit of doing early modern history.

It is heartening that private institutions and foundations continue to sponsor historical research. I first went to Mexico in 1976-77 through the generosity of the Helen and Grace Doherty Charitable Foundation. At two crucial points, the Shelby Cullom Davis Center for Historical Studies at Princeton University, under the direction of Professor Lawrence Stone, provided me with fellowships. The first enabled me to finish the dissertation. The second enabled me to write the book. The American Philosophical Society provided support needed to finish work in Seville, for which I am indebted. The Committee on Research and the Center for Latin American Studies at the University of California, Berkeley, granted funds for travel, maintenance, and copying. Finally, Louis and Madeline Salvucci, who could ill afford the extravagance, did everything they could to help me finish. What more can I say about such wonderful parents?

Now to the point where spouses and lovers protest eternal gratitude. I am never quite sure why Linda Kerrigan Salvucci puts up with me. She interrupted and delayed her own education, traveled second (and sometimes third) class, and lived an existence that only Rand McNally could find pleasing. When it appeared that life had thrown her a lemon she made lemonade, wrote a prize-winning article in my field, and went off to resume her own career as a historian, much to my pleasure but not to my surprise. All of this with grace, style, and a mean left hook. To her, with love and admiration, I dedicate this book.

Textiles and Capitalism in Mexico

No large country, it must be observed, ever did or could subsist without some sort of manufactures being carried on in it; and when it is said of any such country that it has no manufactures, it must always be understood of the finer and more improved, or of such as are fit for distant sale. In every large country, both the clothing and household furniture of the far greater part of the people are the produce of their own industry. This is even more universally the case in those poor countries which are commonly said to have no manufactures than in those rich ones that are said to abound in them.

ADAM SMITH, *The Wealth of Nations*

INTRODUCTION

THIS IS A STUDY of a major economic activity in colonial Mexico: the production of woolen cloth. Its significance is twofold. Until the eighteenth century, the inhabitants of New Spain largely made their own cloth. Until then, colonial textiles were sheltered from competition, since imports—by price or quality, or both—were essentially luxury goods. The establishment of commercial production under relative autarchy, and its inability to survive integration into the world market after 1790, therefore tells much about the structure and productivity of the economy as a whole and, particularly, about conditions of supply. Supply in turn reflects cost, and cost, relative scarcity. Societies face no decision more basic than the approach to scarcity. In the history of Mesoamerica, from the time of classic civilization to our own, adaptation to scarcity has conditioned patterns of settlement and shaped institutions for successive generations of conqueror and conquered. For the inhabitants of New Spain, Spaniard and Indian, scarcity and social choice influenced interaction and perception, behavior and motive. A study of the woolen industry illuminates the range of responses, along with the rationale and consequences, that one kind of scarcity elicited. For apart from the demand for food and shelter, the need for clothing is basic. This book explains how a part of the activity was organized and how environment and colonialism affected it.

Aside from its explicitly economic focus, this book is also an institutional study. Its concern, however, is not primarily state structure or the formal distribution of power but the structure of markets and other allocative devices in the colonial Mexican economy. It is also an account of actors, of principals and agents in economic activity, and of the reasons for their behavior. Because of its dimensions and complexity, the woolen industry offers a lens through which to view nearly all phases of production, distribution, and exchange. The characteristics of supply and demand in the woolen industry compelled its participants to contend with the problem of commercial activity in radically imperfect markets. As a result, an examination of the woolen industry may display the complex and often equivocal nature of colonial capitalism, with its reliance upon *both* free exchange and coercion and upon mobile resources and immobile labor. No one study can adequately capture the twists and turns that

3

developing markets took in New Spain, but an examination of the woolen industry does so better than most.

Within the larger context, however, this work is principally a history of the obraje. Obrajes, used strictly in the sense of textile manufactories, accounted for much of the woolen production in New Spain; they have long fascinated historians. Superficially, at least, obrajes resembled factories in their division of labor and apparently large-scale production. Their activities spanned three centuries of Spanish colonialism in Mexico, and the problems they posed for metropolitan officials were unending. From the control of output to the treatment of labor, few viceroys escaped the responsibility of dealing with obrajes. Many, it is clear, saw obrajes as necessary evils, enterprises whose product figured importantly in the supply of durables, and as sources of income and employment. Yet for all the attention paid them by the architects of policy, both advocates and otherwise, the obrajes failed to survive the colony and seemingly vanished without a trace. If they were so important, why did they disappear? If they vanished so easily, could their disappearance matter? Evidently no obraje in Mexico provided a direct link to technologically advanced forms of production.

But should they have done so? Luis Chávez Orozco's interpretation of obrajes as "embryonic factories" begs just that question and assumes that obrajes and factories shared a common economic basis. It is not at all clear, however, that the proposition is valid. I therefore also intend to explain precisely what the obraje was, and what it was not. I hope to demonstrate why the obraje assumed the form it did, what this implied for colonial markets, and why the obraje's potential for institutional transformation was limited. Moreover, I suggest that technological change, relative factor prices, and the systematic exploitation of labor were all of a piece. What emerged was an institution limited in its potential for productivity increase—an unrealized weakness while the economy remained in relative isolation. As the access of Mexican consumers to cheaper domestic and imported cottons grew during the late colonial period, however, the inefficiency of the obraje was laid bare. The resulting destruction of the textile industry in New Spain placed British capitalism on a plane with smallpox as an imported agent of efficient destruction.

The final purpose of this study is informational. Although a number of articles on the obraje have appeared—some quite useful—there are no monographs and no systematic economic histories. Many articles, particularly in Spanish, tend to recapitulate well-known documents and to mine them for data. I have synthesized much of this literature in drawing my arguments, but the bulk of my study rests on previously unknown or unused primary sources. I have consciously attempted to break with the past in this respect and have concentrated on aggregating data on production, prices, investment, capitalization, and labor force. Most of the results are presented in tabular form, where they may prove useful to other researchers.

The book is divided into five chapters. Most of the descriptive material, particularly that dealing with colonial businesses, covers the years between 1650 and 1830. Nevertheless, I include statistics and material on policy formation before 1650 to reconstruct secular economic trends and to provide a context for patterns that crystallized over more than two centuries. This was particularly true of economic geography and of the repeated transformation of the labor system; I discuss these over the longest run possible.

Chapter One is a description of the variety of textile production in New Spain, with a focus on domestic, handicraft, and artisan arrangements and the ways in which they differ from the obraje. I emphasize family and kin-based systems of production and the advantages these enjoyed in imperfect labor markets. Virtually all artisan industry dealt with cotton rather than wool, and problems in its supply, demand, production, and distribution receive particular attention here. It is in this chapter that the relation between cottons and woolens is first discussed. Drawing on eighteenth-century surveys, I consider the rise of the commercial cotton industry in Puebla in the latter part of the century.

In Chapter Two I define the structure, function, and rationale of the obraje, analyzed within a wider economic context. When understood in terms of market constraints, techniques of production, and seasonality in supply, the obraje may be seen as a forced solution to the problems of commercial supply in imperfect markets. In the discussion I develop data on costs, markets, and market areas and address theoretical issues, including protoindustrialization and economies of scale. Allocative issues, particularly the costs and benefits of the obraje system, are considered as well.

Chapter Three is a collective biography of principals and agents in the woolen trade, that is, of owners, managers, investors, and financiers. The approach is regional, and I focus specifically on business practice. Problems of operation and financing are treated in detail, as are the recruitment, mobility, and persistence of participants in the trade. Family firms and kin-based commercial practices were particularly significant and are explained in terms of transactions costs. Of these, perhaps the most important was the cost of information, a subject whose implications receive detailed attention.

In Chapter Four I consider labor in its many aspects. A portion of the chapter is descriptive and reconstructs work routine, size and demographic characteristics of the labor force, and the relative significance of apprentices, convicts, and slaves. The analytical sections account for the heterogeneity of the labor force and explain regional variations in the significance of coercion. Freedom, indebtedness, and peonage provide the points of focus. Also included are detailed discussions of wages, piece rates, productivity, and the truck system. Two themes unify the chapter: the evolution of the labor system and the shallow and uneven diffusion of the labor market.

Chapter Five covers long-run variations in output, investment, and industrial location. I describe these changes and account for them in terms of trade, population, internal demand, and Crown policy. The growing availability of domestic and imported cottons, and the impact these had on the output of the obrajes, receive special attention. The effects of tariff policy and political instability are considered in the context of a simple statistical model of the "demand" for contraband.

The scope and approach of this study are unusual and perhaps merit a brief discussion. This is above all an economic history, and one strongly influenced by modern approaches to the subject. Theory and measurement are essential to any such treatment, and they figure prominently in this one as well. Of course, measurement involving early modern data is always difficult, and the statistics in this book are correspondingly tentative. As a general rule, the estimates presented, particularly of output, are conservative ones. The same is true for profitability and productivity. Moreover, no calculation should be cited out of context, for qualification is essential in measuring markets whose dimensions fluctuated substantially.

The intellectual foundations of the work are located in price theory. I can think of no better justification for the choice than its explanatory power, since neoclassical economics is concerned with explaining the efficiency of existing institutions. To ask why given patterns of employment occur, or why certain devices for labor recruitment predominate, is to pose questions that price theory is well suited to ask. Moreover, it is impossible to assert that competitive, efficient markets existed in Mexico from the Conquest (or as some anthropologists think, from before). As a consequence, every conclusion here is a limited one whose qualifications must be understood. I emphasize imperfect and inefficient markets and discontinuous, costly economic adjustments rather than instantaneous, costless ones. To do otherwise is to turn New Spain into a world of perfect freedom, mobile resources, fluid social structure, and costless information. Few historians would be persuaded by the result.

The chronological and geographical dimensions of this book are broader than recent colonial historiography might lead one to expect. There are two reasons for this. The first was a lack of guideposts. No study of colonial industry matches the range of François Chevalier's inquiry into the hacienda, of Charles Gibson's investigation of the history of the Valley of Mexico, or of Woodrow Borah's synthesis of seventeenth-century economic development. The sense of context that informs and structures regional studies of land tenure and estate agriculture simply does not exist. It therefore seemed appropriate to provide as broad a focus as possible. Only then would particular variations possess much meaning.

The second reason is methodological but related to the first. The fortunes of the woolen industry varied substantially over time and space. To isolate the causes would clarify the relative strength of market forces, an underlying concern of this study. Yet a scale of measurement requires more than one point of reference. Wages, for example, are neither high nor low but must be judged in relation to another quantity. To account for regional variations in comparative advantage necessarily implied studying more than one region. This was what I did. The benefit is a relatively powerful but nevertheless simple view of the forces of institutional and economic change. The cost is some sacrifice in detail and nuance. The balance between the two I leave for the reader to judge.

ONE

A Web of Weavers

INTRODUCTION: THE CONTEXT OF ARTISAN INDUSTRY

THE EXISTENCE of an artisan textile industry in the Indies was never viewed unambiguously by successive generations of royal officials. For example, in the *Nuevo sistema de gobierno económico para la América*, José del Campillo y Cosío indicated his interest in the "large number of looms in both Kingdoms that not only supplied poor Indians, but also Spaniards of middling means."[1] Although Campillo's treatise, written in 1743, was delayed in publication until 1789 (it appeared as part of Bernardo Ward's *Proyecto económico* in 1762), its concerns were echoed in the thoughts of the viceroy of New Spain in that era, Revillagigedo the younger (1789-94). In his *relación de mando* to the marqués de Branciforte (1794-98), Viceroy Revillagigedo commented that a colony whose industry displaced the manufactures of the mother country would eventually find political subordination unnecessary.[2] As minister of the Indies (1776-87), José de Gálvez had, in 1783, received alarmist reports of weavers financed by merchants who purchased the fine cottons, silks, and taffetas that such artisans made to the detriment of Spanish industry and the China trade.[3] From his intimate, the marqués de Croix, Gálvez had learned of the "considerable prejudice that the obrajes of this Kingdom [Mexico] cause to the Metropolis, and to national commerce." Croix furthermore complained that the "nearly free establishment of looms for woolens and silks [was] directly contrary to and destructive of the most common and simplest textiles from the Peninsula." This should never have been permitted, Croix wrote, if only "for convenience of trade with the Kingdom of Castile."[4] It was scarcely surprising, then, that Gálvez would instruct the crown's attorney for the Royal Treasury, Ramón de Posada, and Viceroy Matías de Gálvez (1783-84) to investigate the substance of the charges.[5]

It was from such concern that an idea of the extent of the artisan textile industry in New Spain began to appear, although the interest was hardly novel. In 1594, King Philip II expressed his concern over the development of a textile industry in New Spain "in such a state of growth as to supply that land and a greater part of Peru with

9

cloth." Since the commerce of Spain was clearly diminished by the existence of a colonial industry in textiles, Philip ordered Viceroy Luis de Velasco the younger (1590-95, 1607-11) "to look deeply into it . . . [and] to send me a report of what has transpired." Velasco's report, which has not surfaced, was surely of interest. On departing for Peru in 1595, Velasco echoed the dangers that the growth of the textile industry in New Spain represented. As a result, there are useful statistics on the production of the obrajes from as early as 1597, even though the interests of peninsular trade rather than industry were more clearly at risk.[6] Of course, the cosmographer José Antonio de Villaseñor y Sánchez made passing reference to textiles in the 1740's, but his observations were more allusive than precise. Nevertheless, it is with the eighteenth century that systematic surveys of weaving appear, so a reconstitution of the industry may proceed most fully from that point.[7] It was not until José de Gálvez advanced plans for the expansion of the colonial bureaucracy that the potential for comprehensive collection of data existed. Even then, the apparatus that Gálvez created moved sporadically in the enumeration of looms and workers.

The most striking example of this process first appeared during the administration of Martín de Mayorga (1779-83). Disliked by the minister of the Indies and impelled by the fiscal burden of Spain's participation in the War of American Independence to find sources of colonial revenue, Mayorga looked to the emerging fiscal bureaucracy for a solution to his problems.[8] Thus, in 1781, Mayorga addressed the administrators of the Royal Excise concerning revenues to be collected from the obrajes. It was clear, wrote the viceroy, that an excise for textiles had never been properly determined, so that "for the lack of a levy, the Royal Treasury has suffered, since the taxpayers have employed this pretext to avoid paying the Crown its proper duties."[9] To increase revenues, the colonial government surveyed the textile industry, finding some success in 1781, but considerably more in 1793 and 1799. These reports provide a detailed picture of the production of woolens and cottons in the final decades of the eighteenth century.

From the point of view of the authorities, there was a distinction between production from looms employed as *telares sueltos* and that from looms in the obrajes. The telares sueltos or "individual" looms existed within a variety of social, institutional, and productive relationships. They mirrored the pattern of *rancheros* in agriculture and *pegujaleros* in tobacco planting, a class ranging from prosperous artisans and petty capitalists to the working poor. In textiles in particular, many people employed by the telares sueltos formed part of a large, informal economy whose precise dimensions were stochastic and fluctuated substantially.[10] There were, for example, looms owned by independent handicraft producers and those operated by cottage and domestic workers tied to merchant financiers. The owners of the telares sueltos were generally described as artisans (*artesanos*) who, whatever their financial condition or social standing, were regarded differently from workers in the obrajes. The latter, in turn, were simply termed *operarios* and *sirvientes*, perhaps best lumped together as "workers." On the whole, colonial observers never went beyond the principle that telares sueltos were looms that operated outside the framework of the obraje: *sin sujección a ninguna oficina*. To understand the significance of the obrajes, then, is to understand the artisanal and domestic context with which they occasionally merged but from which they nevertheless differed.

In October of 1780, well in advance of Viceroy Mayorga's comments, the joint directors of the Royal Excise, Miguel Páez and Juan Navarro, started to investigate the extent and nature of textile production in New Spain. Writing to officers posted to the colony's twenty-eight excise districts (*alcabalatorios*), they requested reports on the number and types of looms operating, the composition of their ownership, and the rate and base of the tax levied on weaving.[11] On the strength of reports from Guanajuato (including Irapuato and Silao), Querétaro, and Celaya, Páez and Navarro felt confident enough to write that "the majority of what are called obrajes are nothing more than 1, 2, or a few looms held by people of the poorer sort whose numbers are in a continual state of flux, sometimes falling to almost none at all when they can no longer keep on weaving."[12] Although Páez and Navarro were ultimately mistaken in their characterization of obrajes, their reports shed light upon the variety of telares sueltos. Trapiches were defined, for example, as "little obrajes . . . that produce wool for cloths . . . bays, serges, friezes . . . and the like." A *consulta* of 1690 labeled obrajes as "factories for wool or cloth . . . that need more then twenty workers, skilled laborers and apprentices. . . ." An *obrador*, on the other hand, "belonged to any sort of master working in woolens who plies the trade in his own dwelling using a few looms or other tools. . . ."[13] Much the same notion emerged in the instructions given an early eighteenth-century inspector of the obrajes: "a complete [*entero*] obraje is one with twelve looms and equipment for dyeing. . . . A trapiche is half an obraje in which fine and common stuffs, says, bays, *palmilla* [very cheap woolens], friezes and serges are woven

11

and dyeing vats are used. . . . An obrador has two looms for common stuffs, bays, and palmilla."[14] Sometimes, the term obrador signified production unit, as in obrador de teñir, cardar or tejer, that is, the unit for dyeing, carding, or weaving.[15] Terminology was inconsistent and reflected the same ambiguity that characterized the definitions of hacienda and *rancho*.[16] In general, observers thought obrajes larger and functionally more complex than telares sueltos, although they regarded differences in productivity as equally important.

WHAT WERE THE TELARES SUELTOS?

In late colonial Mexico, the idea of the telar suelto embraced a variety of productive arrangements, including artisan, handicraft, and domestic or putting-out types. Handicraft or artisan looms were typically the property of small producers who worked at home, but they were also operated in small shops, such as *trapiches* and obradores. The simplest form of handicraft found a weaver and his family operating a loom or two at home and working up the cotton or the wool. This sometimes shaded into a domestic or putting-out system, where the weaver entered into a relationship with a merchant financier or a larger textile entrepreneur, the owner of an obraje who provided credit and raw materials. For example, this was the case with Domingo de Sandoval, a mulatto from Puebla, who lived in Mexico City. Residing in the so-called Casa de Chihuahua, Sandoval, a weaver, borrowed 84 pesos from two other residents of the Casa to weave Puebla-style *manta* in his quarters. He promised to repay his creditors at the rate of 2 pesos per week and to turn over 50 percent of his profits. But he could not and was threatened with a term in an obraje to work off the debt.[17] There was, on the whole, a tendency for weavers to become indebted to merchant capitalists who financed their production. This occurred in Malinalco, not far from Cuernavaca, where the subdelegate wrote in 1805 that "the cloth workers do not own their own looms, and are but wage workers."[18] In the obradores, substantial artisan and petty capitalists employed a small number of workers, sometimes kinsmen, sometimes not. The master weavers were small tradesmen and were invariably found in large cities such as Mexico City, Querétaro, and Guadalajara.

The telares sueltos were of particular importance in Guadalajara, for here the obrajes were of limited development and significance. Throughout Jalisco, and more specifically in towns such as La Barca, Tepatitlán, Tepic, Lagos, Juchipila, and Aguascalientes, the production of cottons among the Indian peasantry maintained a strong continuity with prehispanic traditions. In the sixteenth and seventeenth centuries, cotton cultivated by the Indians and rural peasantry was ginned by hand for weaving into mantas on backstrap looms, primarily within families as an item of domestic consumption. By the eighteenth century, the market for cottons produced by the telares sueltos had grown, and Spaniards, both American and European, as well as mestizos, became involved in marketing and production. In urban weaving centers, poor mestizos increasingly entered the craft, and the remaining Indians were relegated to reselling finished cottons in small towns, haciendas, and mining centers. Evidence from 1792-93 shows some 450 *fabricantes de algodón* within the city of Guadalajara; by 1821, those who worked telares sueltos constituted the single largest occupational group. In other words, although Jalisco was, strictly speaking, independent of the jurisdiction of New Spain, its telares sueltos shared in the larger pattern of development.[19]

Handicraft and domestic industry in New Spain and New Galicia therefore dominated the production of textiles. Although it did not include reports for Puebla, Teposcolula, Mexico City, and Coyoacán, the survey of 1793 nevertheless suggested there were over 7,800 telares sueltos in New Spain as opposed to thirty nine obrajes.[20] In 1807 and 1808, the production of cottons supported some 20,000 people in the province of Puebla and was capitalized at 8.4 million pesos there and in surrounding towns.[21] In the province of Tlaxcala alone in 1780, there were approximately 4,000 looms operating, 3,000 in cottons and 1,000 in woolens. The incomplete survey of 1781 found concentrations of looms in Acámbaro, Guanajuato, and León.[22] Although the survey of 1799 was taken when Mexico was cut off from Spain during the wars of the French Revolution, and was thus unrepresentative, it is nevertheless striking that the expansion of production was termed "astonishing and extraordinary," evidence of a substantial capacity waiting to be tapped.[23]

The prosperity of this industry varied inversely with its extent. The reports submitted by the regional excise officers in 1781 agreed that the handicraft and domestic workers in textiles were poor and "of little substance." In Guanajuato, petty producers were of the "most unfortunate class"; in Celaya, cotton weavers were "a few poor people . . . engaged in manufacturing . . . in their dwellings"; in San Luis Potosí, there were "a few looms for woolens and cottons . . . mostly the property of very poor Indians, some belonging to castes, and the remainder to whites."[24] By far the most convincing description of the state of handicraft labor came from Acámbaro, where the excise officer wrote that there was

> another class of rootless individual who preferred no permanent commitment to the more substantial trapiches. These people would rather set up an ill-shapen loom in their shanties and make woolens or cottons with their families and friends of similar inclination. They sell what they produce in the market on Sunday.[25]

Such activity did not, and could not, absorb more than part of the participants' time if only because supplies of raw materials were seasonal, and inventories were costly to hold. In Guadalajara, for instance, looms operated only part of the year, just as they did in Guanajuato, and to the north, in Monterrey. In the ranching areas of Saltillo, looms worked on a seasonal basis, *por temporada*, and in Zacatecas, they were worked only during the shearing time.[26]

Periods of work were followed by periods of idleness. This goes some way toward explaining why the productivity of telares sueltos was relatively low. In Acámbaro, for example, the average product of a loom in an obraje was 900 pesos of woolens per year in 1781. In artisan industry, a loom would produce about 238 pesos of woolens yearly.[27] A weaver working sporadically on inferior cottons and woolens earned only a small income and could hardly accumulate much capital. Moreover, when demand fell, handicraft weavers abandoned their looms and sought other sources of support. In this way, through loans, merchant capital entered the industry.

In San Luis Potosí, the excise officer wrote that the Indian peasantry and *gente menuda* who wove spent as much time looking for credit as in working.[28] A rural curate from Tlaxcala was more explicit. Writing to Viceroy Iturrigaray in the early years of the nineteenth century, José Mariano Moreno insisted the weavers in his parish had little capital of their own but were financed by merchants, who supplied them with yarn. It was no exaggeration that these persons hired out daily and weekly for a wage. Even in the best of times, they did not earn enough to survive. "They usually get into debt to make ends meet," the curate concluded.[29] The spinners, too, principally women and children, were financed by merchants and shopkeepers who extended goods on credit in return for payment in yarn. Short of force or fraud, such arrangements offered weavers and spinners a chance to produce for the larger market. It was not ideal. Many saw the relationship as exploitative but also as the best that was available to them.[30]

Much the same transpired in Acámbaro. There, the Indian peasants and castes who worked the telares sueltos as *retaceros* or "patchworkers" did a business that the local excise officer termed "without profit, permanence, or utility."[31] The retaceros, said a contemporary, were to be counted neither among the ranks of weavers nor among the makers of cloth. They were rather *mecánicos* "like shoemakers and blacksmiths," wage laborers in reality (*jornaleros*), who, like shoemakers, received raw materials that had been put out. They were nothing more than residual claimants after other costs had been paid.[32] Since retaceros were poor, their only source of supply was the willingness of larger obrajes to act as brokers and financiers. Worse still, the retaceros got only the leavings from the obrajes, and these at double the going market price. Caught in a web of debt and monopoly, the retaceros had few choices. At best, they were pressured to give up an independent, if precarious, existence by the owners of the obrajes. At worst, their patrons' refusal to supply them with wool, cotton, and dye left them without work. "Destroyed, dissuaded from trade, and left to wander," the retaceros took to smuggling tobacco and prohibited liquors, hardly a sturdy, productive existence.

Such limited evidence cannot support more than fragile inference. Nevertheless, a tentative conclusion is warranted. If the productivity of the telares sueltos fell below that of the obrajes, the quantity of labor offered in the telares sueltos (and perhaps its quality) was probably lower. Single-factor productivity estimates are of limited value, but casual employment in the telares sueltos was almost certainly universal. Still, it is not apparent that this productivity difference was decisively disadvantageous. The costs of large-scale production in the obrajes and changes in the demand for cottons and woolens must be considered as well.

Trapiches and Obradores

More complex than the telares sueltos were the trapiches and obradores. The larger of these were small shops divorced from the household economy, and their owners were petty capitalists who employed a few assistants, rather than heads of families working with kin. Nevertheless, there was considerable variance in status among trapicheros, for some were as poor as the domestic weavers of the telares sueltos.

The most valuable sustained evidence on the obradores may be found in the manuscript census of the Indian *barrio* of San Juan in

Mexico City in 1800. Among the records of the wool-weavers' guild, *El Gremio de Tejedores de Lana*, which also included spinners and carders, there were several obradores, such as the one belonging to a self-proclaimed mestizo master-weaver, Juan Ignacio Montoya, on the Calle de Manito. Mantoya, probably a thoroughly Hispanised Indian, employed a creole and his *castiza* wife, an Indian couple, another Indian, and perhaps eight or ten laborers who lived in or near the obrador.[33]

Nor was the obrador of Montoya unique. There were others like it in the city barrios of San Pablo, Santa María, Atizapan, Acatlán, Xihuitongo, Ixtopulco, and Inzahuatongo. Weavers of woolens were also found in connection with religious institutions—probably of an eleemosynary character such as the *casa de recogimiento*—and notably with the *colegios* of San Ildefonso and Cristo and the Casa de los Agustinos. Others worked for secular shops such as the Casa de la Chinampa and the Casa de los Chabacanos. Indeed, most men in the census of the barrio of San Juan who were members of the wool-weavers' guild worked for some casa or obrador and constituted a labor force of journeymen rather than of independent artisans.[34]

A similar situation existed in cottons, where Indian weavers who were members of the cotton-spinners' and weavers' guild, *El Gremio de Tejedores e Hilanderos de Algodón*, frequently lived and worked at some casa in one of the barrios of Mexico City, such as Santa Cruz, Salto del Agua, and San Pablo. Nevertheless, there were also Indians working in cottons who lived as independent artisans, or who had no affiliation with a casa or obrador.

Production in the trapiches and obradores was roughly similar. Both shops were ostensibly prohibited from producing fine cloths and limited to making says, bays, friezes, and "other weavings of lesser account."[35] The difference between them may have been terminological. When used to describe a small textile shop, "trapiche" was common to parts of the Bajío, less so in central and southern Mexico. There, "obrador" was employed, perhaps to avoid ambiguity in the use of trapiche, which could also refer to a sugar press. Real differences were minor, for both shops occupied an intermediate position between artisanal and household industry and the complex organizational patterns of the obraje. The economic significance of the trapiches, however, was evident, particularly in the Bajío. In Querétaro in 1796, there were 327 trapiches whose ownership cut across ethnic lines.[36] Humboldt claimed that the trapiches as a whole employed roughly 1,200 workers in 1793, an average of slightly more than three workers per unit.[37]

The trapiches in Querétaro, sometimes referred to as *obrajuelos*, or little obrajes, worked in cotton and wool outside the guild of the owners of the obrajes, the *Gremio de Obrajeros*.[38] They were explicitly prohibited from producing the heavy woolens or *paño* that the city's obrajes manufactured and specialized instead in serges and friezes.[39] Much of the output of the trapiches was sold locally, either at the place of manufacture, or in the main plaza of Querétaro by license of the *corregidor*.[40] The *trapicheros*, or owners of trapiches, lacked the status of the owners of major obrajes in Querétaro, those "most principal householders of the city," and were never addressed with the honorific "don," even though the usage had become practically universal in the eighteenth century.[41] This makes sense, for the officer of the Royal Excise there thought trapiches belonged mostly to those of lower social and economic status.[42]

The trapiches consumed 5,000 to 6,000 arrobas of wool per year, but it was purchased *en rama* at a higher price than wholesale. Wool en rama had already been sorted and washed by the obrajes and sold, in turn, to the trapicheros for at least three times wholesale. The trapicheros did not buy wool in bulk but simply purchased what was necessary. They were obliged to rely on the larger obrajes for wool. A tax commissioner who dealt with trapicheros in 1773 said that "I have found among the trapicheros [of Querétaro] such misery—it is so obvious—that really, nothing more than a look at them proves their insolvency.[43] But not all were miserable. In 1773, Eugenio Quiterio de Zúñiga, an illiterate *indio principal* and trapichero of Querétaro, petitioned the General Indian Court for a three-year moratorium on his debts. The detailed list of assets and liabilities Quiterio de Zúñiga submitted appears in Table 1.1, and it is possible to surmise something of his affairs from it.

Quiterio de Zúñiga was, perhaps, a good example of a prosperous petty capitalist. He was not a wealthy man, with a net worth of 900 pesos, but was short of cash rather than poor. He probably employed several workers living at the trapiche, since the chapel there indicated a resident labor force for whom weekly Mass was obligatory. If there were residents, however, they amassed no debts to him, for none appear as assets. There were large borrowings for purchases of wool, as well as evidence that this trapichero did not depend on the obrajes in Querétaro for raw materials. Although Quiterio de Zúñiga may not have been typical of the trapicheros, he was better off than the indebted artisans of the telares sueltos. He received relief from his debts through the General Indian Court.

TABLE 1.1
A Balance Sheet for Eugenio Quiterio de Zúñiga,
Indio Principal de Querétaro

Liabilities and Net Worth	Pesos
To don José González, tenant of the hacienda of San Isidro, Querétaro, for wool	480
To don Manuel de Torre, Guanajuato, for wool	240
To don José Manuel Sánchez, Querétaro, for wool	57
Net Worth[a]	923
TOTAL	1,700

Assets	Pesos
A dwelling in Querétaro	700
Four burros	
Twenty arrobas of wool	
A mule for drayage	
A horse, with saddle and bridle	
Five burros	
A chapel, or oratorio (includes everything other than dwelling)	1,000[b]
TOTAL	1,700

[a] Net worth = Assets − Liabilities.
[b] Includes all assets other than dwelling.
Source: AGNM, Indios, vol. 63, exp. 240.

THE INDIGENOUS POPULATION AND THE TELARES SUELTOS

In his *Political Essay on the Kingdom of New Spain*, Baron Alexander von Humboldt placed the population of Mexico at the end of the colonial period at 5.8 million inhabitants, of whom 2.3 million were "Indian." The term "Indian" has proved troubling to historians, for it meant more as a fiscal category than as an ethnic one by the time of Humboldt's sojourn in Mexico.[44] Indeed, modern social historians doubt the utility of ethnic categories; they would agree with J. R. Poinsett's observation that "it [was] difficult to distinguish the African blood . . . after two crosses with the Indians."[45] Nevertheless, the problem of measuring the subsistence production of the Indian peasantry remains, although acculturation and miscegenation make the term "Indian" a vague one. One thing is relatively clear. The market for imported luxury goods was no more than a million persons, or 17 percent of the population in 1817. On the other hand, if what Humboldt termed the Indian population produced cottons and woolens for village use and purchased little, subsistence then satisfied the consumption needs of 40 percent of the population. Since those consuming imports or homespun amounted to 60 percent, the remaining 40 percent of the population formed a market for the obrajes and the telares sueltos, even more if the separation between subsistence and commercial production was less than complete, as there is reason to assume. The diffusion of textiles from the obrajes and telares sueltos lowered their price relative to homespun and enlarged demand for marketed goods. In this regard, recall the observation of José María Quirós. Although he believed that commoners could purchase very little, few of them were without a shawl, sarape, bandanna, or petticoat made of cottons or woolens from domestic industry.[46] If blankets of all sorts are included as well, demand was large indeed.

Nevertheless, the spread of this market was slow and uneven. Peasant production tended to limit its size, even though itinerant traders peddled Spanish wares throughout the countryside. Contemporaries agreed that Indians largely produced their own clothing. Among men, breeches and a shirt of cotton were common, with the woolen sarape finding some use, depending on the locale. Women wore an *enredo*, or skirt, the *huipil*, or long blouse, and the *quechquemitl*, a triangular shawl, the style and material of each varying between ethnic group and region.[47] Of these the *consulado* of Veracruz wrote in 1817, "The Indians spend nothing on cloth save what they make for themselves, and they produce their own raw materials."[48] This was especially frustrating to Viceroy Revillagigedo the younger. He commented with irritation in 1791 that it was impossible to prevent Indians from making whatever they chose, however numerous the prohibitions. "Many produce without looms, and without the equipment believed necessary in Europe."[49] It was consequently difficult to determine the value of indigenous production or to fix upon its pattern of location. Any peasant could become a weaver, for the capital that many of them used was the backstrap loom, "one end tied to a tree, or to something stable; the other, to their bodies."[50]

Though the peasantry produced cottons and woolens for use in huipiles, sarapes, and other common clothing, there were certain textiles, such as *paños de rebozo*, or common shawls, that found a wider market. Revillagigedo was convinced that Catalonian industrialists had failed to seize the potential market that paños de rebozo offered. "Everyone used them," he wrote, "religious sisters, wealthy and prominent women, even the poorest of villagers."[51] Consumed in altar cloths and veils, and in coverlets and sashes, paños de rebozo represented an important link between the village economy and the urban market. In other words, whatever the degree of autarchy in consumption, the Indian peasantry nevertheless produced textiles for a larger market. At the end of the colonial period, conservatively calculated, roughly half the colony's population may have been included. In earlier years, prior to the improvement of roads that linked centers of the telares sueltos such as Valladolid and Sultepec to the *Camino Real de la Tierra Adentro*, this market would have been smaller in extent, and shallower in depth.[52]

As it happens, a clear example of peasant production for the market was provided by weaving in Sultepec and Temascaltepec, both in the intendancy of Mexico. By the end of the eighteenth century, the silver mines of Temascaltepec were in decline, as mercury for refining was progressively diverted to Guanajuato. Weaving rapidly became the principal source of local income, and paño de rebozo from Temascaltepec found a market in Guanajuato, Querétaro, and elsewhere, enjoying a reputation for high quality, despite their crudeness of design and embroidery.[53] A description of Temascaltepec provides a glimpse into its industry, even though it did not typify what Revillagigedo the younger regarded as simple peasant production. In Temascaltepec, paño de rebozo was made of a cotton and silk mix and embellished with metallic strands. The workers included both poor and better-off women, none of whom owned looms or workplaces. They had no fixed quota of goods to send for sale. Everything was done by hand. This made for a finer and more durable weave, with none of the damage to the fabric thought characteristic of the looms of Puebla. Such paño de rebozo thus had a good reputation.

Its marketing was simple. One weaver collected the product of several others, and in her name a family member or trusted employee took the paño and sold it, returning home to divide the profits. In much the same way, itinerant merchants stopped in Temascaltepec to collect paño de rebozo until they had a full load and then went off and sold it.[54]

Peasant weavers with backstrap looms, retaceros at the margins of subsistence, trapicheros adrift in urban markets, artisans with shops and journeymen, and peasants who sold goods in markets beyond the local village or *tianquiz* were all part of a varied network—a web of weavers—that helped supply Mexico with cloth that Spain could not provide. Yet all shared a common characteristic. Although capitalistic, their production approximated artisan and domestic arrangements rather than the system of mill or manufactory. But although numerous and critical to local supply, the telares sueltos were different from the obrajes. Markets were one of those differences.

MARKETS OF THE TELARES SUELTOS

As a first step, I have presented the survey of 1781 on a map of New Spain, followed by a similar representation of the results of the survey of 1793. It would be incorrect to infer growth by comparing the two, for the second survey corrected the deficiencies of the first. As the Director of the Royal Excise, Juan Navarro, wrote, "The officers of the Royal Excise reporting to this office did not adequately respond to the circular orders of April 9, 1781 . . . so that this point had remained in abeyance."[55] Even so, the concentration of telares sueltos in the Bajío, the Puebla-Tlaxcala basin, the valley of Oaxaca, and the Mixteca Alta presents striking evidence of regional specialization.

Population density aside, one reason why cities such as Acámbaro, León, San Miguel el Grande, and Querétaro had so many telares sueltos was the limited area over which woolens and cottons from artisan industry could be sold. The telares sueltos of Acámbaro, for instance, produced mainly for the local market, and there were consequently looms throughout the Bajío and, indeed, throughout New Spain.

Although prices to support this interpretation are scarce, references to the relative prices of paños de rebozo from Temascaltepec and Sultepec may illustrate the market areas for the telares sueltos. Paños de rebozo made in these towns were priced from 60 to 600 pesos the dozen, or from four to ten times as much as paño from Puebla, and circulated north into the Bajío and the Tierra Adentro. Such paños, "especially fine varieties with high silk content and a great deal of hand work," enjoyed relatively extensive markets, for

21

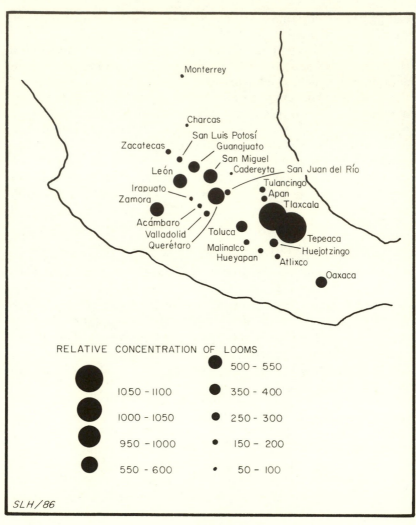

MAP 1.1
Telares Sueltos in 1781

Source: Compiled from AGNM, Alcabalas, vol. 521. For Tlaxcala, see AGNM, Alcabalas, vol. 37.

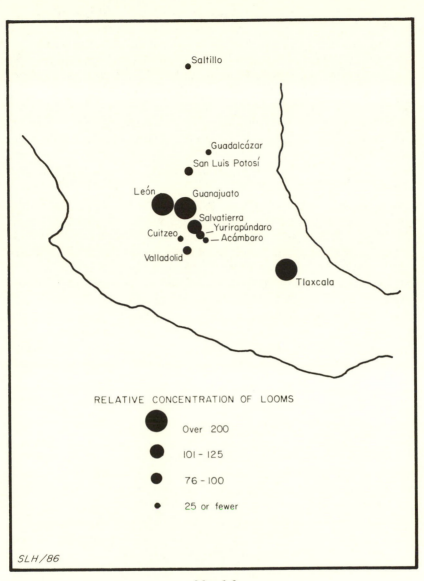

Saltillo

Guadalcázar
San Luis Potosí

León Guanajuato
Salvatierra
Yurirapúndaro
Cuitzeo Acámbaro
Valladolid

Tlaxcala

RELATIVE CONCENTRATION OF LOOMS

Over 200

101 - 125

76 - 100

25 or fewer

SLH/86

MAP 1.2
Telares Sueltos in 1793

Source: Compiled from AGNM, Alcabalas, vol. 37. Some omitted. For Texcoco, see
AGNM, Aduanas, vol. 13.

they were superior goods and highly prized. Yet there were other grades, as Viceroy Revillagigedo the younger noted, "paños of an inferior class woven of cotton only," that had high transportation costs because of their bulkiness.[56] These goods had limited spatial markets and were therefore manufactured quite widely. Moreover, better grades of woolens and cottons were made in far fewer places but possessed broader regional and interregional markets. Well-regarded manta from Cholula circulated north into Tierra Adentro, while less-desirable manta and huipiles produced in Teotitlán del Camino were sold there and in Tehuacán and Puebla, a considerably smaller area.[57] Similarly, an individual wishing to operate a trapiche in Zinapécuaro reasoned that the peasants and the poor who purchased says or sackcloth would respond positively to its licensing. It would be cheaper for them to purchase goods made in Zinapécuaro "with the savings on the costs of bringing goods in from outside."[58] Final confirmation of this point comes from Querétaro, where cottons and woolens made by artisans—manta and *sabanilla* (handwoven sheeting), for example—did not find a market beyond the city itself "because of their very low prices."[59] The evidence thus suggests a complex pattern of local self-sufficiency among many domestic cottons that ran counter to forces that enlarged the scope of the late colonial market in textiles.

EARNINGS IN ARTISAN INDUSTRY

The survey of 1793 provides data on earnings in artisan industry and on the relationship between the weavers, suppliers, and financiers. Many of the reports were imprecise. The weavers of Acatlán, Petalcinco, and Huajuapan were said to be "poor and unfortunate folk." The peasants who made friezes and serges in Charcas "could barely sustain themselves with their earnings."[60] Examples could be multiplied. The data in Table 1.2, however, document the attempts of the fiscal bureaucracy to compute the income from the telares sueltos and yield insight into the nature of their work.

These descriptions require some commentary and explanation. All assumed that a weaver devoted full time to the trade, that is, twenty-four days a month. Fluctuations in the supply of wool, cotton, and credit, however, and seasonal variations in demand made continuous work a rarity for all but the most prosperous.[61] A weaver's income was seldom stable; it moved inversely with the price of raw materials, as did the number of individuals in the trade. The early 1790s were years of very high cotton prices, and the incomes

TABLE 1.2
Described Earnings in Artisan Industry, by District (1793)

District	Earnings
Atlixco	earnings of 2.5 to 3.75 reales per day for cotton manta
Cadereyta	earnings of 12-14 pesos per year making manta
Celaya	income had once been 30-40 pesos per year, but rising cotton prices in 1793 had reduced them to 6
Guanajuato	in Iraputao, woolen looms produced 80-100 pesos per year if employed full time; in Silao, a maker of manta made up to 1 real per day, and those making woolens about the same
Hueyapan	1-2 reales per day for manta
Ixmiquilpan	2-4 reales per day per piece of frieze
Jalapa	2 reales per day in making manta
S. Juan del Río	castas could earn 30-40 pesos per year making cottons and woolens; "Indians" might earn a real per day
Monclova	a weaver earned 40-50 pesos per year
Oaxaca	journeymen weavers who worked the looms of master weavers could earn 20 reales for a "chiapaneco" and 3 reales per day for a "corte chiapaneco"; rebozo-makers earned 1.5 or 1 real per piece; the master weavers got 50 percent of what the journeymen earned for furnishing with looms and organizing production
Tepeaca	a loom making manta produced 60 pesos per year; a loom making "lanilla" and friezes, 40 pesos per year; an "Indian" weaver earned 20 pesos per half year
Texcoco	a master weaver making "manta ancha" could earn 10-12 reales each 2 days; one making "manta judía" earned 1 real per day and a half; a master weaver who made "manta angosta" made 7 reales per day. Extended unemployment common
Tlapujahua	in Zinapécuaro, a woolen loom produced 100 pesos per year
Tlaxcala	an "Indian" making woolens earned about 3 reales per day; others who worked looms made 1 real per day, less if the loom was hired out; the going rate for manta was 5 reales the piece
Valladolid	working daily, a weaver could earn 50 pesos per year
Villa Alta	tributaries earned 4.5 pesos per year making manta
Zacatlán	manta produced 4 reales per day
Zamora	a weaver could earn 13-14 reales per week for a cut of manta; with assistants and a division of labor, he could triple output and earn 15 reales per week in weaving alone

Sources: AGNM, Alcabalas, vol. 37; Zamora [1781], AGNM, Alcabalas, vol. 521; Texcoco, AGNM, Aduanas, vol. 134.

of weavers may have been lower than normal. An example was Celaya, where earnings fell sharply as cotton prices rose, and the same was noticed in Salamanca, Toluca, Valladolid, and Zitácuaro.[62]

A second problem with the data is their lack of homogeneity. The reports of the excise officers measured a variety of different things because their instructions were rather vague. Some discussed piece rates, and others, profits. Still others described a combination of the two. Even simple comparison of piece rates is misleading, for a piece of manta differed in size and composition from a shawl, a Chiapas-style cotton skirt (*chiapaneco*), or a *corte de manga* (another variety of woolen shawl commonly lined with cotton). In other words, the piece rate alone could not determine what a weaver earned per period of employment.

Bear this in mind when interpreting the average daily earnings that appear in Table 1.3. Where available, I cite the daily rate. When yearly earnings are given, I convert them to daily rates based on the twenty-four-day working month. Where a mixed range is provided (i.e., upper and lower limits of daily or yearly income), I report or convert as required. Consequently, the statistics represent expected daily income from the telares sueltos in 1793, other things being equal. If, however, artisan industry absorbed, for example, half its participants' time, the expected values double. In other words, the figures are approximations, at best.

The results are suggestive. On the one hand, earnings in the Bajío cluster at about a real or so a day, as they do in Cadereyta, Huichapan, San Juan del Río, and Valladolid. A slightly higher average is registered in the Puebla-Tlaxcala basin, as in Atlixco, Zacatlán, and Tlaxcala. Such interregional differences may be significant, but no conclusive demonstration is possible. The rough intraregional convergence may indicate greater mobility among artisan weavers than one might expect, for in seeking the best terms offered, some equalization in earnings would necessarily occur. Nevertheless, the possibility should not be exaggerated, for differences of a real were substantial, and disparity in earnings could as plausibly be emphasized. In this case, the evidence points more toward immobility and the weavers' reluctance to migrate for small differences in earnings. Since weaving was frequently supplementary to other village pursuits, the case for limited mobility is more likely.

Some evidence from the survey of 1793 may be offered in support of this interpretation. From Zacatecas, the excise officer wrote the weavers there were not completely tied to the trade for a living, "since they labor in the mines and smelting works as well."[63] The

TABLE 1.3
Average Daily Income in Weaving (1793)

Excise District	Income
Atlixco	2 reales 6 granos–3 reales 9 granos
Cadereyta	less than 1 real
Hueyapan	1 real
Jalapa	2 reales
S. Juan del Río	1 real
Monclova	1 real–1 real 6 granos
Oaxaca	3 reales
Tepeaca	1 real–1 real 6 granos
Texcoco	1 real–7 reales
Tlalpujahua	less than 1 real
Tlaxcala	1 real–3 reales
Valladolid	1 real
Villa Alta	less than 1 real
Zacatlán	4 reales
Zamora	2 reales–2 reales 6 granos

Source: AGNM, Alcabalas, vol. 37; Zamora [1781], AGNM, Alcabalas, vol. 521; Texcoco, AGNM, vol. 134.

same point was made in Valladolid, where handicraft workers with a loom or two never worked more than one or two months per year "since they can make more in another line: as in working someone else's looms; in private business; or in public works."[64]

Nevertheless, was 1 or 2 reales a day in the eighteenth century a plausible income? If the supplementary nature of the work is understood, the answer is "yes." These artisans probably grew their own food and did other kinds of work to cover deficits in subsistence. Moreover, David Brading reports a "strong presumption that the money wages of agricultural laborers [in the Bajío] remained fixed at one and one-half to two reales a day from the mid-seventeenth century until the 1880s," at least in the León region.[65] The estimated returns may be low, but they reflect the weavers' willingness to work for less in supplementary employment.

WEAVERS, FINANCIERS, AND SUPPLIERS

A final point concerns weavers, their suppliers, and financiers. Some weavers had no fixed source of supply or finance, testimony to the casual nature of employment. This was the case in Ixtlahuaca, where villagers with cotton and yarn brought it to the looms to have "such petticoats and sheeting made as their dwellings required."[66] Frequently, however, networks of supply were more formal.

In the far north, where the great ranchers pastured their flocks, those who made woolens went directly to the source for raw materials. In Durango, the holder of the urban meat supply and a few local owners of haciendas furnished weavers with wool. In Saltillo, the woolen weavers "[made] friezes and serges with wool that they purchased from the sheep drovers, the *chinchorros de ovejas*."[67] Further to the south, arrangements such as these were less common, and weavers almost invariably dealt with brokers to procure wool and cotton. Because many weavers had little capital, the brokers, generally local merchants and shopkeepers, often acted as creditors and organizers of domestic systems of production.

At one level, merchants and shopkeepers fulfilled rudimentary functions. In Taxco, the cotton weavers sold their wares "in the shops of this mining town" and "bought their cotton from the same shopkeepers." In Tochimilco, the weavers purchased cotton from shopkeepers who supplied themselves in Puebla."[68]

Nevertheless, supply was generally more formal and complex. In Toluca, merchants mediated the incipient division of labor. They put out cotton to be spun and resold it on credit to weavers "always indebted to these same merchants."[69] A variation existed in Metepec, where artisan weavers either sold on their own account in the plaza of the town, or passed on their products to merchants for resale. Others entered into narrower domestic systems, weaving on merchants' orders for wholesale or retail.[70]

In other words, there were a number of variant relationships between weavers and their suppliers. These ranged from a capitalistic domestic system to traditional artisan industry. Generalizations about the nature of weaving outside the obrajes are thus uncertain.

So too with the supply of raw materials to the telares sueltos. Much took place informally and remained unrecorded. Woolens were essentially the preserve of the obrajes, and the supply of wool is properly considered in relation to them. But a class of itinerant materials merchants did exist and brokered the small amounts of raw wool that artisan weavers demanded.

The situation with cotton was more complicated. The fiber was grown primarily on the coastal lowlands and warm interior valleys and was transported to the highlands for weaving. Until the mid-eighteenth century, preconquest patterns of production were generally preserved, and most raw cotton was drawn from the Pacific coast, on a line running south from Jalisco and Michoacán to Oaxaca, from the Mixteca Baja, and from interior valleys in New Vizcaya.[71] But in the second half of the century, the lowlands of Veracruz, and especially the Costa de Sotavento, emerged as a major source of supply. Two factors caused the shift. The growth of the Catalonian cotton industry after 1750 produced a larger demand for raw materials, and the Crown provided for duty-free shipment of American cotton to the peninsula in 1767, 1794, and 1802. Nevertheless, the quantities of Mexican cotton exported to Spain remained small.[72] More important was the demand exercised by the growing cotton industry in Puebla, a commercial development studied by Guy Thomson in several unpublished works.[73] By century's end, the transition to commercial growing along the Gulf coast was well advanced, and the volume of cotton harvests there exceeded those of the Pacific by about a third. Although vestiges of a pattern in which individuals grew cotton on small plots for their own use persisted, the newer industry tended toward extensive cultivation financed by merchant capital.[74] The growth of cotton output from all sources and the increasing importance of imported cottons would eventually compete with the woolen production in the obrajes. By the end of the colonial period, the cotton industry had become one of New Spain's largest, with an estimated employment of 1.5 million and a product of 3 million pesos. Of its economic significance there can be no doubt.[75]

CONCLUSIONS: TOWARD A THEORY OF MARKET DEVELOPMENT

The production of cottons in New Spain in the colonial period embraced a variety of forms, ranging from domestic and artisanal to the merchant capitalist. Much of this production was intended for the use of producers themselves and was not traded. Perhaps the greatest stimulus to the broad diffusion of cottons was the Conquest itself. In its aftermath, the ostensible prohibition against commoners' wearing cotton, previously brought in tribute as a luxury good within the Triple Alliance, disappeared. By the era of the *Relaciones Geográficas* (1577-86), men frequently wore cotton trousers and frocks, and there was among women a parallel substitution of cottons and some woolens for henequen and other coarse fibres.[76] Logically, the volume of production reflected larger population movements and gathered increasing momentum with the demographic recovery of the eighteenth century.

The telares sueltos meshed closely with the lives of those who drew part of their livelihood from them. For many, weaving was a supplementary occupation, not a profession, and generally only the finer cottons, such as high-quality shawls, entered the larger colonial market. But much output circulated only within local markets and produced a degree of regional self-sufficiency. This was logical. Prices were low and transportation costs were high. For the most part, cheaper cottons could not bear distant circulation and were part of a larger, less formal economy in which levels of productivity were low. Nevertheless, by all evidence, the volume of cottons marketed in the eighteenth century increased, particularly after 1750. In Puebla, for instance, Thomson finds an urban, commercial industry on the upswing that increasingly drew older, rural production into its control. Several factors accounted for this, not least of which was an elastic supply of cottons that were cheaper, lighter, more comfortable, and easier to clean than woolens. Here Mexico shared in a shift in tastes of historic proportions, one evident in Europe as well.[77] Cottons thus posed a source of competition to the woolens of the obrajes, particularly later in the colonial period.

Nevertheless, it would be incorrect to see only competition between cottons and woolens, between the telares sueltos and the obrajes. The process of market development itself is the reason, for self-sufficiency is primarily a matter of relative prices. A simplified version of the expansion of production for the market might focus on the price of cottons relative to woolens. As the woolen output of the obrajes grew, particularly in the sixteenth and seventeenth centuries, its price relative to cottons produced by subsistence weavers fell, and thus the demand for woolens grew. Conversely, the relative price of cottons rose, and weavers could slowly enter the market as suppliers. Weavers either exchanged cottons for woolens (whether money was involved or whether the exchange was direct makes no difference), or consumed fewer cottons and substituted woolens for what they formerly produced. In any event, an expansion of marketed output in both cottons and woolens took place, the source of the increase in telares sueltos recognized by Spanish officials. By the mid-eighteenth century, the growing volume of cottons altered relative prices once again and changed the pattern of consumption. In other words, if domestic and imported cottons ultimately helped displace the production of woolens from the obrajes, they nevertheless (in conjunction with other traded goods) underwrote the demand for woolens at an earlier stage. The telares sueltos and obrajes were therefore linked in development, but significant differences remained in their solution to problems of production. We now turn to these differences and their meaning.

TWO

Embrión de la Fábrica?

THE OBRAJE: INTRODUCTION AND DEFINITIONS

IN 1938, Luis Chávez Orozco published his *Historia económica y social de México*, in which he called the obraje a "factory in embryo."[1] According to Chávez Orozco, the Conquest occurred just as economic institutions in the Peninsula were evolving beyond late medieval corporative forms. Thus, he understood the artisan workshop—in his view, the trapiche or obrador—and the obraje as representing different historical epochs and forms of production. The artisan workshop was precapitalist and essentially medieval. The obraje was an "advanced," if anomalous, institution. It was a factorylike structure that epitomized the leading edge of a modern, entrepreneurial, and capitalistic enterprise. The distinction is an important one, and its implications for the economic history of Mexico are many. If the obraje was a "factory in embryo," did it harbor the potential for sustained industrial development? Was the obraje the primitive forerunner of a factory system that failed to materialize? How and why was its potential lost, assuming that it ever existed? Or was the obraje an institution suited to the peculiarities of the colonial economy, its endowments and constraints? What larger lessons, in other words, can economic historians draw from the obraje?

To answer these questions, we need a working definition of the obraje. We begin with one provided by a trapichero in Mexico City in the late seventeenth century. In an effort to resist its classification as an obraje for tax purposes, Jacinto Romeo said of his trapiche, "Although you may call [it] an obraje, it is not, strictly speaking. Rather, it is a trapiche, for it has neither a perch for inspections, nor a fulling mill, the things that make an obraje complete . . . nor a press, nor cards for carding wool, nor a bench for shearing, which is essential. . . . Its water supply is useless."[2] When Salvador Gueraveo of Zinapécuaro asked to be permitted to operate a trapiche of four looms for making *sayal*, or says, a coarse woolen yardage fabric, he likewise said that his business "cannot be called an obraje because of its small plant" that "employs what is necessary to support [my] family."[3] Some observers defined the obraje in terms of output, leading the jurist Juan de Solórzano to call the obraje "a shop or office in which they spin, weave, and work not only serges, bays, friezes, coarse worsteds, and others requiring little skill, but [also] common cloth. . . ."[4]

Part of the problem lies in translating the term "obraje." One hesitates to use "mill," "factory," or even "manufactory," for these conjure up anachronistic images of industrial capitalism. "Manufactory" is possibly the least inappropriate, for it suggests a process driven by hand or water, rather than by heat or other inanimate sources of power.[5] Logically, then, an understanding of "manufactory" follows from the "factory." Although a formal definition of "factory" has proved difficult for even economic historians, its characteristics include the concentration of numerous workers in one place, the horizontal division of labor, and the close supervision and coordination of work. Machinery is not necessary to the definition, but specialization of the workplace is. People go to a factory to work, not to live. This distinction is significant for understanding the textile obraje in New Spain.[6]

An appropriate observation made by George Kubler for sixteenth-century industrial architecture in New Spain, but equally valid for the later colonial period, is that the divorce of residential and commercial architecture is a modern phenomenon. In New Spain, stores were places of residence; and workshops, the homes of artisans. Thus it is hardly possible to distinguish between domestic and industrial architecture.[7] Kubler was correct. The tendency of many owners of obrajes to call their businesses *casa de obraje* suggests a unity that industrial capitalism ended: the residence and the manufactory. A photograph of the obraje "Posadas" in Coyoacán reveals little more than the conventional Spanish dwelling.[8] The physical structure of the obraje was not radically different from the residence in form, and conversions between the two were not unknown. One took place in Coyoacán in the later 1730s, when Fernando de la Peña sought license to establish an obraje of twelve looms in his dwelling.[9] In the 1740s, the wealthy creole, don Manuel de la Canal, had constructed a residence valued at 30,000 pesos outside the town of San Miguel el Grande; but later, he petitioned to have the structure made into an obraje.[10] Conversions were common enough to appear in advertisement for real estate at the beginning of the nineteenth century. A notice in the *Diario de México* maintained that a residence with six rooms, a large patio, and a well might be turned into an establishment for weaving.[11]

There were logical reasons for a Spanish casa to meet the physical requirements of an obraje. A large obraje might contain twenty-five or thirty looms; a spacious residence could accommodate them. The design of the casa, with its central courtyards or patios, surrounded by large satellite spaces (*piezas* and *galeras*), and topped by a mezzanine and a second story, was well suited to the organization and flow of work that the manufacture of woolens required. There was room for inventories and for the needs of managers and foremen; there were even owners who lived at the obrajes. Some obrajes had secure areas that doubled as prisons for convict laborers, and entry halls and doorkeepers could be turned to the needs of security. In short, although the particular structure of the obraje differed from place to place, and from rural to urban environments, all possessed common features and tended toward thorough but incomplete functional specialization. One can see this on a tour.

Consider, for example, the smallish one owned by Antonio de Leyva, of Mexico City. Even though it was uncertain whether or not the obraje might be more properly called a trapiche, the description is revealing. Leyva owned a

> house with a mezzanine on the Plazuela de Santa María la Redonda, and the street that runs from the church of Santa Veracruz . . . 73 *varas* north and south; 36, east and west. Facing the street is a small obraje, with an entry hall, and a small, dilapidated room; a patio, tiled, for the most part; 2 larger rooms, one for weaving, the other one for carding; 5 rooms, in one, a dyeing vat . . . living and sleeping areas; outside, an attached structure; on the corner, a shop with its living quarters.[12]

Let us compare this description with the floor plan of a slightly larger obraje belonging to Santiago del Arenal, also of Mexico City. The assessed value of Arenal's obraje was 10,000 pesos, including the property it stood on but excluding the value of capital equipment.[13] The obraje was not unlike those described in Puebla and Querétaro; its design might therefore be considered representative.[14]

The floor plans included here are based on descriptions similar to Leyva's. Notice the close integration of the flow of work with the plan of a *casa entresolada*, that is, the residence with mezzanine. The lower floor of the obraje served as the workplace. The area around the *patio principal* was the focal point for weaving and for the stages of manufacture leading up to it. Looms were erected on the patio. Carders and spinners worked up yarn from fleece in the adjacent galeras. Raw materials were stored in the bodegas. *Salas* on

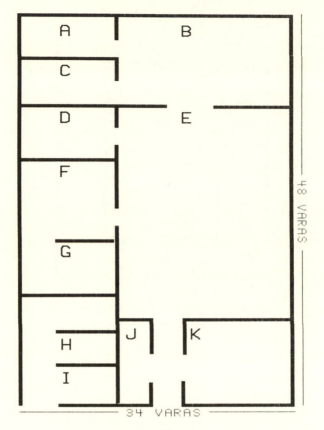

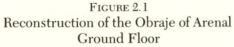

FIGURE 2.1
Reconstruction of the Obraje of Arenal
Ground Floor

KEY:

A: Merced del Agua (Water Tanks)
B: Patio Segundo (Dyeing)
C: Pieza del Tinte (Cauldrons)
D: Prensa (Hot and Cold Presses)
E: Patio Principal (Weaving)
F: Galera (Spinning)

G: Galera (Carding)
H: Bodegas (Inventory)
I: Tienda and Trastienda (Retail Shop)
J: Sala
K: Sala (Finished Goods in Inventory)

Source: Reconstructed from tasación de Joaquín de Torres, México, Oct. 17, 1752, AGNM, Tierras, vol. 856, exp. 2.

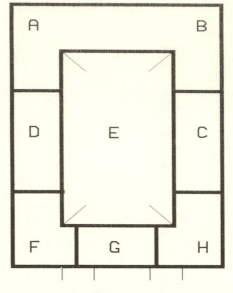

FIGURE 2.2
Upper Floor and Living Quarters

KEY:

A:	Cuarto	E:	Area over Patio Principal
B:	Cocina (Food Preparation) and Washing	F:	Recámara (Sleeping Quarters)
		G:	Sala de Asistencia (Living Quarters)
C:	Sala		
D:	Dispensa (Inventory)	H:	Recámara (Sleeping Quarters)

Source: Reconstructed from tasación de Joaquín de Torres, México, Oct. 17, 1752, AGNM, Tierras, vol. 856, exp. 2.

either side of the entry hall (*zaguán*) served as storage areas for inventories of finished woolens.

From this simple reconstruction, it seems probable that woolens in this obraje were dyed in the weave. The product of the weavers was brought back from the *patio segundo* where equipment for finishing and dyeing—such as the presses, copper-bottomed vats, and so on—was kept. This section had a water supply, since the patio segundo used sewers and conduits to distribute the water and to drain away the effluents of washing and dyeing. Because these effluents fouled the water, obrajes in urban areas were frequently clustered in industrial districts as much to minimize friction with other users as to benefit from external economies.

In theory, the working area was separate from the residence of the second floor. The Arenal obraje demonstrates this, for the second floor contained Arenal's living quarters and the obraje's galley. The living quarters could also be occupied by managers and foremen; this often happened when the owner was an investor rather than a clothier, properly speaking. Many obrajes had a resident population of convict laborers or peons for whom meals had to be provided. So it fell to the galley to prepare what diet the obraje offered. The limited division between living and working areas, however, applied only to the managers and not to the labor force. In the obraje of Balthasar de Sauto in San Miguel el Grande, for instance, a royal inspector discovered conditions of terrible overcrowding. On questioning a foreman about where the laborers slept, the inspector was showed the galera where the spinners and carders worked up the yarn, a room with two barred doors, "like a jail." There, "all together, one atop the other" in the space between the spinning wheels and their seats slept "as many as fit." Those who could not fit slept on the patio. This was not a unique case.[15]

A final description of an urban obraje reveals its generality of design. This one belonged to José Pimentel, to whom we shall return later. Pimentel was having legal problems when the evaluation was done, so the obraje was not in good order. Still, it had a capacity of about fifteen looms when it prospered, and the picture that remains is interesting. The obraje was

> located on the Calzada de la Piedad. Its residence has two rooms at the entryway. You enter either through the storerooms, or through the rooms where cloth made in the obraje is kept. The main body of the obraje has a chapel where they celebrate the sacrifice of the Mass for the workers. There is a room for the press, and a room for the roller. There is a room for the apprentices, and a galera for the carders. There is an arch of the weavers, a storeroom for *tequesquite* [a weak, alkaline soponifying agent], and a masonry stairway leading to the roof. There are three masonry vats in the dyeing room, two with copper bottoms. The retaining walls are all fallen. One passes through the dyers' room to enter the spinners' area, and the place where the unwashed fleece are kept, and it leads down to the corral, or open area, where the fleece are washed. Behind a small door there is another room for the spinners, and above it, one used for the chapel.[16]

Another aspect of the obraje was its size. It would be a mistake to make too much of dimensions, since a larger obraje need not have been prosperous or fully utilized. Still, the evidence yields rough orders of magnitude. By looking at dimensions, and by assuming that space was available for carding, spinning, weaving, dyeing, and finishing, one perceives how large an obraje could be. Statistics are presented in Table 2.1 and range from 5,700 square feet to 39,000 square feet. In other words, if the "typical" obraje resembled any of these, it was larger in scale than the trapiches and obradores, not to mention domestic industry. It brought together the stages of producing woolens and provided residence for a substantial and specialized labor force. On the surface, it resembled the factory in the functional sense, a simpler forerunner, or "protofactory," as these are called.[17] But appearances may be deceiving. The early factory system was based on its efficiency, or ability to produce more for given inputs. The factory's overhead, or fixed costs from the purchase or rental of productive assets, were spread over substantial output. By implication, the system depended upon a tendency for total factor productivity, or overall efficiency, to increase. But there was no important technological change in the obrajes during the colonial period. And while single-factor measurements of output per

TABLE 2.1
Floor Space of Selected Obrajes

Obraje/Location	Dimensions (Varas)	Area in Sq Ft
José Pimentel/México	94 × 55	38,873
Juan Pérez Cota/México	(88 × 33) (60 × 30)	35,369
Mendoza y Escalante/Puebla	62.5 × 70.5	33,130
Frejomil/Querétaro	72 × 55	28,151
Antonio de Leyva/México	73 × 36	19,760
Santiago del Arenal/México	48 × 34	12,277
María de León Coronado/Puebla	27 × 50	10,150
Cecilio de Chávez/Coyoacán	43 × 17.5[a]	5,648

[a] Average dimensions of an irregular building.

Sources and methods: The vara is converted into meters using a factor of .836, and then into feet by a factor of 3.28. See assessment of obraje of Arenal, México, Oct. 17, 1752, AGNM, Tierras, vol. 856; assessment of obraje of Cecilio de Chávez, México, Mar. 26, 1743, AGNM, Hospital de Jesús, leg. 350, exp. 3; assessment of obraje of María de León Coronado, Puebla, Mar. 27, 1736, AJP, leg. for 1732; assessment of obraje of Mendoza y Escalante, Puebla, Apr. 28, 1746, AGNM, Civil, vol. 178, 2d part.

loom favored obrajes over telares sueltos, such differences could not offset the fixed costs the obraje bore. What then drove the Spanish to organize obrajes in New Spain and to bear the costs of their operation? What incentives existed? What, in other words, was the rationale for the *obraje de tejer paños*?

THE OBRAJE: RATIONALE

The obraje produced woolens commercially for a large colonial demand in the face of significant market imperfections. By integrating production, the obraje reduced covariance in supply. It also lowered the costs of transfer or transaction that made commercial production difficult. The founders of the obrajes, the immigrant producers from the Castilian cities of Cuenca, Toledo, and Segovia, faced a difficult situation. In Castile, wool was a commodity of pervasive social and economic importance and had been so since the late thirteenth century.[18] The woolen industry had long offered possibilities for substantial profit. Its commercial potential was also large in a colony whose endowments and climate made sheep, wool, and woolens valuable commodities. Moreover, the market was protected by the tariff of distance. The fine cloths of Segovia, its 22s and 24s (these terms are explained below) for example, cost from 11 pesos 4 reales per vara to 15 pesos between 1530 and 1550, whereas woolens made in New Spain were priced at 2 pesos 2 reales per vara.[19] Equally fine cloths of Toledo and Almodóvar could not compete with inexpensive woolens made in New Spain. Thus, although many early shipments to America consisted of clothing, textiles, and wine, they were necessarily high-quality items that could bear the taxes and freight.[20] Moreover, the transatlantic trade was slow and unreliable as well as costly. The capacity of the *carrera de Indias* was limited, and round trips of fifteen to eighteen months for merchandise were the rule.[21] In other words, the market of the colonial middle sector, the coarse woolen cloth and yardage used for tents, sacks, horse blankets, packing materials, bags, floor coverings, religious habits, military uniforms, and the clothing of the urban poor, could not come in sufficient volume or regularity to meet the ordinary needs of the economy. Thus, between the demand for luxury goods and the supply of cottons produced for the village and province, there was scope for considerable commercial activity.

Whatever the potential demand, the producers of woolens faced complicated problems in supply and marketing. Whereas cotton was indigenous to New Spain, sheep, wool, and the technology used to produce woolens were not. Moreover, although technology could be transferred, there were difficulties in acquiring a stable supply of skilled labor. Although smaller, early obrajes employed some Indian wage labor, the rapid decline of the population of central Mexico between 1532 and 1568, the period when the first obrajes were established, made absolute labor scarcity a problem.[22] This decline was compounded by factors that also induced a relative labor shortage. Specifically, whatever the prior Mesoamerican experience with market exchange in commodities, no significant market for labor had existed.[23] Labor markets have always lagged in development, either because the marginal product of labor is difficult to measure, or because subsistence producers are unwilling to be governed by supply and demand.[24] Whatever the case, the demand for labor in New Spain could not be easily met. The Indians had little or no prior experience with labor markets. They perhaps lacked the calculus of self-interest by which the "hiding hand" of the market operates (although post-Conquest jockeying for positions in the native aristocracy contradicts this). They displayed a limited demand for money and would not work for it. Or the Indians were self-sufficient in provincial villages and unavailable for recruitment through free contract.[25] To the extent that labor *could* be mobilized for other pursuits, early viceroys, such as Antonio de Mendoza (1535-50), favored mining over other industry.[26]

In other words, in the middle sixteenth century, there was no labor market in New Spain. Such a market would grow slowly and irregularly in time and place. A well-studied example is the Bajío, an urbanized, densely populated region, where acculturation was well advanced by the late colonial period and where there were few corporate Indian villages.[27] Even here, the labor market was subject to substantial imperfections. As a consequence, labor in the obrajes was governed by a system that found free, indentured, convict, forced, and slave labor working side by side, often in the same place. To understand this is to grasp one aspect of Spanish colonialism: the use of public power by private parties to obtain labor that market incentives alone could not provide. In other words, the obraje acquired and maintained a readily available labor force, and so avoided costly and repeated recourse to an imperfect labor market.

The internal structure of the obraje can be interpreted in the same way. Economists understand the firm as a device that organizes production more efficiently than the market itself.[28] All firms, in other words, have an advantage over individual agents. When applied to aspects of institutional change, this insight accounts in part for the structure of modern business.[29] Along these lines, the obraje integrated the manufacture of woolens and lowered or stabilized the supply price of factors of production. This was particularly evident in skilled operations such as weaving, dyeing, and finishing, in which the market was thin (having few buyers and sellers) and subject to volatile prices. Where there were more suppliers, as in spinning and carding, dependence upon the putting-out system was less risky, and the obrajes frequently did so. On the other hand, dyers, weavers, and skilled finishers were always the core of an obraje (and well into the eighteenth century, they were often slaves). These tasks were never separated from the obraje, although decentralized textile production was not uncommon in other societies.[30] In other words, the Mexican obraje met the demand for commercial production in a small economy in which markets were thin and imperfect, and the response of supply, uncertain.

The obstacles to the evolution of the labor market affected other markets as well, although less severely. The principal imperfections were related to costs of both transfer and production. Levels of risk and uncertainty were high, in part because information moved no more rapidly than people themselves. This, in turn, induced an adaptive shaping of attitudes, institutions, and business practices typical of less developed economies. Moreover, transportation costs were high and strengthened regional autarchy. For example, on the Mexican plateau, the average mule carried 300 pounds and moved about 12 or 13 miles a day. In Mexico City, where the supply of transportation was relatively abundant, wheat was more than double its price 175 miles away, while wine, unloaded at Veracruz, increased in price by 70 percent.[31] Nevertheless, the evidence suggests stronger markets for many commodities. For maize, the price convergence that defines a market is evident in the later sixteenth century in the *audiencia* of New Galicia.[32] For raw wool, there are no comparable price series for different regions in New Spain, but in 1740, one knowledgeable party wrote that "In the Kingdom, it is usual that there be a common and general price for wool after the shearing takes place, with a difference of a real or two regarding quality."[33] A better definition of "market" could not be had from a classical economist. Finally, evidence that the obrajes as a group responded to market incentives lies in their overall migration from the Puebla-Tlaxcala basin in the sixteenth century to the Bajío in the eighteenth, a movement indicative of sensitivity to changing relative factor prices.

Market forces thus worked more efficiently in some areas than in others. This was natural, if only to continue preconquest patterns in which allocation by markets and by command coexisted. The presence of these opposing tendencies, a result of multiple environmental, ecological, and technological constraints, merged with the commercial capitalism that Spanish settlement entailed. Consequently, the growing demand for labor and resources exercised a paradoxical impact, enlarging the scope for market activity, but reinforcing long-standing tendencies toward nonmarket response. The obraje thus accommodated the demand for resources, particularly labor, that market incentives were not sufficient to provide. The result was capitalistic—obrajes were conducted as profit-making enterprises— even though self-regulating labor markets did not exist. But they hardly existed in Western Europe until the nineteenth century, and no one seriously doubts that economic activity there was capitalistic.[34]

To view the obraje in a neoclassical framework does not exhaust alternative interpretations. Their utility depends upon their ability to account for the evidence. So, for example, one could call the obraje a "protofactory," an organizational precursor of the factory that lacked only machinery, yet realized economies of scale. Although productivity estimates are difficult to come by, one report from Acámbaro in 1781 indicated that looms in the obrajes produced almost four times as much per year (by value) as did the telares sueltos.[35] To what extent did division of labor and learning-by-doing in obrajes account for the difference? On the basis of limited data, the questions are unanswerable. The productive efficiency of obrajes cannot be deduced from evidence of single factor productivity.

Another approach involves direct estimation of a production function for the obrajes. I have compiled statistics on output, employment, and working looms from the records of a *composición de obrajes*, or examination and settlement of licenses, in the Valley of Mexico in the 1690s. There are serious grounds for rejecting the entire procedure, and even so, the estimate does not indicate that obrajes embodied significant productive efficiencies. To the contrary, its economies were easily exhausted and unimportant.[36] Moreover, there is no evidence that obrajes drove smaller producers of woolens, such as the trapicheros of Querétaro, out of the market. If anything, the data suggest that smaller producers, whatever their problems, persisted and expanded into the late eighteenth century. If insignificant economies of scale are not enough to drive out smaller producers, only insignificant economies of scale were present in the obrajes.[37] Furthermore, some contend that technological change contributed more to increase the output of modern industry than did economies of scale. Little or no technological change, however, occurred in the textile obrajes, and their potential output remained limited.[38] Finally, even if obrajes seem like precursors of a factory system—consider their impressive physical dimensions once more—a closer examination of their capitalization belies first impressions. As in other early modern industry, their ratio of working capital (inventories of raw materials and finished goods, and workers' indebtedness) to fixed capital (structures and equipment) was high; it ranged from roughly 2:1 to as much as 10:1.[39] The low level of fixed costs indicates that economies of scale were not the basis of the obraje: why else do unit costs fall as output increases? In other words, the obraje facilitated turnover of working capital, not a centralized array of fixed capital such as machinery. Or the accumulation of inventory in the obraje was a hedge against fluctuations in supply and demand common to thin, imperfect markets. In other words, to see the obraje as a primitive factory is incorrect, because the rationale of the factory was different.[40] Small wonder no entrepreneur turned an obraje into a factory by eventually introducing machinery.[41] The obraje was not a "factory in embryo."

Although the obraje was in some sense inefficient, it was not irrational. It did ensure, for instance, adequate labor and skilled supervision. Moreover, the constant charge that *obrajeros* used power and influence to acquire labor is pervasive evidence of their effectiveness and suggests economies of scale in labor recruitment and supervision. In provincial centers such as San Miguel, Querétaro, and Acámbaro, owners of obrajes were among the wealthiest residents and used their influence to get labor through formal and informal means. Perhaps this accounts for the growing size of successful obrajes between roughly 1600 and 1800, although a redistribution of wealth among their owners might have produced similar results. Yet the control that the obrajes exercised over their workers is impressive. For instance, data from Querétaro (calculated in 1793 prices) appear in Table 2.2. Of the 46 pesos and 7.5 reales of direct costs in a *cuarterón* of *paño de Querétaro* (roughly 39 varas, or 33 meters in length), about 31 pesos 5 reales or 67.5 percent represented cost of materials. Labor costs were only 33 percent of direct costs (overhead, or indirect cost, was understood but not reported) and subject to a variety of manipulations. By contrast, labor costs were 75 percent of total costs in mining in Guanajuato, an industry ostensibly characterized by competitive recruitment of a mobile labor force.[42] Apparently, the prohibitions against competition for indebted labor

TABLE 2.2
Cost of Producing a Cuarterón of Paño de Querétaro

Stage of production	Cost
7 arrobas of fleece at 2 reales per arroba	24 pesos 5 reales
Washing the fleece	.5 real
Carding	4 pesos 1 real
Spinning the warp yarn	5 reales
Spinning the filling	2 pesos 2 reales
Beaming the web with warp	2.5 reales
Weaving	4 pesos 6 reales
Winding the filling	2.5 reales
Perching	6 reales
Fulling	1 peso 1 real
Indigo for dyeing at 45 reales	5 pesos 5 reales
Firewood	2 reales
Panocha, tequesquite, and oil	1 peso 1 real
Charcoal, press, and presser	1 peso
TOTAL DIRECT COSTS	46 pesos 7.5 reales

Source: "Obrajes o fábricas de paños que hay actualmente en esta ciudad de Querétaro y jurisdicción," AGNM, Alcabalas, vol. 37.

among the obrajes (the *sonsaque* laws) had a predictable effect. The owners and their agents received a larger share of surplus than in a free, competitive labor market.[43] The workers, on the other hand, did worse than if a competitive market had existed; they thus bore a significant share of the welfare loss that the lack of a well-developed labor market implied. Nevertheless, the comparison should not be overdrawn. Woolens were not silver—marginal revenue per worker was higher in silver mining than in manufacturing. Miners attracted more labor because they could pay more, and pay more in cash.

Finally, it is worth recapitulating the differences between obrajes that produced woolens and telares sueltos that made cottons. New Spain's cotton industry was governed by rather different conditions. It used an indigenous plant fiber familiar to native artisans that was considerably more tractable than wool. The primary sources of labor in the cotton industry until well into the eighteenth century were family and kin. Their part-time employment in spinning and weaving meshed easily with other activities. Similarly, many weavers grew their own cotton, at least until the commercial orientation of the industry became overwhelming. And, with few major exceptions, the markets for cottons—from local to regional—were directly accessible to the producers themselves. This, too, was different from the geographically broad markets of the obrajes. In other words, the rationale for the obrajes—constraints upon supply and the transactions costs of commercial production—was less evident in cottons than in wool. The need to enter imperfect markets was smaller. Consequently, cottons were produced differently from woolens.

Nevertheless, as the volume of cottons grew in the late colonial period, market imperfections diminished. In the growing commercial sector of Puebla, the *algodoneros*, or cotton merchants, profited from the elasticity of supply that the putting-out system provided and benefited from increased labor productivity.[44] In cottons, the fixed costs of obrajes were thus unnecessary, and the disadvantage that woolens suffered increased. Cotton cloth itself was lighter, more comfortable, and easier to keep clean. Moreover, as conditions of supply improved, some obrajes changed, disintegrated (in a technical sense), and shifted their carding and spinning to the putting-out system, a response that paralleled cottons.[45] The telares sueltos thus had substantial advantages and could capitalize upon them when conditions changed. The smoother functioning of the market helped undermine the obrajes. But more about this later.

FROM FLEECE TO FABRIC

Among the elements the Spaniards brought to America were sheep and the technology to transform fleece into woolens. In the New World, sheep adapted less easily and multiplied less rapidly than cattle and never grew into feral herds for the settlers to harvest. Nevertheless, sheep prospered in the highlands and mountain zones of the *altiplano* of New Spain. By the later sixteenth century, they had spread across the face of the colony and were divided into northern and southern concentrations. In the south, the Mixteca Alta and La Cañada regions of western Oaxaca, and the valleys of Tlacolula and Zimatlán in the Zapotec region south and east of Oaxaca, found the largest numbers of sheep. To the north, the central areas of the altiplano between the Sierra Madre Oriental and Occidental were the principal grazing areas.[46] The division was significant. The southern flocks were run principally for village use and provided wool for huipiles, shawls, and skirts rather than for use in the obrajes. The commercial supply of wool came largely from the northern flocks, which also provided stocks of mutton, hides, and dressed sheepskins for storing mercury in the mines.[47] Here sheep multiplied rapidly and strained the carrying capacity of the land. The climate of the altiplano, seven months of winter drought and five of summer rains, produced a Mediterranean pattern of transhumance, the migration of sheep from summer to winter pastures.[48] By the late sixteenth century, more than 200,000 sheep from the Bajío were driven annually to the meadows of Lake Chapala and to western Michoacán, from whence they returned the following May. Likewise, the flocks that provided wool to the obrajes of Puebla were driven to winter near Vera Cruz, along the moist slopes of the Atlantic.[49] Transhumance was also recorded in the Río Verde of Guadalajara in the early seventeenth century.[50] Coincidentally, around 1635, the plains of New León were opened to grazing; this fueled the expansion of the northern pastoral economy that so benefited seventeenth-century Querétaro.[51] In sum, during the sixteenth and seventeenth centuries, the focus of sheep ranching moved from the overgrazed lands of central Mexico to the new ranches of Sinaloa, Durango, Chihuahua, and Coahuila, as well as to northeastern New Galicia, and northward into Zacatecas.[52] Nevertheless, the growing demand for wool went unmet. By the later seventeenth century, sheep ranching had spread to the Río Grande Valley in New Mexico. There are no estimates of the size of the trade in wool to New Spain through Chihuahua and Saltillo, but by the 1770s, Spanish officials in New Mexico held it responsible for a shortage of livestock.[53] It was, in other words, implicitly a factor of major importance.

Details on buying and selling wool are sketchy, other than from the ordinary dealings of the obrajes. But even if its mechanics and dimensions are unclear, circumstantial evidence warrants a few generalizations about the trade. For example, the production and sale of wool shaped the early growth of Querétaro, an entrepot whose hinterlands pastured perhaps a million sheep by 1630.[54] The haciendas that supplied the obrajes were largely the patrimony of New Spain's wealthiest families. For many, the trade in sheep and wool was the foundation of the enterprise.[55] The ranches, estates, and their owners are well known: "Bledos," "Bocas," "La Erre," "Ciénaga de Mata," "Presa de Jalpa," "Guanamé," and "Santa Lucía," to mention but a few. For these, the wool trade was the key to substantial fortunes. Ranchers and middlemen alike prospered by it. Such were

Duarte de Tovar, a successful wool trader from Querétaro's early seventeenth century, or the Marqués de Jaral, who supplied perhaps 30 percent to 40 percent of the wool consumed there in the 1770s.[56] In San Miguel el Grande, the trade enriched the Unzaga, Lanzagorta, and Allende, who were in turn linked to the puissant houses of the capital operated by the Bassoco and Yermo, among others.[57] Indeed, the picture is of a far-flung network of ranchers, muleteers, and merchants engaged in a very risky business. Coordination between suppliers and demanders was difficult. Shortages of mules and packing for drayage were common. Losses to flocks from disease, predators, and theft were familiar.[58] Nevertheless, well-capitalized participants could realize profits, so many entered the trade. Silver mining may thus have encouraged a wider spatial integration of markets, but it also produced a substantially distorted allocation of resources.[59] To paraphrase an eighteenth-century observer who understood the situation, the wealth of New Spain lay in its sheep and looms, not in its mines.[60]

The obrajes, then, obtained raw wool in a variety of ways. Many ranchers integrated to the limits of profitability and constructed obrajes on their estates, or drew upon adjacent producers. For well-capitalized urban producers, integration was also attractive and entailed the purchase of a ranch to ensure competitive supplies. Although the benefits were potentially large, the costs were commensurate, and not every producer could afford to invest in a ranch. The alternative was to purchase wool on the market. Here the buyer faced a variety of suppliers. The smallest lots could be purchased from itinerant merchants, marginal suppliers chiefly useful to artisan producers. General merchants also handled wool at wholesale or retail, depending on the size and frequency of purchase. And finally, there was a group of specialized brokers, "those who deal in wool, indigo, tallow, and hides," about whom little more is known.[61] Once purchased, the wool was held in inventory for further use, sometimes in an unprocessed state, sometimes worked into yarn. The inventory of the obraje of Don José Negrete in Mexico City describes the varieties and grades held, with quantities of raw, washed, dark, and dyed wools, and various kinds of yarn, all of which accounted for 16 percent of capitalized value.[62]

Working the wool into a finished cloth involved four steps. First came preparation of the raw wool, that is, sorting, cleaning, and drawing out the fibers. Spinning or drawing and twisting the loose fibers into yarn followed. Next was weaving, in which some yarn, the warp, was laid lengthwise, and other yarn, the weft, was run across, over, and under the longitudinal lines to form the rough fabric. At the end was finishing, and it involved fulling, shearing, pressing, and other tasks.[63] The technology employed was drawn directly from thirteenth-century Europe and underwent virtually no change between the sixteenth and nineteenth centuries. This is not to say that its key elements, the treadle loom, or tools to prepare the yarn, for instance, were unsophisticated. When brought to Mexico in the 1530s and 1540s, the treadle loom, cards, spinning wheel, rotary wheel, spool rack, warping mill, cage spools, and reed were relatively complex. They provided further incentive for division of labor and permitted large increases in output.[64] But what was sophisticated in the sixteenth century grew archaic by the eighteenth, and no evidence of technological change, such as the spinning frame, ever appeared.[65] Potential productivity increase in the obrajes was therefore small and confined to driving workers ever harder. The implications grew obvious when consumer demand was opened to foreign trade in the late eighteenth century.

A closer look at the manufacturing process is then in order. The examination provides insight into what obrajes were, how they functioned, the labor they required, the woolens they produced, and the limitations they faced. It also clarifies technical difficulties, the response to them, and the nature and effectiveness of the operative incentives. Finally, it may illuminate the issue of technical progress— or the lack of it—in the obrajes.

Raw wool came primarily from long-staple, *churro*, or common mutton sheep, an inference based on early nineteenth-century calls by Domínguez and Lucas Alamán for importation of larger stocks of the merino variety.[66] The fleece of the churro was well suited for hand-processing; with sufficient care, it could produce an excellent yarn. Short-staple wool was also available from the merino, but it presented greater problems in preparation and weaving.[67] Yet overall quality never seemed important. As don José María Bustamante put it, the common cloth of Querétaro was not esteemed for its yarn, its weave, or its dye, but "only for the amount of wool that every vara contained."[68]

The first step in preparing the fleece was sorting. The sorter was to separate different grades of fleece according to the part of the animal from which it was shorn. A sheep would yield *lana cañonuda* for friezes and sarapes, *lana de buen filamento* for ordinary cloths and bays, and finer wool for *paño 36no*, termed "equal to the best that come from Europe."[69] Sorting determined quality; the mixture of different grades produced a deterioration in the woolen.[70] Although sorting required skill, the obrajes did not promote it. Domínguez complained that preparation of the fleece in the obrajes was deficient and contributed to woolens of poor quality.[71] He recommended that the ranchers sort at shearing, indirect evidence that sorting was a less-practiced art in the obrajes.[72] Once sorted, the dirty wool, known as *lana puerca*, was cleansed in a tepid solution of stale urine (a source of ammonia) and water, then rinsed in cold water to separate from it the "wool fat" (lanolin) and foreign matter that constituted about half the weight.[73]

Dyeing could take place in any stage of manufacture—in the wool, the yarn, the weave, or the cloth—but descriptions of it in New Spain suggest that dyeing in the wool was most common. Because wool does not have an affinity for most dye solutions, it is generally necessary to mordant the wool. The mordant fixes the dye on the wool fibers. With the exception of indigo (*añil*) and cochineal (*grana*), wool was treated with fixatives like alum (*alumbre*) or copperas (*alcaparrosa*) to render it receptive to the dye and to vary its shading. The obrajes made cloths in a host of colors, such as greens (dark, emerald, and lime), and cochineal-based scarlets.[74] Some colors were geographic specialties. Cholula routinely made turquoise, white, black, raisin, and cinnamon brown but created olive, various yellows, and purple only on special order.[75] It was common for the larger obrajes to make dyes from dyestuffs; indigo, cochineal, Campeche, and Brazil woods were frequently found in inventories. Dyeing required large quantities of water and dyestuffs and demanded subtlety, skill, and care—qualities that Domínguez judged largely absent from the obrajes.[76] The entire procedure employed heated, copper-bottomed vats. Standing over a boiling vat and using chemicals such as sulfuric acid or green vitriol made work in an obraje hot, noisome, and dangerous. In addition, large and stable supplies of firewood and alum were necessary to uninterrupted operation; anyone or anything that threatened these could and did become a source of controversy.[77]

Not all wool was dyed, but plain wool could be used only in friezes and ordinary woolens. Once dyed, wool was returned to the inventory as *lana tinta* (dyed wool) to await further work. But all wool, either before dyeing or before use if plain, was "willowed" or beaten with long rods (the verb was *varear* in eighteenth-century Mexico) to untangle the knots and to remove the remaining foreign matter. It was then oiled with tallow (*manteca*) to form long, continuous strips. With short-staple wool, carding would follow in preparation for the manufacture of cloth. Workers used pairs of cards—wire brushes, in reality—to straighten, strip, and align the fibers of the fleece for spinning. Two different types of cards were employed: *cardas de emprimar* produced yarn for finer cloths, and *cardas de emborrar* produced the wool for lesser grades. Proper carding was important, for the evenness of the yarn and the durability of the cloth depended on it.[78] A fleece improperly carded would never yield good yarn, and poor yarn made for inferior woolens. To judge from Domínguez and others, carding never received the training or attention it merited. As a result, the cloth made was inferior.[79]

Not all lana tinta was carded. In particular, there were certain woolens known as new draperies, stuffs, or half-worsteds that combined carded filling, or weft, with a combed warp. What distinguished these from ordinary cloth was the length of the staple, for short-staple wool is carded, whereas the long-staple is combed. The comb differed according to the stuff to be fashioned (i.e., bays, says, serges, and friezes such as *pastora*, *carmelita*, and *camera*), but combing typically used a heated metal comb (*peine*) to separate the long fibers of the fleece. Stuffs, or half-worsteds, had several advantages over "old draperies" made from carded wool, generically called *paño*, or *paño de la tierra*, that is, "country cloth." Worsteds were lighter and cheaper to produce, and final milling, or fulling, was not necessary.[80] These woolens became increasingly popular in Europe in the early seventeenth century and, if terminology is to be trusted, were also made in Mexico at an early date.[81]

In New Spain, paño produced in obrajes such as one located on the hacienda "Gogorrón," in San Luis Potosí, or in another in Tacuba, was tightly woven on broad looms (*telares de ancho*) and was coarse and very heavy, with the felted finish characteristic of woolens that were fulled.[82] Serges (*jerga, jerguetilla*) and says (*sayal*) were also coarse, but were generally lighter and more loosely woven on narrow looms (*telares de angosto*). The diffusion of worsteds was uneven; late in the seventeenth century, most obrajes in the Valley of Mexico were still producing old draperies, particularly 16s (*paño seisceno* or 16no) and 14s (*catorceno* or 14no) that were relatively costly.[83]

A variety of colors, sizes, and styles characterized the worsteds. There were broad and narrow cloths made on looms of different widths (*bayeta angosta* and *ancha*) and different grades and widths of serges. Another measure of the quality of the cloth was the approximate count of hundreds in the warp. Thus, there was *bayeta 14no*, or simply 14s, with 1,400 threads to the warp, 12s, with 1,200 threads to the warp, and many others. The greater the number of threads to the warp, the better the woolen. Thus, the 1633 weaving ordinances of the Marqués de Cerralvo (1624-35) referred to the warp as "what is basic (*lo primero*)."[84]

Carding and combing were followed by spinning, or twisting and drawing the yarn from the web of fibers produced by combing and carding. Combed wool (*iscatel*) and carded wool (*iscapeso*) were spun into different kinds of yarn.[85] Iscatel became closely twisted yarn for the warp; iscapeso was used for looser filling. Some spinning took place in the obraje, since spinning wheels had been introduced. At least some iscatel and iscapeso, however, were put out (*tequio*). The Cerralvo ordinances termed spinning the "principal supply" (*avío*) of the obrajes, and every major center of woolen manufacture had its tequio, in which cottage workers received advances for the task.[86] The corregidor of Coyoacán said that the poor spun all the yarn consumed there in their dwellings. Particular obrajeros confirmed his statement and spoke of "people from outside who enter to get wool to spin, carry it home, and return [the yarn] to be paid."[87] Cottage labor did this as well in San Miguel el Grande. In Querétaro, spinning, other than for the weft, "was done completely outside [the obrajes]."[88] The need for large numbers of spinners—three to four times as many were needed to make yarn as to weave—brought heavy pressure upon the obrajes in times of increased demand.[89] Too few spinners led to a shortage of yarn and brought work to a halt. As one owner said, "[The obrajes] sometimes stop for lack of spinners."[90]

The warp yarn (*pie*) was then wound on the warp beam by a master, sometimes after sizing to strengthen it (*urdimbre*; the entire procedure was called "sizing and beaming"). At the same time, the filling or weft (*trama*) was wound on bobbins (*canillas*) to be placed in the shuttle (*lanzadero*). From this point, the loom allowed the weft to be interlaced with the open warp, producing an unfinished or crude woolen. In the case of broad cloth, the weaver's assistant (*lanzaire*) would help throw the shuttle.

The final stage began with fulling. Fulling, or milling, is a way of tightening or thickening a woolen by cleaning, shrinking, and felting, and thus eliminating its otherwise reedy feel. Although fulling was once done by treading the cloth under foot, mechanized mills were common in New Spain, at least by the late seventeenth century. A turning waterwheel shaft in the mill, studded with projecting knobs or cams, alternately raised and dropped heavy wooden stocks on the cloth—hardly a technique designed to produce fine woolens.[91] Larger, or "complete," obrajes were theoretically required to have attached fulling mills (*batanes*), although some did not, probably due to the expense involved. For such obrajes, access to a fulling mill was important, since crude cloths did not find much of a market. Although access to capital was a prerequisite for a fulling mill, running water was obviously more important and acted as a major influence in the location of the obrajes.[92]

After a woolen had been milled, it was ready for finishing. This was not one but several processes, and each demanded a high level of skill. The nap of the woolen was evened by clipping off the projecting parts of the filling; it was then brushed (*tundido*). The operation could be repeated several times. With hot and cold presses, the woolen was ironed and its finish smoothed yet again. Finally, the cloth was drawn over a board while set in a frame and examined (*perchar*) for the defects, knots, holes, and broken threads that passing through so many hands made inevitable. The final examination was important, since substandard or imperfect goods could be seized by the local *fiel ejecutor*, the municipal official charged with enforcement of standards.

Producing woolens was thus a complicated process, a complexity fraught with implications. Problems of coordinating the supply and quality of inputs were large, and shortages of materials, fuel, labor, or water could bring work to a halt. In the face of constraints upon supply, integration and centralization were effective, if costly, hedges against uncertainty. The inventories of the obraje "Panzacola," for instance, constituted nearly 50 percent of assets; and this figure, not an atypical one, does not reflect the cost of worker indebtedness.[93] Consequently, operating an obraje required substantial capital, more than most individuals could raise. In the face of a rudimentary and inefficient capital market, these requirements shaped the social context of entrepreneurial behavior. Moreover, since the technology was skill-intensive, it left ample grounds for worker sabotage and resistance, particularly when the infliction of pain was employed as an incentive.[94] As a result, the quality of the woolens was poor, just as Domínguez and others attested. And if the necessary skills were unavailable, the owners sought to substitute skilled supervision for unskilled labor. Adequate supplies of woolens for everyday use were therefore available, but through a fragile, complex, and costly system always susceptible to breakdown. The wonder is not that obrajes worked badly, or failed to provide a basis for industrialization, but that they functioned and persisted as long as they did. Obrajes thus responded to and depended upon the peculiarities of colonial markets, a relationship that was both cause and consequence of technological stasis. The words of a nineteenth-century liberal are not unbiased, but José María Luis Mora summarized the issue nicely:

> What progress was there in our factories [?] . . . The colonial system influenced this backwardness [atraso]. . . . Producers who [were] sure of selling their goods and taking a profit without fear of competition regarding quality and price [would] take no interest in improving them. . . . If there are no other producers . . . products will sell, even if they are no good, and [the manufacturer] will profit by them, as if they were good.[95]

Distinct seasonal fluctuations in supply added to problems of coordination, information, and control. Sheep, for example, were generally shorn in March and again in August. Allowing for some lag in transportation, raw wool was most readily available at these times.[96] As a correspondent of the intendant of Guanajuato claimed: "the volume of cloth made in the obrajes is not constant. It depends [not only] on how many spinners and carders there are, but more importantly, upon the supply and price of wool."[97] More evidence was provided by the guild of obraje owners in Querétaro. As it stated, muleteers transported the clipped wool only four months of the year. The remainder of the time they spent hauling the weavings.[98] In other words, important variations characterized the supply of raw wool and transportation. Other factors, particularly labor, reinforced supply constraints. Labor for carding and spinning was particularly important, and carding was slow and laborious. To ready a pound of carded wool for spinning might require a day's labor, so the demand for carders and spinners was necessarily large.[99] In areas where agriculture offered alternative employment to seasonal labor, potential imbalances in supply and demand assumed critical proportions.

In the Bajío, the proximity of a fertile hinterland to the textile industry in Querétaro and elsewhere made the corregidor, Domínguez, remark that perhaps a third of the tributaries from the villages and haciendas moved between the fields, obrajes, and trapiches. During the rainy season, work on the haciendas ceased, and laborers migrated into the city. At sowing and harvest time, they returned to the countryside.[100] In other words, seasonal labor was readily available during the summer, but less so during the spring and late fall. This pattern existed outside the Bajío as well. In 1633, a Tlaxcalan argued that the city's obrajes provided work to the rural people "so that they would not go idle during the dead times in agriculture, and in other occupations that are not continuous."[101] Since water powered the fulling mills and was vital to washing and dyeing, its supply also mattered. A fulling mill could thus operate at capacity for but three months of the year in Michoacán, for example, because of constraints on water supply. Prolonged operation was possible only if water could be diverted from other irrigation purposes.[102]

The evidence presented in Figure 2.3 supports the hypothesis of seasonality. The graph measures monthly entries of cuarterones of paño, or bolts of cloth measuring 33 meters, into the excise district of Mexico City for selected years. These were subject to the so-called "new tax" in the eighteenth century to support the raising of the militia.[103] If the recurring peaks are proxies for increased supply, the months of February-March, June, and September-October-November are times of abundance, allowing for lag between production and delivery. The March peak was a function of the enlarged supply of fleece entering the market with the spring clip. A June peak is also evident, consistent with the hypothesis that production rose over the months of summer. The September-October-November increase is anomalous in terms of supply and may instead reflect the demand from small farmers bringing maize crops to market in the months following the harvest.[104]

The strategy to minimize seasonal fluctuations in supply was sim-

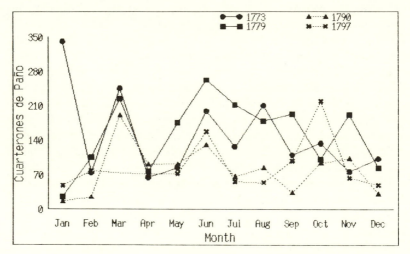

FIGURE 2.3
Entries of Cuarterones of Paño into Mexico City
Selected Years

Source: Yearly account books for the "Nuevo Impuesto de Paños y Pulque," AHINAH.

ilar to holding inventories, but with qualifications. Water, for example, could not be held other than by the construction of a dam, but favorable location could address the constraint. Labor could be held by tolerating underemployment, but this sometimes raised costs beyond recoverable levels. Price elasticity of demand was a crucial consideration here and was determined largely by the availability of substitutes. So the obrajes tried to keep labor readily at hand and to avoid competing for it. But this was difficult, even where the subsistence economy had been thoroughly eroded. The need to compete with agriculture for labor underscores an important issue in industrialization: was it necessary to expropriate the peasantry to create an industrial labor force? In Britain, for example, some think not, since population growth there after 1740 was high, and no labor shortage ensued.[105] In this regard, the record of the obrajes was mixed, but—with a number of qualifications—there was always evidence of labor shortage. Consequently, if obrajes resisted wage labor, it was not for want of rationality or capitalistic ethos. Indeed, obrajes used forced labor *because* of a desire for profit. Under existing conditions of supply, there were few alternatives. The path chosen was costly and inefficient, but the disadvantages could be largely shifted to labor. In the obrajes, to paraphrase Edward Nell, the invisible hand picked the pockets of the poor.

The Obraje: Location

On the whole, the obrajes were concentrated in the Valley of Mexico, the Bajío, and the Puebla-Tlaxcala basin. There were others outside these regions, but they were either few, as in the valley of Toluca, or short-lived, as in Guadalajara after 1780. Confusion over fundamentals has created an impression of obrajes where there were none. Oaxaca is a case in point. There is simply no evidence that obrajes existed there during the period under study.[106] Rather, Oaxaca illustrates the putting-out system in cottons: small masters financed by merchant clothiers, looms maintained in dwellings, and little or no integration of production. In the Bajío, there were obrajes in Querétaro, San Miguel el Grande, Acámbaro, San Juan del Río, and on haciendas such as "La Quemada" and "Puruagua." In the Valley of Mexico, Mexico City, Tacuba, Coyoacán, Popotla, San Cosme, Texcoco, Atzcapotzalco, and Cuautitlán were important. Puebla, Cholula, and Tlaxcala were becoming less significant in the eighteenth century, but there were still obrajes there.

Although models of location are complex, there is no point in pushing modest data too hard. An appropriate location, we might simply say, maximizes access to markets and supply but minimizes transportation costs. So, for example, water influenced location to a disproportionate extent. Water could be transported, but it was costly to do so. Canals, dams, and irrigation ditches could be constructed, but a cheaper alternative was to locate at a river, stream, or canal. So, for instance, a chronicler of Querétaro called it a "well populated city . . . taking water from a common stream that crosses it while watering homes and some obrajes."[107] In San Miguel el Grande, the obraje of Balthasar de Sauto and a local fulling mill were found on an arroyo drawn from a dammed-up stream.[108] In Coyoacán, the obrajes grew up where the waters of the Mixcoac and the Coyoacán streams fell on the way to the Laguna de Xochimilco; the obrajes "Ansaldo" and "Panzacola" were also found there.[109] In Mexico City, an industrial district developed on the southern fringe of the Salto del Agua and along the Calzada de la Piedad, where an aqueduct brought water from Chapultepec, where a canal was situated. The same was true in the barrio of Santa María la Redonda.[110] In Puebla, the obrajes had been established in the eastern part of the city, near the Río de San Francisco.[111]

Other relevant factors of supply were transportation, capital, and labor. Cities such as Querétaro, Mexico City, Puebla, and San Miguel offered the cheapest transportation, given their proximity to major highways.[112] There was some labor migration, but location in or near a population center avoided the costs of financing it.[113] Centers of population were also centers of finance. The rudimentary capital market—the term is nearly an anachronism—was segmented, and the mobility of capital was limited. Cities and towns provided institutions that mobilized the surpluses required to finance obrajes. An urban location also provided external pecuniary economies of scale (not to be confused with production economies). Simply stated, the concentration of business in cities provides firms with supplies at lower cost, due, for example, to economies of scale in transportation or information.

The nature of woolen manufacture itself is equally important from the standpoint of location. Textile manufacturing is a weight-losing or input-oriented process. Since raw wool lost roughly half its weight in manufacture, the obrajes clustered as near to the woolen supply as possible. It was unprofitable to carry the "grease weight" (i.e., unwashed weight) of wool over long distances when half of it would be lost anyway. The concentration of obrajes in the Bajío illustrates the point, close to the colony's ranching centers in Guadalajara and the

Tierra Adentro, and relatively near to markets north and south as well.

On the demand side, the markets of the obrajes were geographically broad. A review of the evidence (drawn from numerous sources) shows that Querétaro's market was quite large, stretching from the colder northern reaches of Saltillo, Parral, Sonora, and New Mexico, to Central America in the south, and from Córdoba in the east, to Guadalajara in the west. Although they were in decline by the late eighteenth century, Puebla's obrajes supplied an area stretching from Guatemala in the south, to Zacatecas and Sonora in the north and to Guadalajara in the west. Acámbaro's obrajes served a regional market, encompassing San Luis Potosí, León, Zamora, and Valladolid. The obrajes of the Valley of Mexico existed to supply the capital. With the exception of some shipments to Guadalajara and to the Tierra Adentro, most product was consumed locally. The contrast with the generally localized distribution of cottons could not be more pronounced.

Perhaps the difference in market areas reflected the higher price of woolens and the strong demand for them throughout the colony.[114] The degree to which some regions paid a premium to obtain woolens provides further evidence. In New Mexico, paño made in Cholula or Querétaro circulated at multiples of four times or more its price in Mexico City in the mid-eighteenth century.[115] This suggests price inelastic demand in a region where substitutes were few, and transportation costs consequently incident more on the buyer than on the seller.[116] On the side of supply, the marketing and distribution of woolens over vast distances and under primitive communications complicated the normal problems of establishing a market, such as finding buyers, providing information on the good, and enforcing agreements on delivery. Doing business under these circumstances required imagination, persistence, hard work, and a great deal of luck.

The Obrajes: Distribution and Uses of Woolens

What was the demand for the woolens of the obrajes? Who used them, and for what purposes? Of common cloth or paño, it was said that "women use them to cover their bodies from the shoulder to the waist; it is because of this that the consumption [of paño] is large . . . [since the garment requires] 2 varas in length and 3/4 in width."[117] In the area of San Miguel el Grande around 1777, the Indians would use the woolen frieze as a blanket when sleeping and as a cloak during the day. "It is usually white, just like the color of the wool," one document explains.[118] Fifty years later the astute (and acerbic) English observer Mark Beaufoy commented similarly on the use of the "universally worn" sarape made in Querétaro. "[It] is usually worn wrapped round the body, hanging down behind as far as the joints of the knees, with one end thrown over the left shoulder, so as to cover the mouth and nose." Castas and peasants used sarapes as blankets and sleeping-mats by night and as protection against the sun during the day. Beaufoy felt sure that the garment grew filthy this way and contributed much to outbreaks of disease. But the area around Tlalpujahua where he lived was 2,600 meters above sea level and very cold at night. Warm clothing was therefore a necessity.[119] The jurist Juan de Solórzano agreed that the obrajes produced woolens "suited for warm outerwear," and it was the need for warm clothing in the cold northern climate that explains the popularity of woolens produced in Querétaro, Puebla, and Texcoco in the mining camps of the Parral district.[120] The same was true of woolens from San Miguel el Grande marketed in the mining district of Guadalcázar.[121] As one informant put it in 1690, "the country people, Spaniards, Indians, and others on the haciendas and in the mines dress in the cloth made in the obrajes."[122] The demand for woolens from the northern frontier is easily explained.

Rural estates were another market, and hacendados were wont to provide woolen cloth as blankets to tenants, sharecroppers, and laborers, or for use as horse blankets, sacks, packing material, and covers.[123] Some erected obrajes to save transportation costs and to reduce cash expenditures. This was the case with the hacienda "Santa Ana Pacueco," near Pénjamo, in León. Owned by the Sánchez de Tagle family, "Santa Ana" was populated by a resident labor force of a hundred mixed bloods and a number of peasants. In 1791, the hacienda operated an obraje with six looms and thirty-three spinning wheels for making cloths, bays, says, friezes, and serges for the peons.[124] Had the woolens not been made at "Santa Ana," they would have been purchased in Querétaro, Mexico City, or Acámbaro. What cost 7 or 8 reales to make at "Santa Ana Pacueco" could, in this way, be priced at 16 or 18, providing an "economy . . . that increased the level of indebtedness [of the labor force]." Had woolens been purchased, freight and commission would have "increas[ed] the cost and reduc[ed] the profit."[125]

Another example is provided by doña Rosalía Gómez de Acosta, widow and sole heiress of don Franciso Antonio Lanzagorta, scion of a wealthy and well-connected *sanmigueleño* family.[126] She inherited two haciendas from her husband, one in the jurisdiction of San Miguel, and the other in Cuencamé, in New Galicia. Together, they employed more than 600 laborers. Doña Rosalía wanted an obraje to produce woolens for the haciendas, especially in view of the savings in transportation costs to and from Querétaro. There were other haciendas and ranchos around the Bajío—in León, Pénjamo, Piedragorda, and in Rincón—that operated looms for similar purposes.[127] An analogous pattern characterized the Jesuit estate, "Santa Lucía." Here, the obraje produced woolens distributed to the employees of the hacienda to minimize cash expenditures or sold commercially to augment income.[128] It is impossible even to guess the volume of production of estate-based obrajes, but their rationale was consistent with the argument here. It was less costly to produce woolens than to purchase them, or to integrate and diversify rather than specialize. The division of labor was limited by the extent and efficiency of the market.

Coarse woolens had other uses in both city and countryside. As Miguel Páez de la Cadena, long the director of the royal Excise, put it, the bays produced by the obrajes were "most common and usual among the poor."[129] Another observer repeated that "the Kingdom and the poor, such as Indians, mestizos, Spaniards, and others are clothed . . . [with] the common cloth, *palmilla* [made in the obrajes]."[130] Members of religious orders also used woolens from the obrajes. In Mexico City, one found "brown and white says for friars from which are woven habits for some of the religions [*sic*] of this Kingdom." The Franciscan Order in New Spain employed just such plain-woven yardage, "natural untreated, undyed, mixed white and black wool, [and] overall grey in color."[131] Coarse woolens were also distributed as slop cloth to black slaves not only in Mexico—on a plantation in Veracruz, probably for winter use when the cold, wet northers sweep down—but in Cuba, where woolens clothed the slaves during the winter months. Says were common material in slaves' clothing and represented significant demand, particularly in the seventeenth century, when Mexico's slave population was large.[132]

There were various ways in which the products of the obraje could be distributed to satisfy urban demand. Merchants, of course, were frequently involved. For example, a one-time prior of the *consulado* of Mexico City, don Diego García Castro, testified that "although he had not been the owner of an obraje, there was a period in which [he sold their cloth] and acted as an *aviador* to two obrajes in [Mexico

City]."[133] Captain Pedro Albarrán Carrillo, the *obligado de abasto de carne* for Mexico City in 1690, "received for a period of 5 or 6 years, the cloths that don Luis Alvarez wove in the obraje he had in Atzcapotzalco."[134] Certain merchants in Mexico City acted as major distributors for *paño de la tierra*, the term for country or coarse woolens. In the early eighteenth century, don Matías de Velasco, don Francisco Paulín, don Miguel Fernández, and don Martín del Castillo were such merchants. Velasco, for example, was the owner of a specialty store that stocked cloth (*tienda de paños*) in the Portal de las Flores in Mexico City. Many obrajes had cloth stores attached; for others, the distribution of product involved the exchange of working capital for cloth. These activities are considered subsequently, so there is no need to detail them here.

Military use of cloth presented a special market. Once military reorganization and expansion was undertaken in the later eighteenth century, the obrajes became intimately involved in military supply and remained so into the early nineteenth century. The contract held by Juan José Pérez Cano, a one-time prior of the consulado of Mexico City, provides an interesting example. By degrees, Pérez Cano was first a captain in the Urban Commercial Regiment of Mexico City, later a colonel.[135] He owned an old obraje with twenty looms on the hacienda "Puruagua," outside Salvatierra, and used his connections to advantage. The woolens he made were sold to the military; some ended up in the *presidio de Nuestra Señora del Carmen*, in Mérida, on the Yucatán peninsula. His *paño azul* was used in capes, dress coats, and breeches, whereas his *paño encarnado*, dyed in cochineal, ended up in the dragoons' uniforms.[136] The same woolens were used for the uniforms of the Provincial Dragoons of Puebla.[137] One wonders about the success of woolens in the climate of Yucatán; some professional soldiers voiced unhappiness about their use in a tropical environment. In 1797, for instance, the subinspector general of the Battalion of Pardos and Morenos on the island of Cuba rejected importing paño from New Spain for use there.[138] "What is made in the Kingdom of New Spain is not paño," he complained, "but very heavy, very ugly *bayetón* that could not be used in this climate." Moreover, "the scarlet cloth made there is in no way suitable for the uniforms of the Blacks." Military regulations stipulated that uniforms were to last from four to eight years, and that the cloth was to be of the highest quality. This could not be expected of paño from New Spain. Nevertheless, military contracts sheltered some obrajes from competition, permitted them to raise prices above competitive levels, and prevented a worse collapse of the industry than did occur in the years following independence.[139]

CONCLUSIONS: THE MARKET PROBLEM ONCE AGAIN

Historically, markets are not given as free goods. They are created at considerable social, political, and economic cost.[140] The existence of the obraje underscores this notion because it absorbed the functions of the colonial market, but it did so at considerable cost. Demand was not the problem. Coarse woolens were suited to numerous urban and country uses in a highland climate, and commercial needs were supplemented by tradeable goods such as cottons produced in the villages. But supply, particularly the supply of labor, was a problem. The obraje integrated manufacture; assumed the supply function of thin, imperfect markets; and forced a solution to commercial production under constraint.

The solution was itself fragile, costly, easily subject to disruption, and often contingent upon marginal devices for acquiring labor. Substantial requirements of capital and political power became basic to the obraje's management and labor supply, the consequence of the imposed solution to the market problem. And to the extent that the system drove labor costs below competitive levels, the incentive for technological improvement was lost. The potential for productivity increase was small, a weakness whose implications were realized only when competition from imports and cheaper domestic cottons appeared late in the colonial period.

Nevertheless, the obrajes enjoyed success in measure. They supplied a wide geographic market within New Spain and exported additional quantities to Central America, Venezuela, and Peru, where the prohibition of intercolonial trade had a major impact.[141] In other words, they contributed to the functioning of a settlement economy, their lack of flexibility notwithstanding. But an inefficient system could not meet total demand, a proposition demonstrated by the market for contraband. The obrajes were not an optimum solution, but they were the best the economy could offer.

At a higher level of generality, we offer two further suggestions. First; the obrajes did not represent protoindustry, much less protofactories. Indeed, virtually any notion of industrialization in Mexico prior to the opening of the railroads is anachronistic, considering the resource immobility that existed. One perhaps resurrects the "axiom of indispensability" for Mexican railroads, but John Coatsworth offers evidence of their important social savings, a very large proportion of total product that implies how costly substitutes for them would have been.[142] The railroads permitted the exploitation and transportation of coal and the internal movement of producers' goods that made modern industrialization possible after 1880.[143] Without railroads, Mexico's cotton factories remained wedded to water power and subject to equipment bottlenecks of the worst sort.[144] Supply and demand are fungible in theory, but the Mexican case appears far less tractable, as Coatsworth clearly suggests. Second, if not a missing link in the chain of development—economists instinctively deny lack of substitutability—the obrajes were nevertheless important. Given the composition of colonial demand, their supply function is self-evident, just as Adam Smith's words at the beginning of this book indicate. Moreover, the obrajes illustrate the uneven nature of market development in New Spain and its implications for the economy as a whole. One implication was in the coordination and control of a complex enterprise, for individuals and families necessarily substituted markets for risk, finance, and information. The other was in the cost to labor of a system that reduced the competitive market for its services. These are the subjects of the next two chapters.

THREE

"Little Wealth
and Considerable Debts"

Introduction: The Business of the Obraje

As businesses that operated under a series of market constraints, obrajes faced three related problems. One, common to all enterprise, dealt with daily operations, accounting, finance, and routine supply. The second was peculiar to the obraje, a consequence of the need to recruit and to retain labor outside well-organized markets, frequently at variance with colonial law practiced in New Spain. This need drew the obrajes into close contact with civil officials, particularly the judiciary, and raised difficult questions of power and influence. The third dealt with the coordination of technically complex enterprise under conditions of uncertainty. It required the creation and adaptation of new institutions to manage strategic problems of raw materials, working capital, and distribution. But despite the complex nature of its operations, the obraje nevertheless functioned in an environment in which limited liability, well-developed capital markets, and the smooth exchange of information did not exist. Its managerial hierarchy remained relatively limited, despite the pressing need for supervision and technical expertise, and it was constrained by limitations on fixed costs that limited productive capacity implied. The pattern that emerged was a hybrid. Some features were common to all colonial businesses, and others were peculiar to the obraje itself. But to see the colonial economy through the obraje is to understand some of the economy's most relevant and determining features.

Another series of questions, more prosaic but equally important, needs to be answered. Who were the participants—the principals and agents of the business? From what classes were they recruited? How did they come to enter the trade, and why? How did they accumulate capital, and what were the sources of reinvestible earnings? What criteria were used in making business decisions, and what separated the successful from the unsuccessful? What was the organization of the industry, and how did one learn its inner workings? Were the actors rational, maximizing agents? Were habits of savings and investment, the necessary basis of economic development, present to a significant degree, and how were they fostered and transmitted? What, in short, was the culture of the textile business?

THE GREMIO DE OBRAJERÍA

The obrajes were organized within ostensibly self-regulating guilds and were subject to the laws imposed by the Hapsburg and Bourbon states. The guild had different titles in various places. In Puebla, it was called the *Gremio y Arte de Tejidos de Lana*; in Querétaro, the *Gremio de Obrajería*; *Gremio de Obrajeros* in Acámbaro; and the *Arte y Gremio de Fabricar Paños*, or simply *Gremio de Obrajeros* in Mexico City.[1] Not every center of woolen production was similarly organized. There is no evidence that San Miguel el Grande ever had a guild, perhaps a cause or consequence of the obvious instability of its entrepreneurial community. Wherever the guilds had been established, however, they exercised analogous functions.

One role of the guilds was to maintain the standards of production for cloths and stuffs established in two separate but related ordinances. The first was promulgated in 1592 by the *cabildo* of Mexico City to regulate the manufacture of says and serges. The second was drawn up by the producers in Puebla in 1676, and modified by the guild in Mexico, by request of the viceroy's *fiscal*, don Martín de Solís Miranda.[2] Both ordinances had wider geographic relevance and clearly remained in force as late as the eighteenth century. Thus, in 1728, when the owner of an obraje in Coyoacán desired a summary of ordinances dealing with the manufactories and fulling mills, he was directed to the ordinances of 1592 and 1676.[3]

In the case of Mexico City, at least, there is evidence that the guild's inspectors, or *veedores*, did perform the duties with which they were entrusted: the overseeing and certification of the quality of cloths and stuffs. A list of some sixty "causas contra obrajeros" in the records of the fiel ejecutor reveals seizures of cloths and bays for substandard, inferior, or uninspected work.[4] As late as 1748, there was a general seizure of bays made in the obrajes of Mexico City for substandard work.[5] But the inspectors themselves had no power to conduct independent searches of the manufactories. Jurisdiction was explicitly given to the corregidor or *alcalde mayor*, and not even a municipal councilman (*regidor*) was expected to usurp this authority.[6] In practice, the inspectors of the guild cooperated with the colonial magistracy in the performance of their duties.[7]

Of more direct interest was the responsibility of the guild to control access to the skills of making woolens by licensing masters and to limit the competition that unregulated producers might pose. The ordinances of 1676 provided that no one should operate looms without examination and licensing by the guilds, and that the freedom to put out manta, bays, and such was limited to masters licensed by the guilds. The purpose was to restrict the unchecked competition of both domestic industry and itinerant merchants.[8] From a strictly economic viewpoint, the need to restrict entry into the field was the most important function of the guild.

Historically, craft guilds in Europe found their statutes difficult to enforce; those in Mexico fared no better.[9] In 1738, two masters of the Gremio de Obrajeros of Mexico City, who acted as inspectors and examiners of broadcloth, complained of the neglect and slighting attention given to the ordinances governing their profession, particularly titles 13 through 17 of the *Nueva Recopilación de Castilla*, prepared in the time of Philip II.[10] Things had reached the point that examined masters went unemployed because unlicensed and unexamined journeymen maintained looms in their residences, or simply operated an unlicensed obrador in disregard of the laws and ordinances. The masters desired nothing less than the authorization to close obradores operating without the direction of an examined master, and without proper licensing. By 1750, the guild was obliged to request a *bando*, or viceregal proclamation, ordering the city's merchants, manufacturers, and commission agents to bring in their woolens for official inspection, since the market had been flooded with uninspected goods.[11]

The inability of the guild in Mexico City to require that the owners of obrajes be *maestros examinados* was chronic and revealing. A list of obrajes and their owners dating from 1719 provides significant information. The table does not include manufactories in the surrounding towns of Coyoacán, Mixcoac, and Tacuba, even though these were in theory subject to the gremio in Mexico City.

Of the owners who can be positively identified, three, at most, were certified masters; the number rises to five if the "uncertain" are taken to be masters. Fewer than half the obrajes within the capital proper circa 1720 had owners whose technical skills and qualifications were certified by the guild. But the guild could not afford to be selective about its membership and permitted those who were not clothiers to join "because they had always wanted to be members."[12]

TABLE 3.1
Masters and Obrajes in Mexico City, ca. 1720

Owner	Location	Master
don Francisco de la Peña	Barrio de San Juan de la Penitencia	?
don Jacinto Romeo	Barrio de Santa María la Redonda	?
don José de la Vega	Barrio de la Santa Cruz	Yes
don José de Collado	Barrio de San Diego, Portillo del Convento de San Diego	No
don Juan de Alva	Barrio de San Lázaro, Puente de San Lázaro	Yes
Juan de Ávila	Plazuela del Hornillo	Yes
don Nícolas García de la Mora	Calzada de la Piedad	No
don Juan Bueno	?	No
don Pedro Antonio de Cervantes	?	No
don José de Escorza	?	No
"Fulano" Velázquez	?	No
Vda. de Bartolomé de Ávila	?	No
Vda. de don José Cansinos	?	No

Source: Petition of don Juan Martínez de Lejarzar y Anieto [n.d., n.p.], and notification of owners of obrajes, México, Mar. 6, 1719, AGI, Escribanía de Cámara 196-A.

By 1757, it was impossible to hold elections for the post of inspector of the guild "since there [were] no masters to vote."[13] At that date, of the thirteen obrajes operating in Mexico City, Tacuba, and Coyoacán, only four had owners who were certified masters.

The data presented in Tables 3.1 and 3.2 suggest several hypotheses about the owners of obrajes in Mexico City and its environs. Those who could purchase obrajes in the eighteenth century were not masters per se; they were investors who had accumulated capital in other pursuits and held interest in an obraje as part of a larger portfolio. They would rely on managers skilled in the craft for day-to-day operation of the manufactory; they acquired their serv-

TABLE 3.2
Masters and Obrajes in the Valley of Mexico, 1757

Owner	Location	Master
don Antonio Traspuesto	Calzada de la Piedad	No
don Pascual de Alos y Vidal (2 obrajes)	Calzada de la Piedad	1 only
don Francisco Carrillo	Portillo de San Diego	No
don Nícolas de la Mora	El Placerito (?)	No
don Manuel de Herrera	Puente de Peredo	Yes
don Manuel de Candía	Mixcoac	No
don Francisco de Ortega	Mixcoac	No
don Francisco Paulín	Coyoacán	No
? Medina	Coyoacán	No
don Balthasar de Soto	Coyoacán	No
don José Canales	Tacuba	Yes
don Juan Fernández de Pallares	?	Yes

Source: "Memoria de los obrajes que hay en esta ciudad" [México 1757], AGI, México 1809.

ices through partnership or hire. Does this imply that, on the whole, skilled personnel such as managers and foremen could not accumulate sufficient capital to enter the ranks of ownership, and that they enjoyed only limited upward mobility? Did a relatively rigid pattern of social stratification and an unequal distribution of wealth produce separation in ownership, management, and direction, leading to the formation of a "professional" group of managers who lived primarily through the exercise of these skills? The ordinary contractual stipulations of the hire suggest that capital was relatively scarcer than managerial or technical expertise, for payment to the skilled partner of an agreement generally did not exceed a third of the profits. Did this signify the inability of skilled managers to bid up the premium on their skills during the eighteenth century? We shall consider these issues shortly.

The guilds were not entirely ineffective. One subject guaranteed to provoke a reaction among the owners of the obrajes in any city was the excise tax. From Acámbaro, the excise officer wrote that the

Gremio de Obrajeros exercised "resistance . . . to paying what had been charged them."[14] From 1777 to 1785, the guild there fought a pitched battle with the Royal Excise and its officers over the rate of the tax to be charged on woolens made and sold within the limits of the excise district.[15] The ceaseless complaining of the guild and the legal actions it undertook before the Audiencia forced the Royal Excise to modify its demands to a charge of 2 percent instead of its original goal of 6 percent.[16] Much the same occurred in Querétaro, where the guild raised "cries of imminent ruin to the very skies" about a proposed 2-percent increase in the rate of excise in 1780.[17] The tax on finished woolens remained a dead letter due to the effective opposition of the guild and its success in influencing the excise officer there. As late as 1791, this official, Pedro Russi, submitted that the finished woolens made in the manufactories paid nothing when sold in the same excise district as their manufacture, not because they were exempt but because "this point [was] still pending."[18]

If the guilds failed in the traditional role of licensing and limitation of entry, they did function as effective vehicles for some types of concerted action. They had become local trade associations and exercised significant legal and economic pressure when sensitive fiscal issues were raised. It is evident that competitive pressures divided the obrajes on issues of competition and quality—output and cost in an economic sense—and limited the effectiveness of the guilds in these areas. But in dealing with matters of mutual concern, such as the level of tax to be paid, collaboration proved more attractive. It is difficult to say how effective collusion among the associations' members was in restraining competition for labor. Cartels are inherently unstable because their members have incentives to cheat, and the evidence is a decidedly mixed record in this regard. On the other hand, wages in the obrajes remained low—an indication of greater effectiveness in restraining competition for labor than the producers themselves admitted. There was a clear tension between competition and cooperation in colonial business practice, a tension embedded in its structural and institutional limitations. It was palpable in manufacturing and in estate agriculture as well.[19]

BUSINESSMEN AND OBRAJES IN THE VALLEY OF MEXICO: MEXICO CITY

In economic history, collective biography and the study of career patterns are risky. They rest on the assumption that the dimensions of entrepreneurial development can be understood through common patterns of action. But that is tantamount to claiming that behavior on the average, rather than behavior at the margin, matters—a proposition few economists would accept. The strongest justification for the approach is that it coaxes most from the data available. And if the individuals under scrutiny are not representative, one nevertheless hopes that their circumstances are. What follows, then, is a series of biographies selected for their analytical or descriptive content. They support the interpretation presented, but how "typical" they are—or even if it is desirable for them to be "typical"—is another matter altogether.

José Pimentel

José Pimentel was probably a licensed master who came to own an obraje; his career is documented rather fully. The earliest notice of him that exists dates to the 1730s. One don Francisco Salazar claimed in 1746 to have known him for fourteen or fifteen years, serving as his *mayordomo,* or foreman, in the obraje "La Concepción," and in one owned by don Roque Andonegui, in Tacuba.[20] Salazar's memory was accurate. In 1734, Pimentel formed a company with Andonegui, who owned the obraje, and who supplied 37,000 pesos in cash, wool, and indigo. For a period of four years, Pimentel was to be *administrador,* or manager, and to provide his "personal attendance, care, and labor" in return for a third of the profits. Moreover, Pimentel was to "eat, drink, dress" and "be shod" from his share of the profits, and to be liable for a third of the losses as well.[21] After about three years, Pimentel's gross share of the profits was 6,728 pesos, or 3,291 pesos net of expenses. In other words, Andonegui's obraje earned 20,000 pesos or so in three years, and his manager drew down about 3 pesos per day for expenses.[22]

In 1738, almost as soon as his contract with Andonegui lapsed, Pimentel was able to purchase an obraje.[23] The manufactory belonged to Nicolas García de la Mora and was located at the base of the Calzada de la Piedad, just below the Salto del Agua bridge. The obraje was an old one, dating to the 1590s.[24] When Pimentel acquired it, he agreed to assume payments on a principal of 9,200 pesos secured by the property (including a bakery that was part of the parcel) assessed at 15,433 pesos.[25] These obligations included a *censo* of 1,200 pesos to the Metropolitan Cathedral and to the religious Sisters of the Conception through their convent of Nuestra Señora de Regina Coeli in Mexico City.[26] The same order had made a *depósito irreg-*

ular, nominally of three years' term, for 5,000 pesos to Nícolas García de la Mora "for the increase of his business" in 1735 through their convent of San José de Gracia, also in Mexico City.[27] Finally, Pimentel also agreed to recognize a debt of 3,000 pesos that the widow of García de la Mora had received from the funds of a *capellanía*, or chaplaincy, toward "the credit and development of the textile manufactory that was left in the goods of my husband" in the form of a *censo redimible* at 5 percent.[28] Given the putative distinction between lien and loan in ecclesiastical finance that Arnold Bauer has raised, the phraseology of the obligations is unmistakable. A loan had been made in both instances.[29]

The significance of pious funds was overshadowed by private sources of capital. In 1738, Pimentel formed still another company, this time with an investor, Licenciado Juan de Brisas y Silva, who was a *compadre* of Pimentel's. Brisas joined heavily in the project, providing about 31,000 pesos in looms, equipment, cloth, slaves, cash, and fleece. Within seven years, Pimentel had managed to amortize almost a third of the sum, evidence of modest success.[30]

Finance is crucial to any business, and the limitations of New Spain's economy made it particularly difficult for the obrajes. No capital market existed in the modern sense. The money market, or the aggregate of traders who lent or borrowed money, was also limited, and there was no equity finance. Given that the direct or variable costs of operating Pimentel's obraje were about 500 pesos per week, credit was absolutely necessary.[31] Pimentel borrowed accordingly. From a municipal councilman of Mexico City, don Cayetano de Medina, Pimentel purchased fleece and accumulated a debt of over 8,000 pesos.[32] When he sent his woolens to be fulled, Pimentel amassed a small debt to María Teresa Montes de Oca, in 1738 the holder of the obraje "Ansaldo" in Coyoacán.[33] He also borrowed from Juan de Ortega, a master of the guild, who had dealings with Pimentel for ten years and who sold his cloth. "What usually happened," said Ortega, "was that Pimentel did not have sufficient cash for expenses and supplies of the obraje." So Ortega provided for these expenses, and Pimentel financed his borrowings by reimbursing Ortega in cloth.[34] Pimentel also had one, and possibly two, *aviadores refaccionarios*, or financiers who provided working capital for the obraje. One of these, Francisco Macario Vetancourt, was a major cloth jobber (*fundidor de paños*) and merchant in Mexico City who maintained financial connections with a certain number of owners.[35] He said, "I am, and for many years have been, aviador refaccionario for the obraje belonging to Pimentel, in return for which he sends me a part of the cloth made in the obraje, which usually amounts to a great deal."[36] Vetancourt supplied cash on a weekly basis, and Pimentel used the cash to pay for raw wool, food, and wages.[37] Pimentel's ability to service his debts in cash was almost completely dependent upon the liquidity of his aviadores, whose status was sometimes of more interest to creditors than was Pimentel's.[38] Private resources provided working capital on a short-term basis. Pious funds, on the other hand, offered long-term borrowing for capital improvements collateralized on the obraje itself.[39] Eric Van Young has suggested a similar distinction for estate agriculture, and the difference may have appeared in other parts of the economy as well.[40]

The absence of a capital market and the incipient but incomplete specialization of the market economy necessarily produced a wide-ranging network of comparable business contacts. The obraje "Ansaldo" relied upon Pimentel for its woolen yarn.[41] Pimentel acted as a broker for other owners and purchased wool from many sources, including the governor of the Marquesado del Valle, reselling it to owners such as Juan de Ortega and José Negrete. Producers were driven together by the demands of business and the constraints of the market, even as competitive pressures pushed them apart.

When in 1743 José Pimentel married doña Bernarda Varela, he received a dowry of 6,280 pesos in cash and goods and made a gift to her of 4,000 pesos before marriage, so Pimentel was hardly a poor man.[42] He owned a small hacienda in Huichapa worth 7,000 pesos, which he was later forced to sell.[43] But Pimentel's resources were not sufficient to prevent him from going broke in 1745, when the heirs of Brisas, his compadre and erstwhile partner, obtained a judgment of 21,000 pesos against the obraje. Misfortune followed upon misfortune. Pimentel was sued as the *fiador*, or guarantor, of two associates who failed to pay their debts, and he suffered the further indignity of being tossed into prison—if only briefly—in 1746.[44] Pimentel's problem was common among producers of textiles. He was illiquid rather than insolvent and could not produce sufficient funds to meet the demands upon him. The remedy was to borrow against future income, but this Pimentel could not do. To avoid further contretemps, Pimentel simply disappeared from Mexico City, and the obraje went into receivership. Sometime between 1750 and 1753, the court-appointed receiver, Cayetano López, purchased the manufactory but fared little better. By 1755, he had also fallen into debt for 9,000 pesos of wool and was petitioning the Audiencia for a stay.[45] He did not get it and was forced to seek refuge in the Monastery of San Francisco as a debtor to the Royal Treasury.[46] The continuing turmoil had done the obraje no good. Between 1746 and 1749, when it was in receivership, the obraje's sales in bays and cloth averaged 28,000 pesos a year.[47] A later inventory reported "11 looms and 12 spinning wheels, very old, and without rods," and the labor force had dwindled from 200 in 1750 to forty two within five years.[48] The situation had grown so bad that the Convent of San José de Gracia apparently foreclosed, even though the property could not have been worth much more than 5,000 pesos.[49]

In the interim, Pimentel again surfaced, first as manager of another obraje in Mexico City, then as partner in operating the obraje "El Placer" in Mixcoac.[50] Initially, Pascual de Alos y Vidal rented the obraje from Antonia de Echendía. When Pimentel joined Alos y Vidal, he brought wool and yarn with him from the obraje of García, and for about two years, the men worked closely together. But Alos y Vidal grew unhappy with the arrangement, and Pimentel tried to take over "El Placer" from him, with what result one cannot say.[51] Pimentel did well enough to acquire yet another obraje on the Calzada de la Piedad but lost it to Alos y Vidal, raising questions about the financial relationship between the two. After this, Pimentel appears once more as manager of the obraje "La Concepción"—ironically enough, the place where his career began.[52] There is nothing more until his death in 1776, when Pimentel lived in the Hospital of the Tertiaries of San Francisco, where he was buried on December 30.[53] Thus the career of José Pimentel: manager, owner, debtor, manager, and owner once again. He experienced considerable upward and downward mobility and displayed a wide range of personal, professional, and financial interests. His success was closely tied to his ability to raise capital, and his failures were almost always the consequence of illiquidity. How representative was he?

José Antonio Negrete

Don José Antonio Negrete lived somewhat earlier than José Pimentel. His early career is obscure, but his marriage brought some prosperity. As executor of his wife's estate, he was entrusted with 13,000 pesos she had designated for the care of an illegitimate child that Negrete fathered in Otumba.[54] Negrete owned or operated several obrajes, such as "El Batancito" and "De los Altos," both in San Angel. He rented another from the Society of Jesus for 700 pesos per year that was located in the Salto del Agua district. In this obraje, known as "Peredo," after its founder, Negrete invested 19,000 pesos in cloth, wool, dyestuffs, and equipment, with an additional 4,500 pesos in laborers' debts as receivable.[55]

Negrete had few large debts to speak of, in contrast to José Pimentel. Negrete's contacts were common to the textile business. He distributed his cloth through shopkeepers such as Lorenzo de Guzmán, a *cajonero* on the Plaza Mayor who specialized in domestic and imported cloths.[56] He borrowed money from the owner of another obraje, Manuel de Herrera Puente (who succeeded Negrete in operating "Peredo") to buy wool.[57] Of greater interest were his dealings with managers and foremen such as don Juan de Bocarrando, an Andalusian from the Puerto de Santa María.[58]

Bocarrando is an example of the ubiquitous group of foremen and managers whose role in supervising and operating the obrajes on a daily basis was crucial. Negrete was not a clothier, properly speaking, and he needed a manager with technical skills to run his investment. Negrete had several before Bocarrando, none of whom gave him any trouble. Bocarrando was different.

Although Bocarrando claimed that he and Negrete had formed a company in which Bocarrando was to receive a third of the profits, this was not equally clear to Negrete. His attorneys argued that Bocarrando was nothing more than a salaried employee, who on a whim had backed out of an arrangement for sharing profits.[59] There were other tensions, for Bocarrando owned his own "obraje"—a trapiche, really—and refused to eat or sleep at "Peredo," where he was first a foreman, then a manager, because he spent most of his time working at his own business.[60] The obraje was located in Bocarrando's dwelling—"within my residence, with people, looms, and the rest"—and he tried to be there as long as possible. Bocarrando's only capital was time and skill, for his three marriages never brought him much money. His ambitions brought him into collision with Negrete.

Despite such conflicts, Negrete's interests were never severely prejudiced. Just before his death, he purchased an hacienda in the jurisdiction of Actopan, and after he died in 1746, his net worth was found to be over 21,000 pesos. This made Negrete neither fabulously rich nor obviously destitute.[61] None of the calamities that visited José Pimentel ever befell Negrete, but his status as an investor made him particularly dependent upon a manager who harbored ambitions of his own.

Juan José Sánchez de Gama

Thus far, these sketches might suggest that none of the textile manufactories in Mexico City was particularly profitable. The problem is as follows. Troubled businesses are overrepresented in litigation, and litigation is the source of most evidence presented here. As a result, the picture of profitability is distorted. But there were some profitable obrajes.

In 1738, Santiago del Arenal y Celis formed a partnership to operate his obraje with a compadre, Juan José Sánchez de Gama.[62] Arenal and Sánchez de Gama each contributed 3,000 pesos, and agreed to divide the profits equally. In twelve years, the company produced 34,000 pesos profit which (under simplifying assumptions) implies a return of between 23 percent and 24 percent to each investor.[63] The capital accumulated was reinvested in the business. In 1751, after Sánchez de Gama died, his widow brought suit against Arenal for the 11,000 pesos owed her husband, who had previously withdrawn 6,000 pesos.[64] Here, again, the regular orders played a role in financing the business, for between 1738 and 1745, Arenal was able to borrow 10,000 pesos in *depósito irregular* from the Agustinian Hospicio de Misioneros de Santo Tomás de Villanova.[65]

Arenal also made money as a middleman. In 1747, he had been empowered to act as an agent for the *poblano* owner of an obraje, Juan Pérez Cota y Madera, in purchasing wool.[66] Arenal, in turn, dealt with Juan de Castañiza, a merchant of Mexico City associated with the Bassoco group, who sold wool as an agent for Antonio Lanzagorta of San Miguel el Grande, while purchasing cloth and bays for distribution from Pérez Cota.[67] Arenal, in other words, was not simply the owner of an obraje but a middleman in the sales of cloth and wool between Puebla, Mexico City, and San Miguel.

The Alvarez-Pozo-Romeo Group

Both Alfonso del Pozo and Gregorio del Pozo were licensed as masters of cloth-making.[68] When Gregorio del Pozo died, his son-in-law, Jacinto Romeo, took over the obraje located in the barrio of Santa María la Redonda. Romeo was in constant trouble; he sought to avoid taxes in general and the great *composición de obrajes* in 1690 in particular. Although not disinterested, the testimony of one of Romeo's associates rings true: "Romeo has been caught short. He has little wealth and considerable debts. He gets the wool he uses on credit, and pays for it in installments. It is well known that the cloth he makes . . . has little value or esteem because it is so cheap. He barely covers his costs."[69] Romeo died before 1719, and when he died, his wife, Úrsula del Pozo, took over. She probably inherited the obraje from her father to begin with and owned several *haciendas de labor* that provided collateral for other loans.[70] Lucas García, a merchant in Mexico City, acted as aviador to the obraje and dis-

FIGURE 3.1

The Alvarez-Pozo-Romeo Network in Mexico City

Sources: Memorial of Miguel de Blancas Belén, México, Apr. 28, 1690, AGNM, Civil, vol. 1435, exp. 1; testament of Úrsula del Pozo, México, Feb, 15, 1716, AGNM, Civil, vol. 223; petition of Bartolomé de Angulo, México, Dec. 23, 1720, AGNM, Civil, vol. 234, exp. 1; obligation signed by Sebastián and Bachiller Antonio Alvarez, AGNM,Tierras, vol. 260, exp. 1; and judgment of the Audiencia in the concurso de acreedores of Sebastián Alvarez at his death, AGNM, Tierras, vol. 261, exp. 1.

tributor of its cloth; another merchant, Domingo Alvares, also traded in its bays, cheap woolen palmilla, and cloths. But Úrsula del Pozo died soon after taking over the manufactory, and her son, Jacinto Romeo, purchased the property at auction for 2,100 pesos.[71]

Jacinto Romeo fell into an established pattern. He borrowed from a brother-in-law, the merchant Bartolomé de Angulo, to finance purchases of wool and indigo. As Angulo became aviador to the obraje, Romeo obtained cash from him too. The business limped along. Only five looms were in operation, and Romeo ran up a debt of 3,000 pesos as he went bankrupt.[72] Angulo tried to obtain the obraje and the Romeo family haciendas de labor, bidding 25,000 pesos for them in 1722.[73] But he failed, for the obraje was ultimately acquired by don Vicente Rebequi (nee Vincent Rebecq), a Parisian who was personal physician to Viceroy Linares—delicious irony— the great opponent of the obrajes.[74]

The Pozo-Romeo group was linked to yet another owner, Sebastián Alvarez. Alvarez's second marriage to María del Pozo made him Jacinto Romeo senior's brother-in-law, who was like him, another small creole businessman in the trade.[75] The familial connection was reinforced by credit. Jacinto Romeo, senior, borrowed 570 pesos against the dowry of María del Pozo when she married Sebastián.[76]

Sebastián Alvarez also dealt with the circle of textile producers in Mexico City and its environs, sending his cloth to Balthasar de Sierra to be fulled, even as Sierra owned an obraje of his own.[77] Alvarez purchased wool from Rafael Rico de Solís, a merchant in the city who acted on the account of Fernando de la Campa, a stockman in Zacatecas, and borrowed from Santiago González de Cubillas, a merchant trading in Antequera.[78] In the later years of the seventeenth century, Alvarez's net worth approached 17,000 pesos.[79]

BUSINESS AND BUSINESSMEN
IN THE VALLEY OF MEXICO: COYOACÁN

The Obraje "Ansaldo"

Coyoacán was a textile town and had been one since the first half of the seventeenth century.[80] There were several famous, not to say notorious, obrajes there. Two of the better-known ones were "Ansaldo" and "Panzacola." "Ansaldo" appears in documents from Coyoacán until the 1740s and was located with a fulling mill in the barrio of San Jerónimo. It was an old obraje. Captain Antonio Ansaldo had purchased it from one Balthasar de Barrera in 1647; its foundation and ownership can be traced back to 1609 or 1595, with the exact date in dispute.[81] "Ansaldo" illustrates well what Richard Lindley calls "kinship and credit," for family resources were shared in financing the business. The data in Figure 3.2 will clarify the discussion. The obraje was indebted to the heirs of don Félix Millán, Ansaldo's first cousin, for 2,400 pesos, and to the heirs of don Nicolás Rosal y Ríos, his first cousin, once removed, for 4,000 pesos.[82] Moreover, both Antonio Ansaldo and his brother-in-law, Tomás de Contreras, were owners of obrajes. Antonio Ansaldo was dead by 1668, and his wife, Contreras's sister, assumed control of the obraje. Tomás de Contreras acted as guarantor for his sister's debts and between 1668 and 1677 assumed obligations on her obraje amounting to 27,776 pesos.[83] This debt was passed from generation to generation among the Contreras. Tomás de Contreras assigned a portion of it to his granddaughter, doña Andrea Millán, while Contreras's daughter, doña María, passed yet another portion of it along to her brother, Diego de Contreras, who ultimately inherited his father's obraje in Coyoacán.

Francisco Ansaldo also tried to aid his mother by lending her 4,600 pesos (2,000 of which had come from his wife's dowry), even as he rented the obraje from her at 4,800 pesos per year.[84] The rental was high when capitalized at 5 percent, even though the obraje had twelve looms and thirty slaves.[85] But Francisco Ansaldo's reasoning is revealing. He paid a stiff rent so that his mother "[might] have enough to meet her obligations with decency, and *so that the obraje not pass on to a third party.*"[86] The assets and liabilities of the kin group were therefore shared, either directly through loans or indirectly through subsidies, and with the explicit end of keeping the family's interests intact. Those who possessed surplus capital financed those who were short, and kinship was the device, the mechanism of intermediation, that substituted for the capital market.

"Ansaldo" passed from the hands of its namesake family. It was later the property of Juan Bautista Salvatierra, and then of his widow, María Teresa Montes de Oca.[87] Unfortunately, Montes de Oca became involved with an unscrupulous financier, Antonio García, and lost the obraje to him. García, a merchant in Mexico City, acted as aviador for the obraje. He first lent Montes de Oca 7,000 pesos for four years, ostensibly at 5 percent, and then provided 200 pesos a week cash to meet the payroll of the obraje.[88] Montes de Oca tried to sell some of the cloth produced by the obraje in its own outlet, or *cajón,* and some through don Roque Andonegui, the early partner of José Pimentel in Tacuba; she also relied on her aviador as

FIGURE 3.2
The Ansaldo-Contreras Group in Coyoacán,
Late Seventeenth Century

Sources: Guillermo Lohman Villena, *Los americanos en las órdenes nobiliarias (1529-1900),* 2 vols. (Madrid, 1947), 1: 29-30; AGNM, Civil, vol. 355, passim.

77

an agent.[89] García's "commission," a disguised interest premium, was 3 percent of what he sold. He also ostensibly agreed to supply wool to Montes de Oca at half its market price and to extend credit without regard to market conditions. By some time in 1740—the exact date is unclear—García had taken over the obraje for debt.[90] He claimed to have provided Montes de Oca with the staggering sum of 21,500 pesos in credit, receiving only 8,900 pesos of cloth in return; there is also evidence that he gouged Montes de Oca for wool instead of discounting it as promised.[91] To round off his activities, García engaged in a *repartimiento de mercancías* with the peasant communities around Coyoacán. So unsavory was his reputation that one petitioner asked relief from the repartimiento: "Do not force me to receive these *novillos* [i.e., bulls of less than two years], otherwise he will do to me what he did to the widow of don Juan Bautista [i.e., Montes de Oca] by having my goods seized (*embargándome*)."[92] Nothing more is heard of García, Montes de Oca, or "Ansaldo" after that date.

The Vértiz and "Panzacola"

Another illuminating case occurs with the infamous obraje "Panzacola," which still lends its name to a street in San Angel. "Panzacola" enjoyed a long and largely unbroken history as property of the Vértiz family from the early years of the eighteenth century through the initial years of the First Republic.

The family's progenitor in Mexico was don Juan Miguel, born in Navarre, captain in the Spanish infantry, gentleman of the Order of Santiago, and one-time consul of the consulado of Mexico City. He was the earliest owner of "Panzacola," perhaps its founder, and was succeeded by his son, Pedro de Vértiz. Pedro was also a peninsular Spaniard and took a creole bride—a cousin, surely—doña Josefa de Vértiz. He survived his first wife and was followed in ownership of "Panzacola" by María Teresa de Vértiz, widow of Pedro de Vértiz; we can say little about her. Pedro de Vértiz, however, had a son by Josefa de Vértiz, Pedro de Vértiz, Jr. (or Pedro de Vértiz y Vértiz, as opposed to his father, Pedro de Vértiz y Oteyza), who also appears as the owner of "Panzacola" and as a member of the commercial firm of Oteyza y Vértiz that underwent a spectacular failure in the early years of the nineteenth century. After this, the obraje passed to Juan José de Oteyza y Vértiz, an associate of Pedro de Vértiz y Vértiz in the merchant house, and his first cousin, once removed. Don Juan Francisco de Lostre, manager of the obraje after 1785, a native of

TABLE 3.3
The Vértiz Family and the Obraje "Panzacola"

Owner	Approximate Dates
Juan Miguel de Vértiz	to ca. 1720
Pedro de Vértiz	after 1720
dõna Teresa de Vértiz, widow of Pedro de Vértiz	after ca. 1745
Various tenants Juan de Torres Roque Andonegui Felipe de Medina y Saravia	
Pedro de Vértiz, Jr.	from ca. 1770 to ca. 1800
Juan José de Oteyza y Vértiz	after ca. 1800
Juan Francisco Lostre and Martín José Iturralde	during 1810s
Juan José de Oteyza y Laurnaga	after ca. 1820

Sources: AJM, Sección de Concursos, various documents on the bankruptcy of the firm of Oteyza y Vértiz, 1804-24; testamento en virtud de poder de Juan José de Oteyza y Laurnaga, México, Dec. 1, 1820, ante Eugenio Pozo, ANM; petition of Juan Martínez de Lejarzar y Anieto, Madrid, Feb. 13, 1721, AGI, Escribanía de Cámara 196-A; bond given by Pedro de Vértiz, México, Apr. 30, 1725, AGNM, Civil, vol. 86, exp. 4; statement of accounts of Juan Miguel de Vértiz, México, Apr. 2, 1714, AGNM, Civil, vol. 335, 2da parte, exp. 6; in general, AGNM, Tierras, vol. 2009, exp. 5; escritura de sublocacíon, Juan de Torres, México, Sept. 9, 1750, ante Manuel López de la Palma, ANM, sworn statement of Pedro de Vértiz, México, Dec. 13, 1781, AGNM, Aduanas, vol. 71; inspection of the obraje of Panzacola [1722], AJM, leg. 71; petition of Manuela del Spíndola, México, Jul. 21, 1746, AJM, leg. 100; petition of José de Iturralde [Coyoacán, Jun. 22, 1768], AJM, leg. 128.

Navarre, and an Oteyza on his mother's side, followed as owner until his death in 1816. He was succeeded by an heir, Juan José de Oteyza y Laurnaga, "household and *labrador* in the town of Tepexi del Río," who resided in Mexico City and was probably another cousin. The retention of "Panzacola" by the Vértiz and their kinsmen for over a century was remarkable and the logical extension of what the Ansaldo and Contreras had attempted.

"Panzacola" was remarkable in other ways. The house of Oteyza y Vértiz offered access to markets; its manager sold cloth on his own account and received 50 percent of the profits.[93] "Panzacola" was

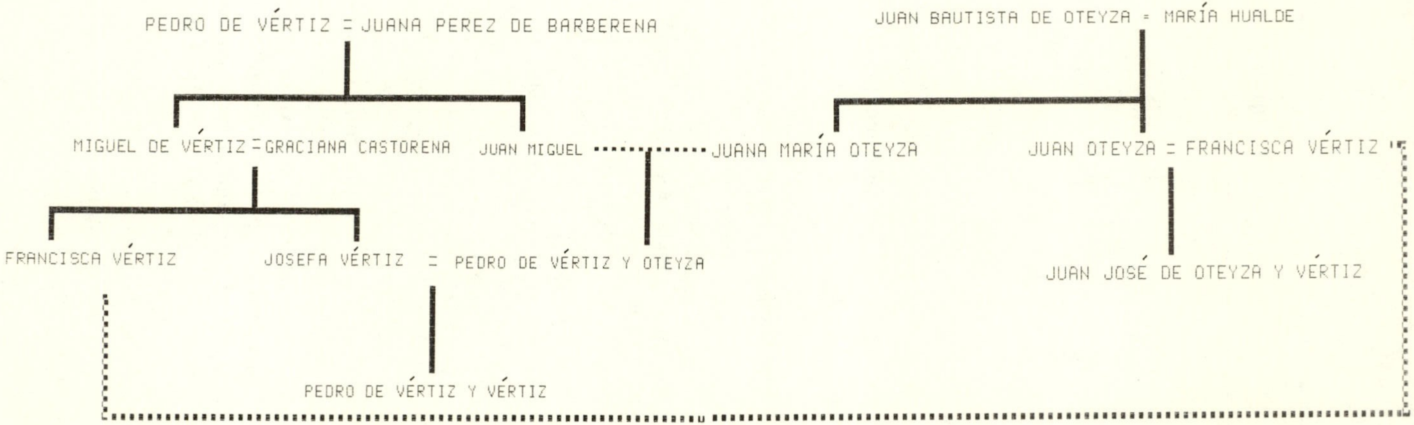

FIGURE 3.3

The Vértiz and Oteyza Families

Source: Ricardo Ortega y Pérez Gallardo, *Historia genealógica de las familias más antiguas de México* (México, 1910), 2d part, 3: Familia Vértiz, 20, 33.

part of the larger operation of the merchant house and acquired wool from an hacienda that Pedro de Vértiz owned in Durango.[94] Although the annual rate of return on equity earned by "Panzacola" is an estimate, but a fairly informed one, its range of 3.6 percent to 4.9 percent is reasonable. The rate of return on equity was roughly equal to the nominal cost of capital, 5 percent on clerical funds; profit on sales was higher, in the range of 11 percent.[95] The scale of "Panzacola" was no less noteworthy. One of the largest for which documentation exists, it was one of the few obrajes that had workers' housing, the *cuadrilla*, attached to it; "Panzacola" had fifteen residences.[96]

What inferences, then, can be drawn about the operation of the obrajes in the Valley of Mexico? For one thing, liquidity rather than solvency was the principal problem. Those who could handle it did well, regardless of the scale of enterprise. Pious funds did finance the obrajes, but secular sources of credit were apparently more important. The merchant-aviador, the fellow tradesman, and the kinsman, usually in combination but sometimes in one person, provided cash and extended credit. Credit was the basis of business activity, and the ends to which indebtedness were incurred were crucial.

TABLE 3.4
"Panzacola": Scale and Profits

Category	1802	1804	1805
Looms	29	32	32
Workers	206	192	185
Spinning wheels	?	98	98
Product (pieces)	1,160–1,305	1,280–1,440	1,280–1,440
Profits (pesos/year)	5,800–6,525	6,400–7,200	6,400–7,200
Equity (pesos)	141,467	147,992	179,814
Return on equity (%)	4.1–4.6	4.3–4.9	3.6–4.0
Inventory (varas)	24,073	33,895	31,364

Sources: Looms, spinning wheels, workers, and inventories taken from the concurso in AJM. Equity for 1804 and 1805 was computed in Tables 3.5 and 3.6. Equity for 1802 is assets less censos. Profits were estimated in José Castañares to the administrator of the aduana of Mexico City, Coyoacán, May 8, 1793, AGNM, Aduanas, vol. 134. Castañares thought that "Panzacola's" profits were at least 5 pesos per piece in current prices and assumed that its looms produced forty to forty-five pieces each per year.

TABLE 3.5
A Balance Sheet for "Panzacola," 1804

Assets (in pesos)		Liabilities (in pesos)	
Inventory of obraje	82,746	Accounts payable	15,933
Magueyal, truck garden, and batán	5,364	Censos	8,200
Equipment of obraje	783	Equity	147,992
Site and structure	13,098		
Chapel structure and ornaments	921		
Cuadrilla and site	426		
Accounts receivable by obraje	67,105		
Inventory and receivables of store	882		
TOTAL	172,125	TOTAL	172,125

Sources: Summary inventory for 1804 in the concurso. I adjusted it to reflect 2 censos totaling 8,200 pesos mentioned by Martín de Iturralde in his 1805 bid on the property.

Investments in productive assets might, in the long run, produce income and enhance liquidity. Indebtedness for working capital was risky; for consumption, it was riskier still. The ratio of working to fixed capital emphasized this difficulty. Investment in inventories was a necessary response to uncertainty. Finance was based on debt rather than equity, and a fall in demand could be disastrous, because debt had to be serviced, whatever the circumstances of cash flow. The financial system thus offered little flexibility, and often produced bankruptcies in which the estate of the owner was at risk. In this context, a merchant rich in cash was invaluable as a financier and distributor. Fellow tradesmen were no less important as brokers, guarantors, and agents, because all faced common problems. In other words, the economy's institutional limitations reinforced patterns of enterprise adapted to imperfect markets. A complex and potentially unstable blend of competition and interdependence was the result. The least costly source of financial stability and insurance

TABLE 3.6
A Balance Sheet for "Panzacola," 1805

Assets (in pesos)		Liabilities (in pesos)	
Inventory of obraje	78,958	Censos	8,200
Magueyal, truck garden	5,364	Equity	179,814
Batán and site	1,614		
Equipment of obraje	1,414		
Site and structure	13,098		
Chapel structure and ornaments	921		
Cuadrilla and site	426		
Accounts receivable by obraje	72,852		
Inventory and receivables of store	656		
Miscellany	80		
TOTAL	188,014	TOTAL	188,014

Sources: As for 1804, I adjusted the inventory of 1805 to account for 65,764 pesos carried as payable after the concurso took place, but not before.

against risk was therefore the extended kin group itself, for it was within the kin group that transactions costs were lowest.[97]

But stability is a relative term, particularly where proprietorships and partnerships are concerned. The liquidation of a successful partnership allowed the participants to seek new opportunities and provided the funds necessary for the venture. Without well-developed capital markets and laws of incorporation, both new even to the advanced European economies of the late seventeenth and early eighteenth centuries, turnover and fluidity were the rule. A successful enterprise in New Spain was therefore as likely a short-term venture as a long-term undertaking. To assume otherwise is anachronistic, even where well-documented evidence of continuity in business ownership sometimes occurs.

Finally, the return to capital was higher than the return to technical skills, a result consistent with the limitations of the capital market. Even so, owners who were not clothiers relied upon skilled agents, mobile professionals versed in the trade whose contacts helped to secure financing. Among the managers, there was some vertical mobility. Foremen sometimes became managers, managers sometimes became owners. But reliance upon managers who sought to maximize their own wealth rather than their employers' could and did lead to conflicts. Nevertheless, the potential for accumulation in the obrajes was apparently restricted. The Vértiz family and "Panzacola" is an exception to the otherwise modest means of owners of obrajes in the Valley of Mexico, whose wealth paled relative to the mercantile patriciate of the capital. The Vértiz pursued integration to its logical conclusion, encompassing all aspects of production and distribution. The family had, in essence, absorbed the functions of the market.

OBRAJES IN THE PUEBLA-TLAXCALA BASIN

Pedro Mendoza y Escalante

By the eighteenth century, Puebla was no longer an important center of the obrajes, although it had been of primary significance earlier in the sixteenth. But there were still a few obrajes there. One was the property of don Pedro Mendoza y Escalante, a *montañés* immigrant. Mendoza y Escalante married well in 1704, taking a creole bride from Tlaxcala, doña María Rosa Yáñez, who brought him a rich dowry. In 1707, Mendoza formed a company with Mario Alvar González to operate Mendoza y Escalante's obraje. Mendoza y Escalante invested about 1,800 pesos in cash and provided workers, wool, and facilities, and Alvar González agreed to contribute his managerial and technical skills for a third of the profits. The company did very well. From 1708 through 1718, it produced profits of nearly 41,000 pesos, implying (under simplifying assumptions) an unusually high rate of return to Alvar González.[98]

Mendoza y Escalante prospered. In 1712, he acquired the hacienda of San Bartolomé and the rancho Guadalupe for 19,500 pesos, and he owned another hacienda, San Diego.[99] In 1709, the title of head bailiff (*alguacil mayor*) was granted to Mendoza y Escalante, evidence of his wealth and status, for the office, known to cost a great deal, was probably purchased.[100] Nor was he alone in this. Another obraje in Puebla, "Apresa," was named after don Domingo de Apresa y Gándara, a captain, municipal councilman, and public trustee (*depositario general*) of the city, in addition to being the owner or founder of the eponymous obraje.[101] The position of public trustee was a favorite with the owners of the obrajes of Puebla, for Mendoza y Escalante ultimately followed Apresa in its exercise. Interest in the position went beyond hunger for honorific titles and reflected the potential for accumulation that the office held. In 1719, the Council of the Indies rebuked Mendoza y Escalante as "bailiff, municipal councilman, and public trustee, concerning the recovery of a considerable quantity of pesos due to the municipal funds [*proprios y rentas*] from the time that he held the municipal meat monopoly."[102] Evidently, Mendoza y Escalante drew on revenues without repaying them. Nor was the trusteeship alone used to advance Mendoza y Escalante's interests. He appointed his son, José, deputy bailiff (*teniente de alguacil*), which was within his powers.[103] More interesting was José's appointment as special judge (*juez privativo*) in Puebla with the power to issue licenses for the expansion of the capacity of the obrajes.[104] One can imagine how useful the office was.

Juan Pérez Cota y Madera

Juan Pérez Cota y Madera was a *montañés* from Gijón who served as head bailiff to the Inquisition in Puebla and as an *alcalde ordinario*.[105] He built his fortune through marriage and inheritance. His parents left him slaves, cash, lands, and personal property.[106] His marriage in 1715 to Margarita Teresa Núñez de Molina brought him a dowry of 12,000 pesos that included an obraje and its license valued at 5,000 pesos.[107] Marriage doubled his wealth.[108]

Although Pérez Cota's obraje was not large and had only about eight looms, his range of business practices was instructive. Pérez Cota drew on Santiago del Arenal in Mexico as a broker for wool from the Bajío, and he sent finished woolens to San Miguel el Grande through him.[109] He relied on owners of obrajes in Mexico City and Coyoacán to transact business. Manuel de Herrera Puente, as owner of the obraje "Peredo," acted as Pérez Cota's agent in charging balances due, and at the time of his death Pérez Cota owed Herrera Puente money.[110] Pérez Cota also borrowed from Francisco Javier Paulín, an owner in Coyoacán.[111] In addition, he operated an outlet for sales of the woolens he made in Puebla, resold smaller amounts of raw wool, and made about 700 pesos per year profit from the obraje.

Seven hundred pesos was not much, and Pérez Cota operated at the margins of solvency. At his death, Pérez Cota had a number of bad debts, and his widow claimed that "[he] was in such narrow straits a little before he died that he was wont to borrow three or four pesos from his neighbors. He usually asked advance payment for orders received since he could not have paid his workers without it."[112]

Tomás Díaz Varela

Don Tomás Díaz Varela was one of the principal suppliers of woolens to the peasantry of the Puebla-Tlaxcala basin.[113] He was a peninsular Spaniard, Galician by birth.[114] He married well in 1772, joining his father-in-law, Lucas de Pineda, as excise farmer in Santa Ana Chiautempan.[115] The obraje he operated came through his wife, so that commercial success was based on a fortunate marriage. Both Díaz Varela and his father-in-law were provincials of some repute. The excise officer of Puebla spoke of their "considerable trade and weight . . . providing householders with their needs in food and clothing," as well as supplying the surrounding villages of the area.[116] Díaz Varela was not fabulously wealthy, but he was comfortable. In 1772, the year of his marriage, his net worth was 25,000 pesos and grew steadily. By 1783, it had increased to 57,000 pesos, and his assets included the obraje, a *tienda mestiza*, the hacienda "San Juan de Bautista," and two rental properties, the hacienda "San Miguel" and the hacienda de labor "San Francisco."[117]

The obraje and fulling mill of the Díaz Varela were very large and capitalized at 300,000 pesos.[118] Drawing on wool from the *llanos* of Apan, San Juan de los Llanos, Huamantla, the province of Tepeaca, and the Mixteca, its twenty-eight looms were reputed to produce woolens as good as any in New Spain, with the exception of San Miguel el Grande. The obraje also made manta from cotton grown around Cosamalapan, but it was very little. With its ninety spinning wheels, numerous looms, and workers' quarters, the obraje ranked with "Panzacola" in size. It continued to 1810, when it was besieged by rebels, ruined, and abandoned. Following the destruction, the woolens salvaged were worth more than 160,000 pesos.[119] Although Díaz Varela dealt with weavers in the Salto del Agua district of the capital, he catered primarily to the provincial market.[120]

What can we say of Puebla and Tlaxcala? Marriage here made a large difference, and creole brides provided substantial resources to their immigrant husbands. The owners of obrajes were more likely drawn from the upper ranks of society than were those in Mexico City, where predominance based on commerce and mining went unchallenged. This pattern repeats itself in the Bajío, to which we now turn our attention.

The Bajío

Obrajes and Elite in San Miguel el Grande

Two days' ride from Querétaro lay the town of San Miguel el Grande. The expansion of its obrajes began after 1740.[121] Local production of wool declined as the surrounding haciendas turned to cereals, and wool was instead purchased from Dolores, which supplied Querétaro as well.[122] The expansion of San Miguel as a commercial center was tied to the increasing prosperity of local haciendas and to the growing demands of the mining camps in Guanajuato.[123] The primary beneficiaries of economic expansion formed a compact and prosperous creole elite composed of families such as the Sauto, Canal, Landeta, Lanzagorta, Unzaga, and Allende.

Progenitor of one of these families, don Balthasar de Sauto, was born in 1710 in the valley of Oquendo, in Alava in 1710. He was present in New Spain by the age of 15.[124] Perhaps it was through don Severino de Jaureguí that Sauto came to San Miguel, for Jaureguí was himself an immigrant and owner of an obraje there. Sauto married his creole daughter, doña Juana Petra, and thereby acquired the obraje.[125] By the mid-1740s, Sauto had become a local magnate, the possessor of haciendas, livestock, and a store in San Miguel.[126] His enterprise was well integrated. Sauto brought fleece from the hacienda to the obraje and used labor from the obraje on his agricultural holdings. By the mid-1750s, the obraje operated a sizable twenty-two looms.[127]

Like fellow provincials who owned obrajes, Sauto held office as a municipal councilman and as an alcalde ordinario. He was a member of the local militia; an excise farmer in San Miguel prior to the incorporation of the excise as a royal bureaucracy; and the local contractor for alum, the mordant without which most textile dyeing could not take place.[128] Sauto was, to put it mildly, well placed and powerful. Perhaps it was inevitable that his growing power and influence should threaten his competitors in San Miguel. His "enemies," and this was Sauto's term, were drawn from the Canal and the Landeta, families as wealthy and powerful as his. Francisco José de Landeta, for instance, was a native of San Miguel, who became first Conde de Casa de Loja in 1753. [129] Two of his daughters, doña Francisca and doña María Ana, married sons of Manuel Tomás de la Canal, another wealthy creole born in Mexico City in 1701, son of don Domingo de la Canal, a powerful member of the consulado. [130] Together, the Canal and the Landeta owned nearly 40 percent of the looms in the obrajes there by the mid-1750s. Moreover, their families held important municipal offices, purchased seats on the cabildo, and occupied the post of *alcalde mayor* for a time. [131] The Canal and the Landeta were also associated with another family, the Lanzagorta, who were wealthy merchants, hacendados, and sheep ranchers near the village of Dolores. [132] Textiles, commerce, and ranching were the pursuits that cemented power and wealth in San Miguel el Grande.

All these families were involved in a major conflict over the conduct of the obraje of don Balthasar de Sauto that lasted from 1758 to 1771. The precise causes of the conflict are not clear, but Sauto thought that "enemies" among the other families conspired against him in competitive spite, although he was formally accused by a *visitador* of gross mistreatment of the workers in his obraje. [133] At the height of the struggle, Sauto was jailed in Puebla, and the young inspector who had been sent to take action against him, don Diego Antonio Fernández de la Madrid, was marrying a daughter of Manuel de la Canal. [134] This inspection culminated in a *cédula* ordering Sauto's obraje closed, but Sauto defied the order and extracted a motion of *obedezco pero no cumplo* from the Audiencia to stop the closing. [135]

The affair blew over, but it demonstrated how rapidly interdependence could turn to chaos when competitive tensions proved overwhelming. In San Miguel, these tensions may well have originated in shortages of labor, resources, and managerial skill as the number of obrajes in operation more than doubled between 1744 and 1755. [136] Moreover, there was no guild to resolve conflicts or to unify producers in the face of hostile civil authorities. From this perspective, Sauto's competitors acted to police a rogue in their midst and to reduce the probability of increased regulation or viceregal retaliation against all of them. [137] Or Sauto may simply have been mentally unbalanced—some of his actions defy rational explanation. But a decade of turmoil clearly did the obrajes of San Miguel no good; only one or two producing finer woolens continued to operate at century's end.

Acámbaro: A Center of Growth

By the 1780s, the output of Acámbaro was in no way insignificant, and its obrajes produced nearly 65,000 pesos of woolens per year.[138] Of eight owners identified in an excise report of 1781, there were three kinsmen: don Nícolas Gómez, don Joaquín Gómez, and don José Alcalá. Accounting for nearly 75 percent of woolen output by value, these were the major producers.[139] Nícolas Gómez and José Alcalá owned retail shops in town and disposed of a portion of their output this way, with more through sales outside the excise district. The brothers Gómez and José Alcalá were principal spokesmen for the guild in its dealings with the Royal Excise, and Nícolas Gómez and José Alcalá had participated in the farm of the excise between 1772 and 1779. In this, they were accompanied by yet another owner of an obraje, don Luis Martínez de Lejarzar, who also owned two shops and a small store in Acámbaro. Although there is little detailed information on the obrajes of Acámbaro, the evidence available does not appear atypical. Concentration among producers there was seemingly the rule in the later eighteenth century. For instance, the obraje of don Mateo Mauricio García produced an annual average of 27,000 pesos of woolens between 1770 and 1772, large by late colonial standards, and relative to the volume of local output.[140] Perhaps Acámbaro grew at the expense of San Miguel or did well by specializing in says for clerical usage.[141] All indicators point to increased prosperity in the later colonial period.

Querétaro: The Center of Woolen Enterprise

The core of the late colonial woolen industry was indisputably Querétaro. "The town was, in days of yore," wrote one visitor, "famous for the manufacture of broadcloth . . . far superior to that made at San Miguel el Grande."[142] Investment and output were large and implied a market of considerable size. But during its heyday before the uprising of 1810, it is unlikely that Querétaro's population exceeded 37,000 to 40,000 people; as late as 1778, it barely approached 20,000.[143] If the extent of the market limits the division of labor, Querétaro's specialization presupposed outside markets. This explains much of the behavior of its textile producers. A common solution was for owners in Querétaro to have retail outlets outside town, as did Juan Antonio del Castillo y Llata, who had a shop in the mining town of El Pinal, in Cadereyta, which he operated in conjunction with his mining interests there.[144] Another strategy was the use of an agent, preferably in Mexico City, who had contacts throughout the colony. Joaquín Valiño and Pedro Garza provide relevant examples.

JOAQUÍN VALIÑO AND PEDRO GARZA

Joaquín Valiño was a merchant, hacendado, and owner of an obraje in Querétaro. Valiño's connections were in Mexico City. He had a continuing agreement there with a merchant, Diego Rodríguez Domínguez.[145] Records beginning in 1703 indicate that Valiño sent serges to the capital, and Domínguez sent specie and bills of exchange to Valiño. The former paid Valiño's expenses and acted as purchasing and collection agent for him.[146] Valiño had a similar relationship with Andrés Rodríguez de Porras, a merchant in Mexico City who sent Valiño yarn, says, serges, cacao, sacks, tallow, hides, books, dyestuffs, and indigo. In turn, Rodríguez de Porras acted as Valiño's agent.[147]

Don Pedro Garza, the owner of an obraje in Querétaro, and don Francisco Sáenz de Escobosa, a merchant in Mexico City, had a similar arrangement.[148] Garza did not receive orders directly from customers but took them through Sáenz de Escobosa, whose contacts in Sonora and whose customers elsewhere ensured Garza continuity in demand. Sáenz de Escobosa also supervised Garza's finances in the capital. He haggled over prices with customers and suppliers, provided information about market conditions and metropolitan regulations, and advised Garza in dealing with the Royal Excise. For this he charged a 2-percent commission on sales outside Mexico City and reciprocity in negotiating bills of exchange. More than an order-taker, Sáenz de Escobosa provided information crucial to the success of the obraje.

THE PRIMO Y JORDÁN

Bachiller don Juan Manuel Primo owned lands and an obraje in Salvatierra, speculated in land in the Bajío, and acted as an aviador to the Querétaro obraje owner don Antonio Camaño.[149] He owned six haciendas in the district of Querétaro and at least one near San Luis de la Paz, apparently moving in and out of the land market with a certain frequency.[150] His family was no less interesting. His brother, Pedro Bernardino de Primo y Jordán, was senior councilman (*regidor decano*) of Querétaro in 1750 and owned two obrajes held in entail on the hacienda "Jurica," near Querétaro.[151] Although don Pedro claimed that these were "very deteriorated" and were valued at only 10,000 pesos, he had a net worth of nearly a half million pesos at the time of his death in 1756.[152] More arresting was the debt of 42,000 pesos that he owed don Francisco de Landeta, first Conde de Casa de Loja, whom he called his "hermano de afinidad."[153] Since Casa de Loja was married to doña Francisca de Primo y Jordán, the meaning is unmistakable.[154] Casa de Loja was Pedro de Primo's brother-in-law, since doña Francisca was surely Primo's sister. Thus were the elite of San Miguel and Querétaro united—the Landeta, Canal, Lanzagorta, and Primo y Jordán—with their investments in haciendas, labores, and obrajes throughout the Bajío. In the absence of a well-developed capital market, the criteria for judging the riskiness of loans emphasized information on the borrower's probable behavior and capacity to repay. It was precisely among such family groups that information was available at lowest cost.

MERCHANTS AND MANUFACTORIES

Juan Manuel Primo y Jordán, and the first Conde de Regla, who owned an obraje in Querétaro, were not clothiers and held obrajes as investments.[155] Throughout the eighteenth century, and perhaps before, merchants became increasingly involved in the obrajes. Although one senses this everywhere in New Spain, the tendency was pronounced in Acámbaro and Querétaro, which overshadowed other woolen centers in the eighteenth century.

One example is the Querétaro merchant, don Tomás López de Ecala. Ecala was born in Navarre in 1740 and came to Mexico to work for a merchant.[156] At 35, he was chief apprentice to don Agustín Carballido y Villerino. By 1783, López de Ecala had become a principal citizen of Querétaro. He purchased and occupied various municipal posts, such as councilman, head bailiff, notary of the Holy Office, and trustee for taxes to support the provincial cavalry regiment. In the census of 1791, López de Ecala called himself an hacendado and a widower living on the Plaza Mayor with his four children. Still, a list of the major obrajes compiled in 1793 does not include him as an owner.[157] It was not until 1811 (at age 71) that he appears as owner of an obraje, an unlikely time to begin a new career.[158] Before then, he had been a valuable ally to the owners of obrajes, for he exercised authority over the distribution of municipal water rights.[159] López de Ecala also made peace with the Royal Excise, eternal *bete noire*

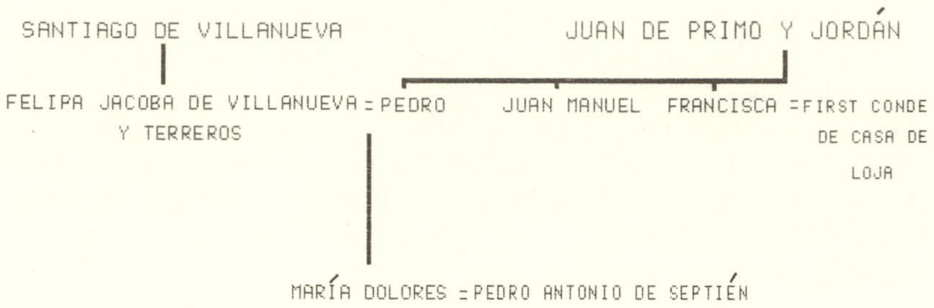

SANTIAGO DE VILLANUEVA   JUAN DE PRIMO Y JORDÁN

FELIPA JACOBA DE VILLANUEVA = PEDRO   JUAN MANUEL   FRANCISCA = FIRST CONDE
         Y TERREROS   DE CASA DE
                                                                    LOJA

                MARÍA DOLORES = PEDRO ANTONIO DE SEPTIÉN

FIGURE 3.4

The Primo y Jordán in Querétaro and San Miguel el Grande

Sources: Petition of Pedro Bernardino de Primo y Jordán to the Council of the Indies [ca. 1742], AGI, México 644; petition of don Juan Manuel Primo y Jordán before the Inquisition, AGNM, Civil, vol. 1526, exp. 11; testament of María Josefa de Landeta y Primo, México, Aug. 21, 1805, ante Ignacio José Montes de Oca, ANM; poder para testar of Pedro Bernardino de Primo y Jordán, Querétaro, Apr. 4, 1750, ante Felix Antonio de Araujo; poder especial of Juan Manuel Primo y Jordán, Querétaro, Nov. 10, 1756, ante Manuel de Rosas; certificación de censo, Querétaro, May 4, 1753, ante Vicente de Llano, with this and the two preceding protocols from Querétaro to be found along with evidence of a depósito irregular en don Juan Manuel Primo y Jordán, México, Mar. 20, 1758, ante José Pérez Cancio, ANM; Brading, *Miners and Merchants*, p. 352.

of the trade, as guarantor for the excise officer in Querétaro.[160] López de Ecala invested in an obraje only late in life.

Although mercantile capital and textile manufacturing had long been linked in Querétaro, the eighteenth century witnessed a qualitative change in the phenomenon.[161] The corregidor of Querétaro petitioned in 1743 that no new licenses for obrajes be issued or new looms permitted. He further requested "that the Royal Law of Castile be enforced, in that the merchant not be an obrajero; or the obrajero, a merchant."[162] Moreover, the data in Table 3.7 show the domination of the guild in Querétaro by merchants and particularly by *montañeses*, who were heavily overrepresented in ownership by the century's end.[163] Only two owners lived at or near their obrajes, suggesting that most, as simple investors, did not administer them. Three owners lived on the Plaza Mayor, traditional center of wealth, prestige, and administrative authority, rather than in the barrio of San Roque, or in industrial districts near the river. Almost all of them had servants, and one, don Juan Antonio del Castillo y Llata, was a colonel in the militia who had made his fortune in mining.[164] By contrast, Querétaro's artisan and handicraft weavers, its trapicheros, spinners, carpenters, muleteers, and cigarette rollers, also

TABLE 3.7
Major Owners of Obrajes in Querétaro, 1793

Name of Owner	Birthplace (Age)	Residence (N Servants)
Melchor de Noriega (h)	Asturias (54)	Plza. San Francisco (1)
Francisco Gómez	?	?
José Gorres (o/c)	Valencia	Calle de la Tenería*
Domingo Fdez. Iglesias (c)	La Montaña (26)	Calle del Beobo (2)
José Martínez (defunct)	?	? (2)
Francisco de la Llata (o)	La Montaña	Bajada de Guadalupe (3)
María Hidalgo (h)	?	?
Juan Martínez de Lejarzar	?	?
Francisco de Carballido	?	?
José Cerrón (c)	La Montaña	Calle del Beobo (2)
Manuel González de Nícolas	?	Plaza Mayor
Mauro Barriero (o/c)	Galicia (50)	Calle del Beobo (2)
Pedro Garza (o/c)	Galicia (50)	Calle de la Tenería* (2)
Juan Antonio del Castillo y Llata (m)	La Montaña (45)	Plaza Mayor (1)
José Gómez	La Montaña	Plaza Mayor (5)

Note: h = hacendado; o = obrajero; c = comerciante; m = minero; * = barrio of San Roque, site of obrajes.

Sources: "Obrajes o fábricas de paño que hay . . . ," AGNM, Alcabalas, vol. 37; for name of owner, place of birth, age, residence, and number of servants, ms. census of Querétaro [1791], AGNM, Padrones, vol. 39. Occupation before slash is from this census; after slash, from "Padrón de españoles de esta ciudad de Santiago de Querétaro . . ." [1794], AGNM, Civil, vol. 2085, exp. 4; Pérez Velasco, *Elogio Histórico*, pp. 11-13.

lived together but in less fashionable districts, giving physical expression to their distance from the business elite of New Spain's leading industrial city.[165]

CONCLUSIONS: MARKETS AND PATTERNS OF ENTERPRISE

The conduct of the obrajes was characterized by adaptation to the market structure of New Spain. Access to capital was a major prerequisite for success. Obrajes, like rural estates, operated with high ratios of debt to equity. Problems with liquidity were chronic, and significant in view of the uncertainty that existed. Capital markets were small, thin, imperfect, and unable to meet demand. The church provided long-term loans but required substantial collateral. Consequently, little credit was supplied through organized financial markets.[166] Aviadores furnished working capital but intruded on control during downturns. It was therefore natural for families to play a major role in development. Although the cost of capital could be high, borrowers were more easily constrained and risk more readily reduced.[167] But capital scarcity and relatively high real rates of interest would hinder efforts to stimulate textile production well into the nineteenth century.[168] Reliance upon debt to secure funds would be risky in the face of business and lifetime income cycles, for it was relatively inflexible. Nevertheless, the pressure of debt service brought an element of market discipline to the obrajes and reinforced adaptation to transactions costs. Why it did not serve to induce technological change is an issue discussed later.

The evident division of ownership and management was another consequence of the limited market for funds. If lifetime income patterns were similar to modern ones, younger entrants who most needed capital were at the greatest disadvantage. By forming partnerships with wealthy investors and moving when another opportunity arose, managers accumulated financial capital. Even less rewarding positions offered experience and good reputation—enhanced human capital—against which managers sought to borrow. Some did so successfully, and others did not. Life for the managers and foremen was a constant struggle; their attitudes and behavior confirmed it. They were often rough characters, at odds with their workers and frequently brutal in their treatment of them. Racism no doubt explains much of this, but opportunism, cynicism, and callousness born of personal experience also played a role. No one, least of all Adam Smith, ever thought that competition bred gentility. Those who married into the business, on the other hand, had the means but not the skills to operate an obraje. The managers were partners and agents of the Canal or the Landeta, but they were not their social equals.

Another constraint upon the obrajes, and upon other colonial businesses as well, was the high cost of information. There were no company reports, financial pages, trade papers, or any of the other modern devices that produce efficient markets. Information not only was hard to come by, but it moved ever so slowly as well. The isochronic lines constructed in Map 3.1 make this point quite forcefully.

Querétaro and Puebla were a week's post time from Mexico City in the beginning of the nineteenth century. San Luis Potosí and Oa-

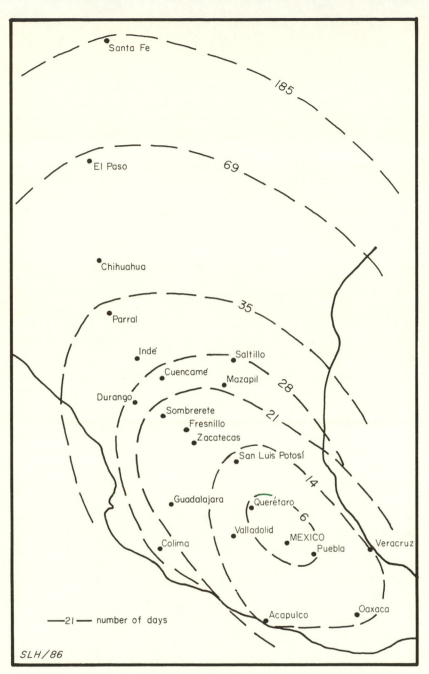

Santa Fe

185

El Paso

69

Chihuahua

Parral

35

Indé

Saltillo

Cuencamé

Mazapil

28

Durango

Sombrerete

21

Fresnillo

Zacatecas

San Luis Potosí

14

Guadalajara

Querétaro

6

Valladolid

MEXICO

Colima

Puebla

Veracruz

——21—— number of days

Acapulco

Oaxaca

SLH/86

Map 3.1

An Isochronic Map of Mexico in the Early Nineteenth Century

The isochronic lines represent the time necessary for a letter from Mexico City
to reach a given point and to be answered promptly. A "round-trip" from Mex-

95

xaca lay two weeks away. The mining districts of Fresnillo, Zacatecas, Saltillo, and Parral were three to five weeks away. These
were major markets for the woolens of the obrajes and were adjacent
to their source of wool as well. The distance between Querétaro and
Alta California was as great as that from the Alleghenies to the Pacific
Ocean, and it required three to four months for freight to pass from
Mexico City to Parral.[169] Coordinating supply under these conditions demanded a network of trustworthy, reliable, and knowledgeable agents and forced competitors to work together even as the
need for labor might drive them apart. The collective nature of family enterprise is easily understood as a response to these conditions,
although the potential for bickering was heightened as a result.
Feuds and genealogical obsessiveness were more than cultural
traits: they reflected the overwhelming economic role that kinship
implied.

Such levels of risk and uncertainty in the colonial economy thus
shaped every aspect of business practice. Risk, a subjective or objec-
tive measurement of the probability of loss of assets, drove the vertical integration of obraje, hacienda, and retail shop, sometimes producing an undifferentiated and unspecialized entrepreneur whose
functional identity was equivocal.[170] But uncertainty, which cannot
be measured (or, at least, measured consistently), was equally important. For one thing, not all risk-averters diversify, so it is insuffi-
cient to claim that patterns of diversification were a necessary response to risk. For another, the similarity of business practice among
the successful is strong evidence of imitation, and imitation is a common response to uncertainty.[171] The entrepreneurial group, the firm
of family and kin, was born of the same constraints that produced the
obrajes. The reasons for its persistence under changing economic
conditions are an invitation to the history of Mexican business.

MAP 3.1 (cont.)
ico City to Puebla or Querétaro required, by this standard, about a week. The
other destinations may be similarly interpreted.

Source: Based on Pedro Gómez de la Peña, "Para escribir a todas las ciudades de Nueva
España y Guatemala . . ." (1802). New York Public Library, Obadiah Rich Collection, no.
45.

FOUR

"Nor More Servitude Than in Other Work"

Introduction: The Heart of the Matter

IN HIS RELACIÓN de mando to the Marqués de Valero (1716-22), the Duque de Linares (1710-16) wrote that the obrajes recruited labor through "deception by the peso." "[The obrajes] hold [the workers] in such violence," Linares wrote, "that if one of them should happen to die, or to flee, they seize their wives and children as slaves." "Poorly instructed in the faith, and worse fed," he concluded, "they suffer in a Christian land what is unknown among barbarians."[1] Linares's view was not a new one. The labor problem was coeval with the obraje and was its reason for existence. Without a well-developed market, the obraje recruited, retained, and maintained the labor force necessary for sustained production. The costs of the resulting system were distributed according to the relative power of owners, laborers, and colonial officials. Owners and their agents sought adequate supplies of cheap labor but faced a radically imperfect market. Such a market—with its bargaining, negotiation, and mutual adjustment—generally characterized labor recruitment during the colonial period.[2] Yet obrajes were particularly unpleasant places, and free laborers often avoided working in them if they could. Consequently, the obrajes were generally under pressure to raise wages. But their ability to do so was limited. On the one hand, substitutes—cloth from the telares sueltos and imports—limited what people would pay for domestic woolens, so their cost could not easily be increased. On the other hand, owners of obrajes argued that raising wages—even if possible—would not increase the supply of labor, since the workers' demand for money income was limited. The owners neither could nor would raise wages, even in the face of a chronic shortage of labor. As a result, bargaining and negotiation for labor frequently gave way to force.

Various types of coercion were used, depending on political and demographic circumstances. The enslavement of blacks and Indians, the *encomienda*, debt peonage, and informal *repartimiento* all played a part, sometimes in conjunction with free, wage labor, occasionally in the same obraje. The profusion of devices and names should not conceal the heart of the matter. Free wage labor and market incentives could not bring sufficient labor to most obrajes. Beyond this, it is hard to generalize, since the labor force varied from place to place and time to time. Yet the interpretation matters. If the owners were correct, coercion was efficient—the obrajes could acquire neither more nor better labor through free hire. If they were wrong, coercion amounted to little more than theft.

Still, one theme emerges time and again: the way power and influence were used to get labor. When the obrajes were first organized, Indians were their source of labor and they presented a substantial legal and moral problem. In theory, Indians were wards of the Crown, minors to be protected. Yet they were also expected to support the Spanish settlers by labor and tribute, much as they had supported their own rulers before the Conquest. Nevertheless, the balance proved difficult to strike, particularly when settlers lived among the Indians while the Crown governed from afar. The many exploiters—and agents of the Conquest—were near at hand while the source of protection and authority was far removed.

For this reason, early indirect governance in the Indies failed, and the government of Philip II undertook a direct, if bureaucratic, approach. Yet even officials sent from the Peninsula viewed the Indians as both a source of emoluments and a burden to be protected.[3] The view was a monument to self-deception, but it became prevalent and deeply engrained. As the Indians disappeared, the authority of those entrusted to govern and protect them became increasingly valuable (and salable). Royal officials made the most of limited tenure in the Indies by selling exceptions to the laws they were to enforce. As a result, men and women who needed labor got to know officials and took their demands seriously. For the owner of the obraje in particular, labor was very scarce; small wonder that venal magistrates and obrajes went hand-in-hand. The outcome was subtle and complex, and individual need, power, and psychology each played its part. Some owners got labor, some officials got rich, and some workers got protection, but in distinctly different proportions. How the system functioned in theory and in practice is the story that follows. We begin with one view of work in an obraje.

THE WORK ROUTINE AND WORKERS

The carders came to work first, generally around 4:00 A.M., in the company of the foreman, his assistant, and crew leader.[4] Each pair of carders, the *emprimador* and *emborrador*, was given a measure of fleece to willow, moisten with tallow, and then reweigh. The spinners in the obraje came two or three hours later and received the warp and filling for the yarn. If cottage spinners were employed, they generally received yarn for the warp and came to the obraje once a week to pick up wool and deliver what they had spun.

The carders and spinners did piecework. A carder generally picked up about eight pounds of wool, and allowing for shrinkage (prescribed by law) they would be paid 1.5 to 2 reales per pound (at rates in 1759, when this description was given). The spinners were assigned three or six pounds, depending on whether they spun for filling or warp, and the piece rate varied from 1 to 2 reales per pound. The same rate ostensibly held for cottage spinners. But carders and spinners who worked in the obraje also prepared wool for dyeing, washed it, and wrung it out when dyeing was finished. They were not compensated for these jobs and frequently had too little time left over to fulfill their primary tasks.[5] Consequently, the wage that a spinner in an obraje actually received was probably less than what a cottage worker received.

The bobbin boys, master warper, weavers, shearers, pressers, and perchers all did piecework. The bobbin boys wound the yarn for the warp and were paid for each ten pounds measured. The master warper "beamed the web" before passing it to the weaver and was paid by the cloth at 1.5 reales per piece. The rate for the weavers depended on the kind of cloth made. For example, six days were sufficient to produce "half" a cloth or new drapery, and the rate was 3 pesos for the cloth and 2.5 pesos for the drapery. The weavers' assistants were also paid by the piece, with rates ranging from 2 pesos 2 reales to 1 peso 7 reales. Bobbin boys were not paid until the weavers were. Their rate was much lower, at 3 reales per "half" cloth. Perchers had a set piece rate, which varied from 2 to 3 reales per cloth, but they were also obliged to help in dyeing. The shearer and his assistants were to do three "half" cloths a day and were paid 2 reales each. The same rates held for the presser. Relatively high rates for skilled workers such as master warpers, weavers, shearers, and pressers did not necessarily imply high earnings. In this particular description, the warper, shearer, and his assistants were slaves, whereas the status of the weavers varied. The details are unclear, but the slave may have received a wage and paid a fixed sum to the owner on payday. If so, high piece rates are less impressive.

All work was done under supervision of a foreman. Weavers, for instance, had the weight of the filling noted before work began and the weight of the cloth registered after they finished. In theory, weavers and their assistants had job cards. The foreman recorded the day the master and his assistants began to weave the cloth, the day they delivered it, and its weight, so that the manager could pay them. Close records were supposed to be kept. Supervision was especially necessary for the apprentices, who had terms of three to five years, according to age, ability, and prior agreement. Apprentices were in the obrajes to learn a trade; some were forbidden to leave "to keep them out of trouble." They were paid a real a day and were to receive a new outfit of breeches, cloak, shirt, undergarment, frieze, and hat per year. Although apprentices were legally free to leave after their indenture had expired, the owners extended their terms to remedy "imperfections . . . in work due to laziness or flight."

The obrajes operated truck stores and kitchens. Each played a role in the work routine. As long as there were slaves or peons, they needed to be fed. In practice, resident workers "hired" a cook and were expected to pay 4 reales a week each, plus three pecks of maize. In return, they received three meals a day consisting of six tortillas in the morning, plus chocolate and *atole*; six tortillas at midday, plus beef or pork; and six more tortillas, a plate of beef *mole*, and atole at night. The truck store operated alongside of a system of cash advances, and "with the exception of trusted workers . . . the others are asked to have sureties should they fail to meet their obligations, or give cause for being fired, because they owe the amounts they have been given." In the truck store, a worker purchased cloths, stuffs, friezes, shawls, manta, Rouen cloth, and serge. Records were kept of whatever workers purchased, and accounts were settled on Saturdays.

The crew leaders of the carders, spinners, perchers, shearers, and pressers were called in by the foreman and were told what each worker had earned. The workers were then brought to the store, and a comparison was made between what they earned and what they owned according to their own and the manager's records. "If the worker earned 12 reales and is in debt, he receives half—6 reales—in cash, and the other 6 remain for repayment of what he owes, and the manager notes in his ledger only the 6 reales." The same system applied to the weavers, but they were paid on Saturday afternoon rather than on Sunday morning.

Finally, the religious obligations of the workers were ostensibly considered. On holy days of obligation, the obrajes were to have chapels suitable for the celebration of the Mass, and a priest was to be available for confession and the sacraments. Owners were obliged to provide cash advances for sacramentals and for baptisms, weddings, and funerals.

All this seems unobjectionable in theory. But theory it was, and an owner's theory at that, complete with workers chanting prayers to the Virgin Mother at appropriate moments of the day. In practice the operation of the obrajes was something else.

SIZE OF LABOR FORCE AND DEMOGRAPHIC CHARACTERISTICS

How large was the labor force of a "typical" obraje? An unequivocal answer is impossible because size varied over time, place, and the business cycle. The evidence is frequently incomplete, particularly regarding free laborers hired on a casual basis.[6] Nevertheless, a few observations are possible, considering first the obrajes in the Valley of Mexico. A report of 1604 indicates that obrajes in Mexico City could have as many as 120 workers, whereas those in Texcoco averaged 44.[7] Fuller information for the Valley of Mexico in 1690 implies a mean of 41 laborers, with a standard deviation of about 28. A few obrajes in the jurisdiction of Coyoacán, notably the eponymous "Ansaldo" and "Posadas," were at least 1 standard deviation above the mean, and "Contreras" was quite large at over 2. Most fell within a range of 1 deviation.[8] By the middle of the eighteenth century, a different picture had emerged. As the data in Table 4.1 indicate, existing obrajes had grown to as many as 200 workers, apprentices included.

Outside the Valley of Mexico, the data are thin, as the statistics presented in Table 4.2 indicate. The evidence for Querétaro is especially disappointing. John Super reports a few figures, derived mostly from inspection records.[9] Where data are available, the variance of estimated employment is large. The obraje operated by don José Escandón, the Conde de la Sierra Gorda, had approximately 200 laborers according to inspection records. But Francisco Quacho, one-time manager of the obraje, testified "he saw that . . . about 800 laborers [worked] inside and out," an enormous figure that likely included cottage spinners.[10] Another put the labor force at an improbable 1,000. The most plausible calculation for Querétaro comes from Juan López Cancelanda, who thought that the average size there was 180 at the beginning of the nineteenth century.[12]

The obrajes of Puebla, important in the sixteenth century, averaged approximately 100 workers in 1588.[13] Figures reported between 1583 and 1655 by Hans Pohl, Jutta Haenisch, and Wolfgang

TABLE 4.1
Labor Force of Selected Obrajes, Valley of Mexico

Obraje	Year	Workers	Looms
MEXICO CITY Obraje of José Pimentel, Calzada de la Piedad	1745	176	12
	1750	209	?
	1755	42	?
Jesuit obraje, Puente de Peredo	1746	173	?
	1751	84	?
	1753	190	14[a]
	1758	123 (inc)	?
Obraje of Manuel Durán de Otero, Salto de Agua	1800	210[b]	?
JURISDICTION OF COYOACÁN "Mixcoac"	1757	69 (inc)	12
	1792	121 (inc)	14
"Posadas"	1690	108	?
	1792	109 (inc)	16
"Panzacola"	1792	51 (inc)	22
	1802	206	29
	1804	192	32
	1805	185	32
Obraje of Fernando Sotabarria	1766	200	?
JURISDICTION OF TACUBA	1799	200	18[c]

Note: (inc) = incomplete; [a] number of looms in 1755; [b] "Indians" only; [c] number of looms in 1793.

Sources: Pimentel: 1745, list of workers and debts, AGNM, Tierras, vol. 676; 1750, 1755, petition of Juan Antonio de Paz, México, Jan. 20, 1750, AGNM, Tierras, vol. 677. *Jesuit obraje*: 1746, list of debts, Jul. 1, 1746, AGNM, Tierras, vol. 680; 1751, list of debts, Mar. 5, 1751, AGNM, Tierras, vol. 681; 1753, list of debts, AGNM, Tierras, vol. 1034; 1758, inventory of Oct. 25, 1758, AGNM, Tierras, vol. 1034; *Durán de Otero*: matrícula de barrio de San Juan, AGNM, Padrones, vol. 105; *Mixcoac*: 1792, AGNM, Padrones, vol. 6; 1757, liquidation of accounts and other testimony, Jul. 5 and Feb. 16, 1757, AGNM, Tierras, vol. 2016, exp. 2; *Posadas*: 1690, inspection, AGI, Contaduría 806, Ramo 3; 1792, AGNM, Padrones, vol. 6; *Panzacola*: 1792, AGNM, Padrones, vol. 6; 1802-5, documents relating to the bankruptcy of the house of Oteyza y Vértiz, AJM; *Sotabarria*: report of Diego Cornide, México, May 24, 1766, AGI, México 1366; *Jurisdiction of Tacuba*: Mariano de la Peña to the director of the excise district of México, Tacuba, Apr. 12, 1793, AGNM, Aduanas, vol. 134.

TABLE 4.2
Labor Force of Selected Obrajes, Other Centers

Obraje	Year	Workers	Looms
TLAXCALA			
Obraje of Díaz Varela	1783	78	28
QUERÉTARO			
Obraje of first Conde de la Sierra Gorda	1769	198	?
PUEBLA			
Obraje of Francisco de Briuega	1583	117	?
Obraje of Pedro de Ita	1608	136	?
Obraje of Alonso Gómez	1610	257	?

Sources: *Díaz Varela*: list of indebted workers, AJM, leg. 146; *Sierra Gorda*: inspection record, AGNM, Civil, vol. 1435, exp. 7; *Puebla obrajes*: Hans Pohl et al., "Aspectos sociales . . . de los obrajes textiles en Puebla," 42.

Löske imply a similar mean, but with considerable variance.[14] Elsewhere, obrajes making says in Tepeaca employed between 50 and 70 laborers each.[15] For Tlaxcala, David Szewczyk finds that the first obraje was probably erected in Apizaco in the 1560s. The labor force of obrajes in Tlaxcala could be as large as 40, but "a force of half that number was more common."[16] The statistics for the obraje of the Díaz Varela are limited to indebted laborers, but the total must have been larger, since it had 28 looms and 90 spinning wheels.[17] In San Miguel el Grande, the number of workers in the obraje of Balthasar de Sauto (ca. 1750) was reported to be 500 laborers, which certainly included cottage spinners.[18]

The demographic characteristics of the work force were equally varied. Its composition varied over time and place, but in a messy way. The ethnocultural meaning of terms used to classify workers, "Indian," "mestizo," "mulatto," and "español," are far from clear. Woodrow Borah, for example, has argued that "Indian" was more a fiscal than an ethnocultural category over time. When did the change occur? Borah thinks it was plainly visible (or plainly confusing) in urban areas such as Mexico City by the late seventeenth century.[19] Yet decrees to obrajes in Coyoacán appeared in Nahuatl into the 1740s, and Borah agrees that "listing people who speak an Indian tongue gives us a fairly firm category."[20] Obviously, there were mon-

olingual Nahuatl speakers in Coyoacán affected by royal and viceregal decrees, but how many, and how important were they? The
famous inspection of obrajes in Coyoacán in 1660 required inter-
preters, so the timing of the change is ambiguous, and a certain fuz-
ziness in terminology remains.[21] The issue is significant, because ac-
culturated Indians were more likely to work for wages and less likely
to be coerced than unacculturated ones. Bilingualism (and accom-
modation to Castilian legal institutions) may then be the best measures we have for native adaptation to market culture in the colonial
period.[22] The issue also points toward a classification of the "disutility" that work in an obraje implied for social status.

Sixteenth- and seventeenth-century legislation was intended to
benefit that Indian, and the phraseology of the law changed only
with the ordinances of 1767. Contemporary reports for Mexico City
find Indians in the obrajes, just as do studies of sixteenth-century
Puebla and Tlaxcala.[23] By about 1650, however, a change is underway. The inspection of Coyoacán in 1660 reveals a significant number of black slaves in the obrajes.[24] In 1654, the obraje at Apizaco in
Tlaxcala was "described as 'filled with low-life people, blacks and
mulattos' "; slaves and castas also grew in numbers in Puebla.[25] The
growth of a heterogeneous work force continued into the eighteenth
century. By 1792, large numbers of mulattos descended from slaves
who inhabited the obrajes "Panzacola," "Posadas," and "Mixcoac."[26]
A similar variety worked for Balthasar de Sauto in San Miguel,
where "mulattos, *lobos*, negros, and other mixtures [formed] the
bulk of his labor force."[27] Only in Querétaro was there much evidence of a laboring population in which blacks, mulattos, and mestizos continued in the minority. According to the Bucareli census,
"Indians" still constituted nearly 90 percent of the over 1,600 workers counted, a finding discussed below.[28]

Eighteenth-century ordinances regulating the obrajes recognized
the change that had occurred. Although "indios" figure in the lan-
guage, "sirvientes," "operarios," and "jornaleros" are more prominent. In other words, it was the castas, whose numbers increased
into the eighteenth century, that ultimately populated the obrajes.[29]
The original Indian population, which declined in the century after
1532, was progressively displaced. This displacement was a consequence of changing demographic realities, but it also reflected the
incessant pressure of legislation in forcing substitutes for Indian labor.

Data on age and sex composition of the labor force are scarce. Certain obrajes, such as "Panzacola" in Coyoacán, had a well-deserved

reputation for abusing children; textile work among children in poor societies is not uncommon.[30] The age distribution of "Panzacola's" population in 1792 shows individuals under age 15 as the largest proportion counted. But neither "Mixcoac" nor "Posadas" shows a similar pattern.[31] In the obraje "Otero," in Mexico City, there were many children, with the just-under-tributary age (*próximos a tributar*) at about 11 percent.[32] But since it is difficult to distinguish between apprentices and children simply living at an obraje with parents, the evidence for child labor is inconclusive.

A similar difficulty characterizes the role of women. Under the Velasco ordinances of 1595, women were permitted in the obrajes, and married couples were to remain together. Single women could work in an obraje, provided they were free to leave at night. The inspection of Coyoacán in 1660 suggests these provisions were sometimes ignored, and that women served as cooks and *tortilleras*, perhaps under compulsion, as they did in "Posadas." Many of the women of "Posadas," however, were married to men working there and were but a small part of the total population.[33] Women were also few in the obraje of Francisco de Briuega, in Puebla, in 1583.[34] They continued in small numbers into the eighteenth century. The obraje of José Pimentel had no identifiable female workers. There were 8 women out of 80 workers in the obraje of María Teresa Montes de Oca, and but 9 out of 173 workers in 1746 in an obraje owned by the Society of Jesus. On the other hand, in the obraje of the Díaz Varela in Tlaxcala in 1783, there were 39 men and 38 women, a ratio that suggests the participation of married couples. A similar pattern emerges on the hacienda "Jurica" during the ownership of don Santiago de Villanueva y Oribay (ca. 1725). There were two large obrajes on the hacienda, and both functioned with a family-based labor system. Men, women, and children all worked together at "Jurica."[35]

APPRENTICES, CONVICTS, AND SLAVES

Three groups of varying significance should be considered separately: apprentices, convicts, and slaves. They worked under various terms and with different degrees of willingness, and each group offered particular problems and advantages.

Apprentices

The ostensible purpose of apprenticeship was to teach the craft to younger workers. Parents or guardians signed the indenture (*escri-*

tura de aprendiz) before a corregidor or alcalde in the presence of a notary. Its terms were usually specified at signing. Apprenticeship was very common. Poverty compelled the poor to apprentice their sons, and orphans sought apprenticeship when it offered survival. Apprentices could accumulate earnings for payment at the end of indenture, a form of forced savings as well as a device to keep them to their agreement. In 1804, "Panzacola" owed apprentices on five- and six-year terms an average of 14 pesos each. By 1805, the figure had risen to more than 17 pesos as three apprentices completed terms.[36]

Sometimes, an apprentice would remain to pursue the trade. In "Mixcoac," the mestizo apprentice Juan Antonio Barrios had been seized for vagrancy and apprenticed at 14. He served seven years and continued for three more, even though he wished to return to Ocuila. A mulatto weaver, Juan José García, had been apprenticed at 11 and spent eighteen years. Another weaver, Tomás Antonio, came to the obraje at 8 and remained for fourteen years. In other words, for some, life in an obraje, whatever its hardships, was better than starving.[37]

But not all apprentices came freely or stayed willingly. María Cecilia Rivera claimed that her 13-year-old son had been shanghaied by the corregidor of Mexico City and apprenticed to "Panzacola."[38] A 12-year-old servant, José Tiburcio Alfaro, was apprenticed to "Panzacola" for five years for stealing a sheet. His mother took legal action to gain him release.[39] In 1660, Francisco Flores, the mayordomo of "Posadas," was prohibited from keeping apprentices "behind closed doors like slaves." Flores replied that "if he let them leave, none would return."[40] In the obraje of Balthasar de Sauto, there were forty boys between ages 5 and 15, equivalent in age to apprentices, who were there to work off the debts accumulated by their fathers and grandfathers. A royal inspector thought them little more than chattel. An apprentice who completed a term for Sauto with unfinished or imperfect work was made to stay on. Ostensibly free skilled workers, the former apprentices worked at a reduced rate and earned no more than *jornaleros*, a difference of 1 peso per half cut of cloth.[41]

What economic role did apprenticeship play? The data in Table 4.3 indicate that apprentices constituted from 6 percent to 20 percent of a given work force, a visible to substantial component of the total. Given their status as dependents, the obrajes could shift to them the cost of training in the form of lower wages. When apprentices received payment as a lump sum at the end of their terms, man-

TABLE 4.3
Apprenticeship in the Obrajes

Obraje	Year	Apprentices (N)	Percent[a]
Jesuit	1758	22	17.9
Montes de Oca	1739	10	12.5
Mixcoac	1757	4	5.7
	1792	12	9.9
Posadas	1792	10	9.2
Panzacola	1792	12	23.5
	1802	16	7.8
	1804	35	18.2
	1805	32	17.3
Sauto	c. 1750[b]	40	8.0
José Gutiérrez de Castro	1690	4	8.0
Juan Pérez de Mata	1690	2	9.0

[a] defined as (apprentices)/(apprentices + other workers).

[b] assumed by virtue of age.

Sources: *Jesuit obraje*: 1758, inventory of Oct. 25, 1758, AGNM, Tierras, vol. 1034; *Montes de Oca*: list of workers and debts, México, Nov. 16, 1739, AGNM, Tierras, vol. 1181; *Mixcoac*: 1757, liquidation of accounts and other testimony, Jul. 5 and Feb. 16, 1757, AGNM, Tierras, vol. 2016, exp. 2; 1792, AGNM, Padrones, vol. 6; *Posadas*: 1792, AGNM, Padrones, vol. 6; *Panzacola*: 1792, AGNM, Padrones, vol. 6; 1802-5, documents relating to the bankruptcy of the house of Oteyza y Vértiz, AJM; *Sauto*: AGI, México, 1047; *Gutiérrez de Castro* and *Pérez de Mata*: inspections of Dec. 6 and 7, 1690, AGI, Contaduría 806, Ramo 3.

agers discounted the cost of their labor, which was yet another incentive to employ them.[42] Moreover, delayed payment enforced the indenture—the carrot at the end of a very long stick. Those who fled before the end of their term lost the carrot.

Convicts

Convict labor was unpopular with the owners of the obrajes, or at least with those in New Spain. Only in Guadalajara were convicts acceptable, even desirable, because the obrajes there remained largely inchoate and were very short of labor.[43] The sale of convict services had a long history in New Spain and became standard punishment for serious offenses by Indians after 1555.[44] Convicts were sold and distributed through both the Real Sala del Crimen and the Acordada, and owners were sometimes unable to distinguish between these jurisdictions.[45] What made convict labor unappealing was that convicts were dangerous as well as unwilling. For example, fifty criminals sent from the Royal Jail in Mexico City in coffles to the obrajes represented a catalogue of horrors. They were guilty of nearly everything: rape, battery, homicide, incest, and weapons' offenses. One prisoner had already escaped from an obraje, and another prisoner had wounded the foreman in an obraje to which he had been previously sold.[46] This obviously made the owners nervous about receiving convicts. Both indebted workers and convicts may have been reluctant laborers, but convicts knew how to fight back, and often did so. Many had been transported far from their homes; they were always looking for ways to escape.[47]

In 1733, all but two owners in Querétaro banded together and refused to accept chain gangs of sixty-four and twenty-three convicts sent by the Sala and the Acordada.[48] Individual owners deluged the Council of the Indies with complaints. Don Bernardo de Pereda Torres, who refused to join the mass action in 1733, claimed that the convicts made him fear for his life. His obraje was two leagues outside Querétaro, and he feared the possibility of an uprising.[49] Don Pedro de Primo y Jordán said his obraje had walls of adobe (not uncommon), and that convicts were expert at breaking through them. Worse, a convict had murdered the owner of "Jalpa," don Antonio de Mier, whose obraje stood just outside Querétaro.[50] Thus, the owners resisted the *repartimiento de reos*, and one made a serious legal challenge to the system. The only obraje that could safely hold convicts was a closed one (*cerrado*), but the Velasco ordinances of 1595 and the *Recopilación* had outlawed those in which the workers were not free. The system enmeshed viceregal administration and owners in a substantial contradiction.[51]

The impetus for convict labor came not from the private sector but from the government. The distribution of convicts was a lucrative business. The proceeds of sales were divided among municipal authorities, court and police officials, and conductors of the chain gang.[52] At the tariff in force in 1733, the chain gang the Querétaro owners refused was worth about 3,100 pesos, a tidy sum.[53] By the late 1760s, the distribution of criminal labor was worth from 10,000 to 12,000 pesos a year.[54] Moreover, officials in places like Querétaro saw the system as shifting the costs of incarceration to textile producers, especially given the shortage of facilities for imprisonment.[55] The owners resisted the transfer, particularly when added security produced no increase in profits.[56] Indeed, one reason the guild in Querétaro resisted convict labor was that it implied an economic loss.[57] Forced labor was not inexpensive in any case, but the additional costs of convict labor made owners resist it more than they resisted peonage. Not only was productivity lower, but the risk was intrinsically higher.[58] Consequently, opposition to the repartimiento de reos led to its formal abolition in 1767, although changing priorities also influenced the decision. Convicts were henceforth sent to presidios rather than to obrajes.[59]

Slaves

In 1588, Licenciado Santiago del Riego reported on his inspection of the obrajes of Puebla and Tlaxcala to the Marqués de Villamanrique (1585-90). The ordinances of Martín Enríquez (1568-80) did not curb abuse and had become "irrelevant" in the intervening decade. In Puebla, Riego had found "many of the Indians injured . . . imprisoned in perpetual hunger [and] worked inhumanely." What was at stake, he thought, was nothing less than "the liberation of the Indians."[60] Yet the obrajes played a major role in the economy, and Riego was afraid to interfere with their smooth functioning. Riego therefore resolved to "speak softly . . . [and] to find a remedy appropriate to what had happened and was to come. To temper rigor with mercy, and to so avoid the sudden destruction of work that was, in sum, necessary to the republic."[61] Riego openly broke with Villamanrique's advocacy of the destruction of the obrajes, writing that "it [was] very useful to have [them]."[62]

This tension presaged much dispute over the next two centuries. The obraje was corrupt and corrupting. Almost inevitably, it exploited first the Indian, then the casta. But the woolens produced were vital to the interests of the colony. In 1572, Martín Enríquez, a viceroy of considerable character and intelligence, stated that Mexico could not do without the production of the obrajes.[63] Thirty years later, the Conde de Monterrey (1595-1603) wrote: "Their supply and cheapness is much greater than could be had from Spain." Obrajes were, then, "most useful to these provinces, and to those of Peru, where [their goods] are sent."[64] The low cost of abusive conduct was a further difficulty for reformers. "The penalty the ordinance provides is slight. The obrajeros ridicule it, and lock up the Indians as they please."[65]

Attempts to curb abuse of Indian labor and to contain obrajes in certain locales gave way under the Conde de Monterrey to efforts to oblige the obrajes to employ black slave labor. In 1601 and 1603, the obrajes were told to obtain slaves, for Indian labor would be prohibited.[66] Monterrey had no illusions about the probability of success: "To prevent the Indians completely from entering the obrajes seems to me very difficult."[67] Obrajes, like sugar mills, could not afford slaves, and a subsidy for their purchase seemed necessary.[68] Historians generally assume, for reasons given by Monterrey, that the measure was unsuccessful.[69] But additional reflection suggests otherwise. In Puebla, castas and black slaves grew in importance to the obrajes, ultimately replacing the Indian peons in the sixteenth and early seventeenth centuries. By 1661, slaves represented nearly 60 percent of their capital stock.[70] David Szewczyk finds a similar substitution in Tlaxcala, where the Indian wage labor that had dominated until 1618 became black and mulatto by 1654.[71] The inspection of "Contreras" and "Ansaldo" in Coyoacán in 1660 revealed numerous black slaves—nearly 200 between them.[72] Before 1630, Indians were the principal source of labor in the obrajes in Querétaro. After that, black slaves supplanted them; some obrajes were run exclusively by slaves.[73]

It is logical to ask whether demographic necessity, or the measures of 1601 and 1603, or both, drove the acquisition of slaves by the owners of the obrajes. Their sale to Mexico accelerated after 1605, even as the native population reached its nadir, and substitutability between the two seems reasonable.[74] But slavery was expensive. Charles Gibson estimated that the labor force of an average seventeenth-century obraje required an investment of 15,000 to 20,000 pesos; "Contreras" or "Ansaldo" in 1660 could easily have cost much more.[75] Of course, investment in slave labor was justified by its greater productivity relative to "free" Indians, particularly as the costs of acquiring Indians were rising rapidly. Some evidence supports this, since sugar planters in the seventeenth century assumed that a black slave could do the work of two Indians.[76] But it is impossible to prove in conventional terms. We might simply infer that with fewer Indians available for work, the owners of obrajes purchased slaves, and that pressure from viceregal authorities induced them to acquire still more.

A significant number of black slaves was still in evidence in the later seventeenth and early eighteenth century. "Ansaldo" in Coyoacán continued with 30, and "Contreras" with 100.[77] Slaves were not unusual in other obrajes in the Valley or in Puebla, where

"Apresa" counted 93.[78] But the eighteenth century witnessed a diminution in the number of slaves reported. Demand for them fell sharply in eighteenth-century Querétaro. By 1777-78, few blacks and mulattos remained.[79] The same happened in Coyoacán. In 1792, "Posadas" reported only one.[80] This closely coincides with Dennis Valdés's finding that the slave market in Mexico City collapsed during the eighteenth century.[81] His regressions show a dramatic fall in the estimated price at birth for a black slave after the 1750s, evidence of the diminishing profitability of raising them.[82] Valdés argues that the recovery of the Indian population induced users of labor to substitute relatively cheaper, free Indian labor for black slave labor: "[an] increasingly numerous, inexpensive supply of Hispanized Indians displaced the slaves."[83] The factor of the British South Sea Company in Veracruz in 1736 reached the same conclusion, noting a "smaller demand for slaves owing to the vast number of tributary Indians with which the Kingdom of New Spain abounds, who perform all labor at easy rates."[84]

In short, the obrajes experienced a series of transitions driven by demographic change and abetted by a legal preference for nonindigenous labor. A fall in the use of "Indian" labor in the strict sense was followed by black slavery and then by the ostensibly free labor of castas. But what could "free" labor mean in light of such imperfections in the labor market?

FREE LABOR AND PEONAGE: DEFINITIONS AND DISPOSITIONS

Contemporaries understood free labor to mean work without compulsion. "He came freely from Querétaro to work in this obraje." "He is in this obraje voluntarily, because he had nothing to eat where he came from."[85] Free workers presented themselves or came looking for work. One could not compel them to do what they were unwilling to do. Nor did debt make a worker unfree. A royal official, for instance, defined free workers as "those who voluntarily go into debt."[86] A free worker could borrow against his future earnings by advances: "He works in this obraje voluntarily, indebted for ten pesos."[87]

Besides volition, free labor presupposed physical mobility. It was impossible to impair the mobility of free laborers without altering their status. When asked the whereabouts of other spinners of the obraje "El Placer" in Mixcoac, Juan García answered: "The rest aren't here, because as free, they come and go as they please."[88] Another owner in Coyoacán testified: "There are more or fewer laborers according to what has to be made," whereas don Sancho de Posadas qualified his labor force as "more or less"—"some days more show up, and some days less."[89] The roll of an obraje in Querétaro owned by the Conde de la Sierra Gorda named various individuals who were absent during an inspection. "They come and go freely," the *visitador* concluded.[90]

These comments yield the colonial definition of free labor. Slaves, of course, were unfree. So were convicts. Apprentices unable to come and go had no freedom. Anyone locked up in an obraje (*encerrado*) for any reason was unfree, past or future status notwithstanding. The formal term for such involuntary servitude (slavery excepted) is peonage, or debt peonage, if implemented to secure repayment of cash or credit. Peonage also characterized the unofficial, illicit assignment of minor criminals to the obrajes in what Herbert Nickel terms the "informal repartimiento."[91] Informal repartimiento could become debt peonage, if economic entrapment ensued.[92] The extent to which peonage and informal repartimiento occurred must modify any notion of free labor employed.

DEBT PEONAGE AND INFORMAL REPARTIMIENTO: THE CLASSIC VIEW

The view of peonage expressed by Linares finds echo in the literature of the obrajes. Above all, Humboldt's description of Querétaro is famous:

> The obrajes of Querétaro employ the same trick which is made use of in several of the cloth obrajes of Quito . . . They choose from among the Indians the most miserable, but such as show an aptitude for the work, and they advance them a small sum of money. The Indian, who loves to get intoxicated, spends it in a few days, and having become the debtor of the master, he is shut up in the workshop, under the pretence of paying off the debt by the work of his hands.[93]

This process concerned viceregal administrations from the sixteenth through the nineteenth centuries. The Velasco ordinances of 1595 regarded indebtedness contracted without intervention of a local magistrate as unenforceable. Advances were to be made no more often than quarterly.[94] Cédulas of 1609 and 1627 "abolished" indebtedness based on advances and viewed such contracts involving Indians as unenforceable.[95] An *auto acordado* of 1656 specified that

Indians held for debt should not receive further money, and that indebtedness could not be subrogated.[96] Ordinances of 1767, subsequently repeated and modified, prohibited the truck store of an obraje (*tienda de raya*) from advancing more than 1 real weekly to finance purchases. No worker was to be indebted for more than four months or to receive more than two-thirds of his salary in advance.[97]

During the administrations of Linares, Amarillas (1755-60) and Iturrigaray (1803-1808), there were substantive discussions of peonage. Yet over nearly a century, their terms and vocabulary remained virtually unchanged, and their reports were indeed interchangeable. Thus, in 1714, Linares wrote that owners made advances "in amounts beyond the capacity of the workers to repay" so that "they expired before the debts did." Caught in a state of perpetual servitude, workers seeking freedom found that "reprisals [were] made, and [that] their own wives and children [were] taken." The fear of reprisals to their families discouraged many from fleeing, although some were hardened to the consequences and fled anyway.[98]

Forty-five years later, the royal inspector, Diego Antonio Fernández de la Madrid, also concluded that peonage was widespread. On their own, owners and bosses had taken to apprehending debtors or their guarantors. Making no distinctions, "they locked all of them up in obrajes to discharge debts. There they remain until the debts are extinguished." Even more alarming was peonage without debt, the informal repartimiento. Acting as "correspondents" for owners, ecclesiastical and secular judges sent petty criminals to obrajes to serve sentences, although the practice had been outlawed in 1632.[99] Others impressed labor on trumped-up charges, seizing victims "as if they had in reality freely and voluntarily incurred a debt." The obrajes of Coyoacán and Querétaro were equally guilty in this regard. In both jurisdictions, magistrates racketeered in selling drunks and vagrants to earn "supplements." Once in the obrajes, the unfortunates became peons. Debt was a thin excuse. Fernández de la Madrid concluded that a venal judiciary was the basis for peonage, with or without debt.[100]

Half a century later, officials undertook similar discussions, saying that "owners of obrajes have sought and, indeed, succeeded . . . [by] means of advancing . . . earnings [and making workers] incapable of paying [them] off in the normal life of . . . working in an obraje."[101] Words written almost ninety years after Linares's indictment were virtually indistinguishable from his own. Apparently, little had changed.

Evidence of this sort, however, is problematic. To demonstrate that successive generations of bureaucrats took note of peonage proves only that. It cannot establish that peonage was common, permanent, or even important. Over the years, bureaucrats read the same reports and reviewed the same cases. Successive *informes* based on the same evidence in the files of the viceregal secretariat— and biased at that (no one broke the law by obeying it)—are not behavioral evidence; they may even be regarded as alarmist or contentious documents based on a few instances, magnified by repetition.

This line of reasoning may be partially validated. For many causes, peonage became less prevalent in the Valley of Mexico than in the Bajío. Once formal slavery had largely disappeared, some free labor, as contemporaries understood it, appeared in a number of obrajes. Yet we must be careful. Peonage did occur in the Valley of Mexico. One can easily find specific instances of advances for payment of tribute or for sacramentals.[102] Their frequency and importance, however, are uncertain.

The demand for peonage also varied throughout the business cycle. Woolen manufacturing was cyclical. Its demand for labor was tied to the cycles of agriculture and weather. There were, in short, peak and slack demands for labor. Peonage reflected this and was therefore generally temporary. Since manufacturing was cyclical, it was irrational to maintain a permanent force of indebted peons. The cost was high when measured in terms of alternative uses of working capital. A peso used to retain a peon, for example, could not be used to purchase raw materials. So, in José Pimentel's obraje, the workers' indebtedness was as large as the value of wool held in inventory.[103] On the hacienda "San Francisco Paula" in Querétaro, the ratio of workers' indebtedness to the value of the obraje was nearly 30 percent.[104] In other words, one could tie up a great deal of capital in creating indebtedness, so there needed to be good reason for doing so. Owners and their agents were always forced to choose between hiring more labor and getting more raw materials. The cost of one was measured in terms of the loss of the other. Peonage, to use a modern phrase, offered no free lunch.

Thus, peonage could circumvent an imperfect labor market, but only at a cost and not without risk. Some workers could beat their debts by flight and death, much to the chagrin of the owners, who found the tables turned. The workers understood this and always tried to use the system to their advantage. What often stopped them was the power of the law, exercised by magistrates on behalf of managers who bought their services. The result was endemic struggle, mountains of litigation, and an appalling record of violence, abuse, and venality. What often brought labor to the obrajes was not the invisible hand of the market but the long arm of the law.

So, for example, in the obrajes of Querétaro, peonage succeeded slavery and was important. In late summer of 1802, the guild there admitted that from 1,500 to 2,000 peons were locked up (*encerrado*) in obrajes. Given the guild's incentive to minimize the extent of an illegal practice, the real number was probably higher.[105] The stated figure implies that 30 percent to 40 percent of the labor force in Querétaro was unfree in the eighteenth-century sense, at least at that moment.[106] Indeed, the guild protested that the obrajes would vanish without peonage. "The prosperity of this beautiful city . . . is held together by the reprehensible conduct and character of the workers in the obrajes," it wrote. "The instant their subordination is lost, a link in this tightly woven commerce will be broken." The guild concluded: "No matter how prodigal nature has been in its gifts, nothing can be undertaken *if there are no hands to do the job.*"[107]

Yet one could also conclude from this that 60 percent to 70 percent of the labor force in Querétaro was free. Biased though the evidence is, it does not point to universal servitude. The figure of 30 percent to 40 percent may well have represented the demand for labor at a seasonal peak of production. As the guild argued, peonage was a "temporary confinement" lasting "8, 10, 15 [days], a month at most."[108] It would be naive to accept this at face value, for most owners also claimed that they never made any money, even as they expanded production. Yet the assertion makes economic sense. It also explains how a limited number of supervisors could control 200 or more ill-disposed, potentially violent men. Coercion, force, and brutality *were* employed to cow workers, but only some of them were prevented from leaving, and for these, the loss of freedom was temporary.

Who did the obrajes seize in the short run? The evidence points to the spinners and carders, since shortages of yarn appeared first, with a consequence of excess looms.[109] The ordinances of the Marqués de Cerralvo (1624-35), written in 1633, noticed that sufficient yarn was vital to operating obrajes: "If this is not lacking, all else is abundant." Yet it was in making yarn that workers were "most skilled and least willing." Thus, owners were inclined "to lock them up if they did not work."[110] Other indications also imply that indebtedness was used mostly to recruit makers of yarn. In "Panzacola" between 1802 and 1805, the average debts of the carders and spinners exceeded those of the weavers. The same was true in the obraje of the hacienda "San Francisco Paula" in 1804.[111] This is a fragile inference—we have no probability sample here—but it indicates that spinners and carders were more often the victims of oppression than were the weavers, who worked from yarn held in inventory.

How could the obrajes prevent individuals from leaving? Quite simply, they had the secure physical structure that the hacienda, for example, lacked. In the Querétaro obrajes, the foremen and crew leaders marked the hands of free workers, so the doorkeeper would know who could and could not pass.[112] For the particularly troublesome double doors were a formidable obstacle, and Humboldt thought the Querétaro obrajes looked like prisons.[113] He was not exaggerating. In 1811, Miguel Domínguez reported that a thousand prisoners from the Hidalgo uprising were in obrajes converted into jails, impressive evidence of their suitability for confining human beings.[114] Truly horrendous obrajes, such as "Posadas" or Balthasar de Sauto's, had not only barred doors but also pillories, shackles, and hand and leg irons.[115] An inventory of "Panzacola" listed "2 shackles, 2 hobbles, and a fetter." The inventory of another mentions "shackles, chains, and other devices of imprisonment for the security of the criminals brought to the obraje."[116] These were ways to keep the footloose in line.

Yet such impediments were not always necessary. Even small debts could be effective if properly enforced. The method left no bruises and produced no complicated account books, but its dimensions were cunning. Enforcement was based on the *fianza*, or bond, secured on a friend, relative, or child. Such bonds definitely existed. Debts from the obrajes "Santa Cristo de Burgos" and "Nuestra Señora de Guadalupe," both on the hacienda "Jurica" in Querétaro, reveal that physical compulsion may have been unnecessary. Consider these entries, drawn from an assortment of similar ones:

Santiaga Pascuala, wife of Blas de los Ángeles, her guarantor, the husband named, and Juan de los Ángeles, her son. A debt of 50 pesos, 2 reales

Juan de los Ángeles, and María de Guadalupe, his wife, their guarantors, Blas de los Ángeles, his father; Félix de la Cruz; Antonio Lázaro; Lázaro Martínez; and José de Mendoza y Jimena. A debt of 114 pesos and 5 burros, charged to him, with Francisco Juárez Jurica, Lázaro Juarez, and Francisco Mesoia[117]

Husbands and wives were jointly indebted, children acted as guarantors, and the family was linked. The point is easy to grasp. It was not necessary to compel physically Juan or Blas de los Ángeles to stay at "Jurica." Should Juan go without repaying his debts, his wife and father were responsible. If Santiaga Pascuala left, her husband and son were accountable. The only way to leave, short of repayment, was mass migration. This was not impossible, but it was not simple. An inspection of Puebla obrajes in 1700 also gives examples of families broken by escape and wives left to extinguish debts of husbands and kin.[118]

In other words, peonage was complex and subtle. It sometimes required force, but occasionally did not. Perpetual servitude was generally absent (there were exceptions), but freedom and mobility were fragile and easily abridged. Peonage effectively dealt with an imperfect labor market, but it did so only at a cost. On the one hand, owners tied up their capital in recruiting workers with payments made in advance of production. On the other, laborers generally earned less than they would have in a free-wage economy. The owners got workers whose productivity was suspect. The workers got bosses with a taste for violence and fraud. Colonial consumers got the cloth they required, but not much more. The system generated some surplus, and there was always a struggle to see who got the largest share of it. Although the owners, who had police power, usually came out ahead, some workers could find room to maneuver. These workers—who came and went as they pleased—were still badly paid. Yet their willingness to work for less (perhaps much less) induced the owners to accept their irregular pattern of labor. Here there was escape from the all-or-nothing offers of employment that obrajes frequently made.

DEBT WITHOUT PEONAGE

To recapitulate, not all workers were peons, and not all peons were slaves. Not even the infamous obraje of Balthasar de Sauto was guilty of perpetual enslavement. Sauto was accused of holding "*most* of the workers slaves for many years . . . with the growth of the debts they were born with."[119] At least sixty families of workers lived in cottages provided in the adjacent barrios of Presa and Carrocero.[120] Even here there was mobility in some sense, although families could be exploited as easily as single people.

Indebtedness without peonage was common in obrajes of the Valley of Mexico in the eighteenth century. Aside from Fernández de la Madrid's report on Coyoacán, there were few complaints of systematic peonage, even though indebtedness was universal. The results of specific instances of indebtedness are displayed in Table 4.4.

Although "Panzacola" reputedly abused workers, their collective debts were modest in 1802-1805. For "Mixcoac," the data are incomplete, perhaps unreliable, but they indicate a similar tendency. Mean indebtedness in the obraje of Leyva was higher, but it is calculated on a small sample. The obrajes of Pimentel and Montes de Oca disclose substantial indebtedness, but it is below those levels considered excessive by contemporary standards. Only in the obraje of Otero were average debts high, but these were held by workers who had fled. Those deepest in debt gained most by repudiating it.

An interesting finding appears for an obraje owned by the Jesuits and rented out. The pattern is one of sensitivity to cyclical change between 1746-58, for the obraje naturally hired workers when business was good and fired them when it was bad. Average indebtedness varied in the same way; it rose when profits increased and fell

TABLE 4.4
Indebtedness in Selected Obrajes

Obraje	Year	Mean Debt (in pesos)	SD (in pesos)	N
Mixcoac	1757	8	11	41
Leyva	1747	16	21	27
Panzacola[a]	1802	10	?	196
	1804	11	?	157
	1805	11	?	153
Otero[b]	1807	50	?	100
Montes de Oca	1739	26	21	80
Pimentel	1746	28	21	177

Note: SD = standard deviation, N = number of workers.

[a] apprentices not included.

[b] average indebtedness of delinquent workers.

Sources: Mixcoac: liquidation of accounts and other testimony, Jul. 5 and Feb. 16, 1757, AGNM, Tierras, vol. 2016, exp. 2; *Leyva:* list of debts, México, Feb. 10, 1747, AJM, leg. 101; *Panzacola:* documents relating to the bankruptcy of the house of Oteyza y Vértiz, AJM; *Otero:* petition of Manuel Durán de Otero [México 1807], AGNM, Civil, vol. 987, exp. 11; *Montes de Oca:* list of workers and debts, México, Nov. 16, 1739, AGNM, Tierras, vol. 1181; *Pimentel:* list of workers and debts, AGNM, Tierras, vol. 676.

when business was poor. A 10-percent increase in average indebtedness accompanied a 4.5-percent increase in the obraje's labor force.[121] The interpretation is obvious. To get increasing numbers of workers, the obraje was compelled to lend more—to move up the labor supply curve. Because demand was strong and profits were good, the cash needed to make advances was available. The workers used the advances for various purposes, particularly to finance births, baptisms, and funerals.[122] As a business expansion slowed, the cycle was reversed. The demand for woolens fell, cash became tighter, and creditors clamored for repayment. The obraje could extend no further cash to its workers and demanded repayment of past advances. As a consequence, the average level of indebtedness fell.

The evidence appears in accounts of individual workers. From the list of names in Table 4.5, half the workers of this obraje typified the population, with debts that rose, fell and rose again. One succeeded in reducing indebtedness over the entire period. The reduction in some debts was surprisingly large. Between 1753 and 1758, Tomás Santos and Juan Santiago repaid about 23 pesos. Manuel de Santiago

TABLE 4.5
Selected Debts, Obraje of the Society of Jesus, 1746-58

Worker	Year			
	1746	1751	1753	1758
Tomás Santos	45/6	28/5	30/2	7/1.5
Juan Esteban Chacón	58/1	35/4	16/7	6/1
Manuel de Santiago	59/5	49/1	54/4	5/5
Miguel Francisco	17/7	7/5	26/2	5/7.5
Vicente Evaristo	13/1	2/1	28/2	17/1
José Santiago	28/2	22/3	34/2	11/5.5
Juan de Dios Sobrerito	20/0	10/6	6/0	30/7
Blas de Candelaria	23/2	12/3	21/7	?
José Borjas	38/6	33/5	21/7	?
José Soto	25/4	6/2	34/2	?

Note: To be read N pesos/ N reales, i.e., 1/1, 1 peso, 1 real.

Sources: 1746, list of debts, Jul. 1, 1746, AGNM, Tierras, vol. 680; 1751, list of debts, Mar. 5, 1751, AGNM, Tierras, vol. 681; 1753, list of debts, AGNM, Tierras, vol. 1034; 1758, inventory of Oct. 25, 1758, AGNM, Tierras, vol. 1034.

repaid almost 49 pesos. In part, repayment could reflect the effort of entire families, as workers borrowed fleece for daughters, sisters, or wives to work on and sell.[123] This enabled them to pay off substantial sums and made even larger debts tractable. But, again, this is not a probability sample; all we can say is that some workers could amortize substantial indebtedness.

This, however, was not always to the good. A decline in indebtedness was not necessarily evidence of a worker's free choice or willingness to pay. Recall that the description of the work routine at the opening of this chapter documents the owners' practice of "discounting" 50 percent of current earnings to repay advances. Owners in Querétaro practiced discounting and defended it as "rational and just."[124] An obraje that cut off credit and advances to its workers brought real hardship to them. Those obrajes that demanded repayment of past advances—rather than allow the employee to work off the debt—were literally turning the screws. If the indebtedness of the labor force fell, workers were quite possibly worse rather than better off, assuming of course that the debts were freely and fairly incurred.

The last test to show that indebtedness and peonage were not the same thing is the proportion of workers with debts in excess of 40 pesos. In the labor ordinances of 1767, debts of 40 to 50 pesos were considered large enough to warrant action against peonage.[125] Consequently, I use 40 pesos as a proxy for the proportion of workers unable to repay a debt—the "threshold" of peonage as eighteenth-century observers measured it. These proportions are displayed in Table 4.6. In the Jesuit obraje, the proportion never exceeded 16 percent, even at peak demand for labor. For the obraje of José Pimentel, the proportion was 22 percent; and for the obraje of Montes de Oca, 21 percent. Frequency distributions also indicate that very large debts were unusual. In the Jesuit obraje in 1746, only eight workers of 173 had debts more than 2 standard deviations larger than the mean. Over the next decade, the proportion was never much greater than 5 percent. In other words, large debts in the Valley of Mexico were more the exception than the rule.

The Basis of Peonage and Indebtedness

If peonage was more prevalent in the Bajío than in the Valley of Mexico in the eighteenth century, why was this so? Most important, the obrajes of the Bajío prospered during the eighteenth century. Consequently, the demand for labor in Querétaro, San Miguel, and

TABLE 4.6
Workers at the Threshold of Peonage

Obraje	Year	% with indebtedness ≥40 pesos	N
Montes de Oca	1739	21.3	17
Pimentel	1746	22.0	39
Jesuit	1746	14.4	39
	1751	8.3	7
	1753	16.1	27
	1758	1.6	2
Mixcoac	1757	1.5	1

Sources: *Montes de Oca*, list of workers and debts, México, Nov. 16, 1739, AGNM, Tierras, vol. 1181; *Pimentel*: list of workers and debts, AGNM, Tierras, vol. 676; *Jesuit*: 1746, list of debts, Jul. 1, 1746, AGNM, Tierras, vol. 680; 1751, list of debts, Mar. 5, 1751, AGNM, Tierras, vol. 681; 1753, list of debts, AGNM, Tierras, vol. 1034; 1758, inventory of Oct. 25, 1758, AGNM, Tierras, vol. 1034; *Mixcoac*: liquidation of accounts and other testimony, Jul. 5 and Feb. 16, 1757, AGNM, Tierras, vol. 680.

Acámbaro grew or remained stable while employment and investment elsewhere fell. Consider peons in the obrajes of Querétaro. In 1777-78, they numbered around 1,600, regardless of the term of confinement. In 1802, the guild admitted to having 1,500 to 2,000 peons in the obrajes. These figures are similar and imply a stable demand for labor. There were also alternatives for labor around Querétaro, where the number of haciendas increased from 58 in 1743 to 82 around 1800.[126] Consequently, although population in the Bajío grew in the eighteenth century, a labor shortage was more likely there than in the Valley of Mexico or in the Puebla-Tlaxcala basin, where the obrajes were in decline. Peonage was most common in the Bajío, because labor was scarce there and coercion, as we have seen, is evidence of shortage.[127] The same situation had existed in the Puebla-Tlaxcala basin in the later sixteenth and early seventeenth century, where peonage accompanied the prosperity of the industry. To find a hundred Indians locked in an obraje there was not unknown.[128]

Yet a labor shortage does not exist simply because there are not enough people available to fill jobs. A shortage may occur if too few people are willing to work at a given wage, or if the wage is not enough to compensate for the disamenities of a particular job. It may even be that raising the money wage still does not bring forth the desired supply of labor.[129]

The guild in Querétaro used just this reasoning in explaining the need to shut up laborers. Arguing that most obraje labor there was "Indian," an assertion supported by the Bucareli census, it claimed that money incentives could not attract more labor. "What good would it do the Indians to increase their wage?" the guild asked. "What would they spend it on?"[130] Still, one must ask how "Indian" these workers were? Some studies indicate that significant acculturation was underway in the Bajío by the eighteenth century, especially in urban areas.[131] Yet even significant acculturation in an unevenly developing market may involve limited preference for commercial goods. Withdrawal from the labor market at a low wage—the complaint voiced in Querétaro—is a predictable outcome. Other societies in which a subsistence peasantry slowly enters the commercial economy—South Africa, Ireland, and the postbellum United States South—come to mind.[132] The relevant questions are how much money income was needed, and how long did it take to earn it? In Querétaro, it appears that, even in the early nineteenth century, the answers to these questions were still "not much" and "not long." Or, at least, not long enough to satisfy the ongoing labor demand of a commercial industry. To this extent, from the owners' standpoint, coercion was efficient.

In thinking about coercion, it is easy to overlook the "disutility" the obrajes created. Obrajes were considered degrading, dirty, and inappropriate for *gente de razón*. One mulatto resisted being sentenced to one, stating "it does me much harm and prejudice, considering that I am of *calidad española*."[133] Others complained that "the punishment was envisioned only for Indians, mulattos, and *coyotes*, since the presidios were marked out for [Spaniards]."[134] A carder confined to the obraje of Francisco Gómez argued that no free man would work under the onerous conditions of an obraje.[135] Miguel de los Santos spent twenty-four years as a peon in a Puebla obraje "doing the hardest and most dislikable work a human being can experience." "[They] made me work continually . . . without pay . . . [and] they whipped me," he said.[136] The manager of "Panzacola" spoke of the atmosphere of "subordination and fear" necessary to keep workers in line.[137] Small wonder that the foremen of the obrajes were called "cruel and angry men."[138] One worker in San Angel begged to be released "from that hell [of the obraje] and sent to any presidio." An official inspector remarked: "I confess . . . that although the cases I read tell me the same, it did not impress me as much as seeing it with my own eyes."[139] Better to be in a presidio in Africa, he later concluded.[140]

These conditions persisted over three centuries, efforts to reform them notwithstanding. For example, an inspection in Puebla in 1632, nearly fifty years after Riego's, found conditions unimproved. Indians were systematically imprisoned, flogged, beaten, enslaved—indeed, bought and sold. One owner threatened to drown them in the Atoyac river if they refused work. Others hustled workers out of sight on hearing of impending inspection. Royal officials were furious. They sentenced one owner to be hanged, his mayordomo to be executed, and several others to be flogged or transported from the colony. But the death sentences were overturned on appeal, and nothing other than fines were levied.[141] Three centuries and innumerable cédulas later, similar reports continued.[142] "Posadas," the eponymous inferno of the seventeenth century, still attracted attention. A letter from the town council of San Angel published in *El Águila Mexicana* December 14, 1826, complained that Cosme Damián, a 10-year-old boy, had been whipped to death in "Posadas," that four workers had been clubbed to death, and that another had committed suicide. It could have been 1660 as easily as 1826.

Notoriously poor conditions exacerbated repressiveness. Noxious chemicals and vats of boiling dyes caused accidents.[143] Crowding 150 to 200 workers into confined areas threatened disease, and one owner refused convict labor on the grounds that her obraje could hold no more people without danger of "some sort of plague breaking out."[144] In general, obrajes were simply perceived as hellholes. The chronicler Cayetano de Cabrera y Quintero wrote that the epidemic of *matlazahuatl* of 1736-39 broke out in an obraje in Tacuba: "[In] that vaporous obraje, within its wool, the fruit matured that put an end to so many around Atzcapotzalco."[145] Cabrera's version of the etiology of the epidemic was pure fantasy, but its symbolism is striking. What place was more likely to hatch an epidemic than a crowded, stinking obraje? Mortality in obrajes in Mexico City was high, and work halted during the epidemic.[146] Can there be any question why some laborers would not willingly work in the obrajes? If the purpose of colonial legislation was to ensure that their laborers, to quote the Conde de Monterrey, found "nor more servitude than in other work," the effort failed.[147]

WAGES AND RATES IN THE OBRAJES

It is difficult to generalize about payment in the obrajes. On the face of it, the wages seem low, even when "whole pay," or the sum of monetary payments plus other income, is considered. In a competitive labor market—one in which workers are both mobile and knowledgeable—the expectation is that "net advantage," the sum of money income plus other amenities of employment, is equalized. Yet it is difficult to measure the "whole pay" of obraje workers, and there is no reason to presume that "net advantage" equalized where mobility and information were imperfect. Indeed, in an economy characterized by imperfect labor markets, wide variations in wages would be expected, more so than for other commodities. So we are faced with a problem. What do variations in obraje wages mean?

The answer depends on looking at a variety of numbers and in exercising common sense. Try as one might, it is hard to find examples in which workers in obrajes were paid *better* than their counterparts in other occupations of similar skill. In fact, the opposite usually holds true. Since the difference is biased in one direction rather than randomly scattered, money wages in the obrajes were almost certainly lower than what productivity would have justified. If we can find no way of explaining the difference other than coercion, we are justified in calling the workers exploited. However imperfect the evidence, workers in the obrajes were, on the average, exploited.

In 1802, for example, the guild in Querétaro reported that "most [textile workers] were happy to earn 1.5, 2, and some, 4 reales," but it admitted that wages were, in general, low.[148] Nevertheless, wages were higher than in the early seventeenth century, when laborers earned from 2 to 4 pesos per month.[149] In the obraje owned by the first Conde de la Sierra Gorda, spinners and carders earned 2 reales per day, bobbin boys received 1 real, and the percher 2 to 3 reales per day in the late 1760s.[150] Since common laborers in construction in Mexico City earned about 3 reales daily between 1698 and 1804, a skilled percher was, by that standard, underpaid. The only way around this would be if the percher enjoyed the amenities of working in an obraje—a dubious proposition—or if the percher routinely pilfered the difference in cloth and raw materials. There was, according to owners and their agents, a constant problem with workers stealing in the obrajes, so the notion of compensating theft is by no means outrageous. Robbing the obraje, however, would have been a cottage industry itself to make up for the disparity in wages; there is no credible evidence that theft ever reached those proportions.

Similarly, spinners and carders made less than day laborers in construction, the opportunity cost of semiskilled labor in the later 1700s. Unskilled labor in mid-eighteenth-century Mexico City could earn 1 to 2 reales per day, and arduous or skilled would fetch 3 to 4 reales.[151] Only weavers, the best paid of the workers in the obraje, earned a competitive wage. In other words, peonage reduced the elasticity of labor supply (that is, reduced the sensitivity of quantity supplied to reductions in real wages) and shifted its costs to spinners, carders, and most skilled labor as well.[152]

In the eighteenth century, textile earnings were roughly equivalent to day labor in estate agriculture, a range of 1.5 to 2 reales daily, or 4 to 6 pesos monthly in the Tierra Adentro, with a weekly maize ration. Even bakers in Mexico City did better, averaging roughly 2.5 reales per day (although .5 real was given in bread).[153] Although there is no way to measure change in real wages, money wages had nevertheless risen. In the early 1600s, average earnings in an obraje did not reach 2 reales per day.[154] Spinners, regarded with carders as the worst paid, improved their wages slightly. Although the nominal daily rate in the late 1760s was no more than a century earlier—1 real daily—the workload had fallen from fifteen to eight pounds per week, which implied a near doubling in money earnings.[155] In Coyoacán, money wages also drifted upward. In the early 1700s, a carder doing ten pounds a day earned 20 reales per month, slightly less than a real daily.[156] By the later 1750s, carders were getting 2 reales per day.[157] In the 1730s and 1740s, the earnings of unspecified workers fell within 1.5 to 2 reales per day, although a general payment of one real daily was recorded into the 1750s in Mixcoac.[158] Weavers earned the most, 4 reales daily based on rates of 14 reales for a narrow cloth, or 18 reales per broadcloth.[159]

Earnings elsewhere varied. In the obraje of Balthasar de Sauto in San Miguel el Grande, workers made about 2 pesos monthly, less than a real per day.[160] Even the indigo miller, a skilled worker, made but 1.5 reales per day in the 1760s.[161] In Puebla, piece rates from 1629 seem high. Carders received 3 to 4.5 pesos per month; spinners, 4 reales daily for a pound of wool; cooks and millers, 4 to 6 reales; and dyers, 3 to 4 pesos per month. Weavers also did well, earning as much as 14 reales per piece of say. By the early eighteenth century, rates had fallen sharply in response to the decline of

125

the obrajes there and to the demand for labor. Spinners of warp yarn did two pounds per day in 1709, earning 2 reales, a reduction of 75 percent relative to rates eighty years earlier. Carders did somewhat better, earning 2.5 to 3 reales per day for eleven pounds of wool in the first half of the eighteenth century.[162]

To reiterate, these earnings were low by any standard. Yet earnings too low to attract adequate labor in the Bajío seemed sufficient in the Valley of Mexico, and labor there was freer besides. Figure 4.1 illustrates why earnings consistent with "free" labor in one re-

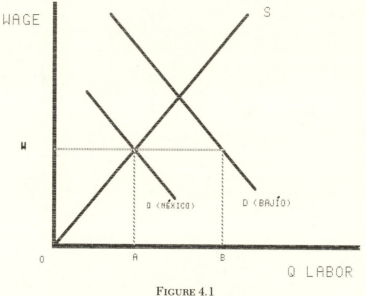

FIGURE 4.1
Peonage in the Valley of Mexico and the Bajío
in the Eighteenth Century

Daily wages (based on productivity and piece-rates) were essentially the same in the obrajes of the Valley of Mexico and the Bajío, from 1 to 4 reales, depending on the task. Yet peonage in the aggregate was less significant in the Valley of Mexico than it was in the Bajío. At w, OA laborers are demanded and supplied in the Valley, but peonage is unnecessary—there is no shortage. At the same level w, OB laborers are demanded in the Bajío, whereas only OA are forthcoming, and a shortage of AB exists. The demand curve reflects different levels of demand for labor derived from different levels of demand for woolens. The labor supply curve is drawn to assume unit elasticity. A similar model could be used for other regions at other periods.

gion were consistent with "unfree" labor in another. On the one hand, the demand for labor is derived from the demand for the woolens it produces. On the other, the labor supply is drawn with deliberate simplification. Here, the increase in quantity supplied is exactly proportional to the increase in the real wage. If labor was relatively immobile and poorly informed, a persistent difference in wages between the Bajío and the Valley of Mexico would not have been unusual. But if migration did take place, and wages tended to equalize, the problem of explaining different degrees of coercion exists. Our hypothetical answer is simple: the demand for labor in the Bajío exceeded the demand in the Valley of Mexico. The quantity of labor offered at the existing wage was sufficient to clear the market in the Valley of Mexico but not enough so in the Bajío. The consequences for Querétaro were twofold. In part, the obrajes there reacted by bidding up the wage, if only by providing workers with advances in excess of the present value of their expected earnings. They also implicitly raised wages by investing in added security. This was needed to handle the second consequence of the shortage: forced labor. In other words, Querétaro responded with a combination of carrot and stick.

All this seems complicated. Would it not have been simpler—or cheaper—for the obrajes in Querétaro to offer a higher wage in a free-labor market? As we have seen, the owners and their agents denied this was possible. On the one hand, they claimed that labor there had a backward-bending supply curve. It was impossible to get more labor by simply raising wages, because money income was subject to rapidly diminishing utility. This, we might recall, is the "primitive needs–primitive market" argument. On the other, they said they could not raise wages, because they could not raise prices high enough to cover the increase in costs.[163] In other words, the demand for woolens had become price-elastic, and the obrajes were unable to pass along the increased cost to consumers. Contraband, legal imports, and domestic cottons, particularly in the late eighteenth century, provided alternatives to woolens made in the obrajes. From the owners' standpoint, the only costs they could control were labor costs. They tried to reduce them while continuing to produce. They used coercion, kidnapping, and other tactics to finesse the resulting shortage, at least in Querétaro. If these were not enough, there was always the weapon of the truck store, a particularly insidious device.

The Truck System in the Obrajes

The "truck system" is a set of arrangements in which some form of consumption is tied to employment.[164] The system has taken many forms but is generally associated with payment of wages in goods, such as groceries, cloth, or the product of an employer's business. Another variation found employers paying workers in scrip or tickets redeemable only at the employer's store. The truck store (*tienda de raya*) is customarily associated with Latin America, but it was also found in England through the nineteenth century. Alfred Marshall produced an analysis of the system there in which he argued that the truck store allowed the employer to recapture part of the expenditures on wages and to reduce real income.[165] The system functioned in this manner in Mexico and reduced real wages in the obrajes by 25 percent to 50 percent.

In the obraje of Balthasar de Sauto, for instance, workers were paid partially in cloth. An inspector estimated that this cost them a third of their money earnings, and even Sauto admitted that the cloth could be sold for, at most, half the price.[166] The same official reviewed the system in Coyoacán. Workers were paid in cloth credited at inflated prices, or in *tlacos* (*clacos* is a variant form), private copper coins used only in the truck store.[167] "At the end of the week, [they] pay workers and spinners in goods [charged] at a very high price," said one informant. "At more than they would be worth anywhere else," said another.[168] The obraje "Panzacola" provided that workers desiring payment in cash rather than in tlacos would incur a penalty of 25 percent of their earnings (2 reales per peso, or *una cuartilla*).[169] The same occurred in "Mixcoac" in 1751, where laborers were paid in *tejoletas* "[and] these miserable people lose half their work."[170] The same charge was leveled at Manuel de Candía, owner of an obraje in Mixcoac, of whom the corregidor of Coyoacán wrote, "I have had repeated complaints that don Manuel de Candía and his managers treat the workers roughly, and tyrannize them, paying them in tejoletas."[171]

The ostensibly humanitarian practice of the food ration was related to the operation of the truck system.[172] But providing workers with food was not a universal practice. In Querétaro, the owners of obrajes contended that it was impossible to satisfy the varying tastes of numerous individuals (one is hard pressed to determine what exotic cuisine peasants might demand); they were better left to their own devices.[173] In Puebla, one study finds that the food the workers received "did not correspond to the ordinances," and that some owners simply paid .5 real per day for food.[174] Indeed, some charged for food they distributed or deprived workers of the ration when their work was unsatisfactory.[175] In San Miguel el Grande, Balthasar de Sauto provided married workers with five half-pecks of maize per week and bachelors with four. Both groups were "given" salt, candles, and soap but were charged for beans. The meat given was very bad.[176] In Coyoacán, workers subsisted on atole, tortillas, lima beans, and "rarely" meat. Bread, candles, and soap were available, but their quality was reputedly low.[177] In the obraje of Manuel de Candía, workers were sold, not given, bread, sugarloaf (*panocha*), and chile, all of poor quality and at high profits for Candía.[178] A baker said that bread sold in the obraje was of "such poor quality [that it was] not even fit for dogs."[179]

It is also possible to view the system in other ways. For one, paying in cloth was a means of dumping surplus when inventories grew large. For another, the truck system was also associated with a shortage of specie.[180] For example, in 1768, the guild in Querétaro complained that "making owners pay workers cash forces them to stop half their looms, because some are in no position to spend the money their operation demands."[181]

On the whole, it is not clear how much value the goods provided by the truck stores had or how much they added to the workers' "whole pay." At most, the goods were worth market value, but most were probably worth far less. The argument that people needed food, clothing, and shelter, and that obrajes provided them, is largely specious. Given the choice between income in money and goods, the workers chose income. Why else did the obrajes penalize them for demanding cash instead of cloth, or candles, or other goods? The fact is, the tienda de raya was of greater benefit to the owners than to the workers, and that is why it was maintained. Few owners or managers did more than was necessary to keep their workers at the job.

Nevertheless, it is significant that workers put up with the system. Had they been free to migrate in search of less oppressive employment, the tienda de raya could not have persisted. Competition for labor would have eroded the system and forced the stores to provide goods on better terms. If a mobile proletariat truly existed by the late eighteenth century, how could the truck stores persist? For that matter, how could any systematic departure from a competitive equilibrium coexist with a mobile labor force?[182] The answer is probably threefold. First, a great deal of purely local mobility existed. Individuals may have drifted around a given locale, but they were naturally less able to migrate over long distances or even to "commute" regularly in search of better employment. Second, high and persistent rates of unemployment and underemployment enforced a rigorous discipline on potential migrants. Even if people could move around, they knew from long experience that work was hard to find. As a consequence, they did not routinely search for better opportunities, even though physical migration was possible. Finally, information about other opportunities was hard to come by, and information was costly. The services that provide information about jobs in a modern economy did not exist. Together, these factors explain why an ostensibly mobile population did not create a competitive labor market. Or—equally likely—historians may have exaggerated how rapidly a mobile proletariat was emerging at the end of the colonial period. Mobility and persistent exploitation cannot coexist easily.

CONCLUSION: MARKETS, LAW, AND REFORM

If obrajes remained outside the law, it was not for want of effort to the contrary. Attempts to regulate and reform them were frequent. On the face of it, detailed regulations bred inefficiency, raised costs, and drove producers into bankruptcy, or so they often claimed. Municipal and guild regulations dictated standards of quality and design for woolens, and the corpus of royal law, everything else. Meanwhile, the production of cottons proceeded unhindered and, indeed, was ultimately encouraged. Regulated woolens grew costly relative to unregulated cottons and were eventually displaced. Or so opponents of regulations argued then—and now.

From this standpoint, regular *visitas* were an unmitigated evil that did little more than line the pockets of inspectors. In theory, nothing could have been further from the truth. The visita allowed officials to take testimony, weigh evidence, suggest remedies, and punish violations of the law. The process was a formidable one. Much of what we have known until now about the obrajes is drawn from sixteenth- and seventeenth-century visitas. Only a reckless person could disregard their findings, for the record—whippings, beatings, murder, an encyclopedia of human abuse—is appalling. How could the same system—indeed, the same men—who established the General Indian Court over the protests of obraje owners have permitted such conduct?[183] Could the owners of obrajes, wealthy and powerful suppliers of a vital commodity, simply blunt reform? Or was it, as Severo Martínez Pelayo argues, that royal officials were more concerned with enriching themselves than with the desires of the Crown?[184] Necessity and venality went hand-in-hand.

Substantial attempts to reform the obrajes began during the administration of Martín Enríquez, fourth viceroy of New Spain, in 1569. An ordinance that addressed working conditions, wages, indebtedness, and forced labor was the result. In 1579, the existing ordinances were supplemented by others specifying the need for clear records of indebtedness and an adequate diet for workers.[185] The ordinances of 1569 and 1579 were confirmed by the Marqués de Villamanrique (1585-90) in 1586. Yet little headway was made, and Luis de Velasco the younger was obliged to provide new ordinances in 1595. Similar to those of 1569 and 1579, these specified again the limits to advances, treatment of Indian workers, and internal living conditions.

Churchmen such as Jerónimo de Mendieta leveled equally serious charges against the obrajes. Mendieta, in his suppressed *Historia eclesiástica indiana* (1596), reiterated the findings of the visitas and proposed that the obrajes be destroyed. Yet the needs of New Spain could not be extinguished by decree. Most royal officials understood this. Some advocated a regulated public monopoly in woolens, an idea that found few adherents. In 1599, the Conde de Monterrey ordered the removal of all obrajes to Antequera, Mexico City, Puebla, and Valladolid, but the scheme failed. Monterrey's preference for black slaves in the obrajes found less opposition. Abetted by royal decrees of 1601, 1609, and 1627 that "abolished" or restricted Indian labor in the obrajes in favor of black slaves, Monterrey's proposal enjoyed some success.

But the use of force was a function of labor shortage. Like the demand for cloth, it could not be abolished by decree. Inspections undertaken in the 1630s revealed abuses similar to those discovered by Santiago del Riego in the late 1580s and produced an analogous response. A cédula of 1632 again prohibited placing Indians in obrajes.[186] Ordinances were once more issued by Juan de Palafox (1642), and an *auto acordado* of 1656 defined acceptable wages as well as restrictions on indebtedness and coercion.[187] In an action reminiscent of Monterrey's "quarantine" of 1599, a cédula of 1680 ordered unlicensed obrajes in Querétaro to be destroyed; it was, however, suspended without effect in 1684.[188]

Events surrounding the visita of the obraje of Balthasar de Sauto in San Miguel between 1756 and 1771 produced another wave of reformist legislation.[189] The findings of the royal inspector, Diego Antonio Fernández de la Madrid, were distressingly familiar and generated a large volume of evidence and testimony. The accumulated intelligence shaped the ordinances of the Marqués de Croix (1766-71), published first in 1767.[190] Croix's ordinances were a blend of old and new, an injunction against novel forms of ancient abuse. Owners were forbidden to operate taverns, *pulquerías*, and *vinaterías* within or adjacent to their obrajes or to advance workers more than 1 real per week to finance purchases. Wages were to be paid weekly in cash. Workers had to be properly fed, allowed to come and go freely, and given periods of rest. The obraje was held responsible for the welfare of workers who took sick; observance of the sonsacarse laws (the prohibition against competing for indebted labor) was again enjoined. The ordinances were repeated by Mayorga in 1780 and 1781, and again by Berenguer de Marquina (1800-1803) in 1800. Iturrigaray's (1803-1808) final revision and restatement of Croix's ordinances in 1805 was provoked by the clash between Miguel Domínguez and the owners of Querétaro over the issue of advances and indebtedness.[191]

Here, then, was 250 years of law, and good law at that. With a few exceptions, the law was far from unrealistic. Its evolving corpus reflected conditions discovered through countless visitas, and it accurately summarized existing abuses. Why did it fail?

The first reason lay in the tension between law, labor market, and social imagination. The Spanish attitude toward Indian society was uneasily poised between economic necessity and paternal responsibility. There was no question that Indians were free, but their status was limited by the obligation to contribute an economic surplus. Such freedom, as John Parry put it, was "the kind of liberty which a legally free peasant enjoyed in Spain."[192] The logical corollary of "legal freedom" was the necessity of coercion, a theoretically moderate repression that recognized the legitimacy of exploiting Indians within tolerable levels.[193] Acceptable exploitation was legal exploitation, regulated and defined by law. With the exception of the principle of sonsacarse, however, the law aimed to create free wage labor in an economy structurally unprepared for its emergence. Free labor could not be legislated into force. Given such a constraint, the assumption that Indians were unwilling workers was not strange, for too few behaved as the law prescribed. The principles of "legal freedom" and permissible exploitation left open the possibility that force alone would secure labor for the obrajes. From this point, repression was only a short step. Who could better say how hard arms needed twisting than those who demanded the arms?

Two factors complicated the situation. First, obraje workers resisted compulsion. Although at a disadvantage, the laborers were not passive. Their opposition to exploitation produced a deliberate slowdown and occasionally outright sabotage. This infuriated the owners, who applied still greater force. Their characterization of the workers bears witness to their persistent frustration.[194] The laborers were brazen vagrants "wanting nothing more than to sustain their miserable habits." "They leave their jobs and ridicule their bosses. . . ." They lived in "abandon, vices, and nudity." Given any freedom, workers thought themselves permitted "to commit with impunity the most enormous evils." "Theft is almost inseparable [from them] . . . in a word, they are possessed of the most detestable vices." "The workers are in general people without truth, honor, or a sense of shame." Rough characters all, to be sure, but with plenty of reason for acting as they did.

In resisting compulsion, the laborers found themselves confronted by the power of the legal system. For them, law was the local magistrate, not a compilation of ordinances and cédulas. Owners used the law to their advantage, or blunted its disadvantage. In Querétaro, for example, they were close to Ignacio Ruíz Calado, the immediate predecessor of Miguel Domínguez.[195] The owners detested Domínguez, a distinguished and upright jurist, accusing him of an "extraordinary desire to denigrate the owners of the obrajes."[196] Yet "denigration" was Domínguez's determination to see peonage restricted and his unwillingness to be bought. This *corregidor de letras* understood the game. If laws limiting advances and peonage were obeyed, Domínguez thought "the owners of the obrajes [would] lose a great deal of money."[197] For such reasons, even a latter-day Querétaro historian has judged the laws "stupid."[198] To the extent that they presupposed and encouraged a free labor market, the laws remained unenforceable and dangerous to the owners' interests. Their potential for mischief was illustrated in San Miguel el Grande, where the alcalde mayor threatened Balthasar de Sauto with an inspection costing far more than the "loan" of a thousand pesos he demanded.[199]

In short, numerous factors frustrated regulation. Owners needed labor and the power to acquire and to retain it. Magistrates needed income; thus they supplied labor and suspended laws limiting peonage. Only owners with direct authority to acquire labor could avoid the logic of supply and demand. The Conde de la Sierra Gorda took rebellious Indians for an obraje in Querétaro through the colonization of New Santander, whereas Cortés drew upon encomienda labor to operate his in the Marquesado.[200] Nevertheless, these avenues were open to very few. Most made the customary, if indirect, arrangement. The resulting failure of enforcement was unintentional, a typical problem of agency in the early modern state.[201] Nevertheless, its occurrence guaranteed that laborers in the obrajes endured "more servitude than in other work."

FIVE

A Business Much Diminished

OVER THE LONG RUN, the volume and distribution of woolen production in New Spain changed dramatically. By the later 1820s, some observers found the industry in a state of decline. Of Puebla, William Bullock wrote, "[it] was formerly celebrated for its manufactory of coarse woollen cloth, but . . . has now fallen off in this branch of industry."[1] Descriptions of Querétaro were equally pointed. Although the British minister to Mexico was "struck with [its] busy look, which has quite the air of a manufacturing district," others were less enthused.[2] "The town was, in days of yore, famous for the manufacture of broadcloth," said R. W. Hardy. "But at this present writing," he continued, "it is only celebrated on account of corn and potato fields."[3] The American consul at Veracruz echoed the sentiment. "I was much disappointed in visiting the manufacturing establishments at Querétaro," he wrote. "They have now fallen into ruin."[4] Nor were hard times limited to Puebla and Querétaro. As Brian Hamnett writes, "The fundamental problems of the Mexican textile industry were structural [and] affected not only Querétaro, but also the other main woolen centers, León and San Miguel el Grande."[5] But what were the structural problems of the industry? Had business much diminished from earlier years, and if so, why? If woolen output had fallen, what replaced it? Why did the industry prosper in some areas and decline in others? Did output fluctuate regularly, and what were the determinants of its cycles? Can prices provide information on the mechanisms of change? How did contraband affect the obrajes? These questions, and more, we now address.

THE PUEBLA-TLAXCALA BASIN

A logical starting point is the Puebla-Tlaxcala basin, early the center of New Spain's woolen industry. The first obraje was ostensibly established in 1539 by Francisco de Peñafiel, an immigrant from Segovia.[6] By 1579, forty obrajes were in existence. But their numbers soon began to shrink. As the data in Table 5.1 indicate, their number had fallen to thirty-three in 1588, a figure roughly constant for the next two decades. The decline was arrested somewhat until 1620-21, but by then the obrajes were already described as "ruined."[7] Woolens from Puebla were important in exchange with Peru, and the growing restriction of the trade after 1590, coupled with the development of the Peruvian woolen manufacture, hastened the contraction.[8] Investment fell throughout the seventeenth and eighteenth centuries. By 1800, Puebla no longer counted for much in woolen production, just as Bullock had observed.

The value of woolens—fine cloth, paño 18no, bays, and says—was approximately 250,000 to 300,000 pesos in 1597, near maximum for the period and, by virtue of Puebla's decline, for the colonial era as a whole. Most of its obrajes were small (many were trapiches), containing an average of about six looms (with a standard deviation of roughly 3). By this measure, only three large obrajes operated in 1597 (more than 2 standard deviations above the mean); most, twenty-six of them, were average (within a standard deviation of the mean).[9] By contrast, one obraje that did well in eighteenth-century Puebla, belonging to Pedro Mendoza y Escalante, and then to Ana de Nava, was rather large at twenty-one looms. In other words, in Puebla, many small woolen producers ultimately gave way to a few larger ones.

Cholula did not fare much better. In the middle 1700s, the *cabecera* had a few dozen telares sueltos but no obrajes. By century's end, the intendant, Manuel Flon, could report that "there were in other days more than 100 looms for woolens [but] today there are only 6, and they are disappearing moment by moment."[10] Looms for cottons had diminished to a lesser extent, and spinning, too, was in decline. Tlaxcala also witnessed a sustained loss in the seventeenth century. An informant from Santa Ana Chiautempan wrote that there were thirty-three obrajes (undoubtedly some were trapiches and other artisan shops) in Santa Ana in 1635, of which five remained in 1674. Consumption of wool had fallen from 920,000 kilos to 172,000. The entire economy had suffered; domestic spinning and carding were failing here as elsewhere.[11] Although there were eleven obrajes in Tlaxcala making says and cloth in 1604, only the obraje of the Díaz Varela in Santa Ana Chiautempan remained active into the eighteenth century.[12]

The Valley of Mexico

A long swing of expansion and decline also occurred in the Valley of Mexico, although it lagged behind the Puebla-Tlaxcala basin. The

TABLE 5.1
Obrajes in Puebla, Coyoacán, Tacuba

Decade	Puebla	Coyoacán	Tacuba
1580s	33		
1600s	35		2
1620s	37		4
1660s	12		
1680s		10	2[a]
1700s			4
1760s	2[b]	5[b]	1[b]
1800	3	3[c]	1

[a] 1690s [b] 1750s [c] 1790s

Sources: Puebla: inspection reports of 1588 and 1599 in AGI, México 71 and Indiferente General 2987; "Relación de los obrajes de paños que hay en este Reino . . . ,"AGI, México 26; Bermúdez de Castro, *Theatro Anglopolitano*, pp. 69-70; Manuel Flon, "Noticias estadísticas de la intendencia de Puebla," in Florescano and Gil Sánchez (eds.), *Descripciones económicas regionales*, pp. 158-81; petition of Pedro de la Sota et al. [February 1800], AGNM, Industria, vol. 8, exp. 12; Villa Sánchez, *Puebla sagrada*, p. 113; "Mapa de los obrajes . . . ," AGNM, Civil, vol. 1628; Hans Pohl et al., "Aspectos sociales . . . de los obrajes en Puebla," 41.

Coyoacán: It would be impractical to list all of them. A valuable source is Francisco Fernández del Castillo, *Apuntes para la historia de San Angel*; the entire body of documents relating to the composition of 1690 in AGI, Contaduría 806, Ramo 3; "Memoria de los obrajes . . . ," AGNM, Civil, vol. 1628; numerous inspections, of which those in AJM, legs. 170 and 182, are most valuable; report of the excise officer of Coyoacán, AGNM, Aduanas, vol. 134.

Tacuba: cédula of Jan. 16, 1621, AGNM, Civil, vol. 477, exp. 5; report of Pedro de la Bastida, México, Apr. 1, 1690, AGI, Contaduría 806, Ramo 3; various documents in AGNM, Civil, vols. 742, exp. 11, and 1604, exp. 8; history of the obraje "San Nícolas Quisquilaca" from 1692 through 1766, AGNM, Tierras, vol. 1798, exp. 2; "Memoria de los obrajes que hay en esta ciudad . . . ," AGI, México 1809; report of the excise officer of Tacuba, AGNM, Aduanas, vol. 134; dowry brought to the marriage of Julián Adalid, México, Jun. 21, 1804, ante Juan Manuel Pozo, ANM; poder para testar de Julián de Adalid, México, Jun. 21, 1804, ante Francisco Calapiz, ANM.

dates of establishment and licensing of obrajes were not always identical, but obrajes that did not exist could not be licensed. Licensing may have taken place with a lag, but it should nevertheless reflect the relative chronology of establishment. Consequently, it is significant that, of the obrajes in Tacuba and Coyoacán in 1690 licensed in the seventeenth century, half were licensed before 1649 and half after (that is, the median date was 1649). Six of these, however, were licensed between 1640 and 1679, indicating a strong incentive for investment then.[13] Moreover, since none appear in a count of obrajes operating in the Valley in 1597, the woolen industry in Coyoacán and Tacuba was most likely a product of the seventeenth century and particularly of its central decades.[14] The maximum number of obrajes reached approximately eight to ten and persisted as late as the 1690s. But, as the figures in Table 5.1 show, both jurisdictions witnessed a fall in investment in the eighteenth century, despite proximity to Mexico City and favorable treatment by the excise collectors. The scale of the survivors is equally impressive. All were large. The obraje "Adalid" in Tacuba had a capacity of 19 looms, and in 1793, "Panzacola," "Posadas," and "Mixcoac" had capacities of 22, 16, and 14 looms, respectively. Smaller rather than larger producers fell by the wayside.[15]

Textile obrajes in Mexico City followed a similar pattern. In 1604, there were 25 obrajes producing various grades of cloth. By 1720, their numbers had shrunk to around 10, and by 1757, there were 6. Observers thought the period between 1769 and 1781 particularly critical, and one estimated that the 18 or so obrajes in the Valley that served Mexico City and its environs were reduced to some 6.[16] By 1800, only 1 obraje, belonging to don Manuel Durán de Otero, remained in Mexico City.[17]

In terms of output, the obrajes of Mexico City produced a minimum of 330,000 to 375,000 pesos worth of woolens in 1597; the actual figure may have been twice as much. If so, maximum output reached at least 750,000 pesos at the beginning of the seventeenth century, only to fall steadily afterwards, particularly so after 1700.[18] Indeed, in 1711, don Francisco Pérez Navas, owner of "Molino Blanco," wrote that the obrajes of Mexico City were "lost" and that the "back-up in their sales" was "notorious." Five had been abandoned, and others had gone bankrupt because of limited demand.[19] Texcoco was equally affected. In 1604, there had been eight obrajes dating to the end of the sixteenth century.[20] By the eighteenth century, two or three diversified producers remained. But between 1732 and 1792, they "disappeared from indolence or some vicissitude of the times for which people do not give much justification."[21] Other sites with long histories—Tecamachalco, Cuautitlan, and Xochilmilco—had also vanished by the beginning of the nineteenth century.

THE BAJÍO

The situation in the Bajío was different. In Acámbaro, the late eighteenth century was a period of growth, as 8 obrajes with 71 looms in 1781 grew to 10 with 141 looms in 1793. Moreover, gross margins (unit revenues less unit costs) were slightly lower than 12.5 percent.[22] By comparison, obrajes in the Valley of Mexico in 1690 reported "profits" per piece of woolen ranging 3.3 percent to 9.5 percent, with most in a range of 8.3 percent to 9.5 percent. Since these "profits" were gross of labor costs and interest payments, the gross margins of obrajes in a declining area were dignificantly lower than in Acámbaro.[23] In San Miguel el Grande, there was a short, sharp expansion after 1744, and an increase in production until about 1755, as the number of obrajes grew from 1 or 2 to 4 or 5.[24] Although the boom was not sustained, the obrajes that survived there and in Dolores were also large, with 17 and 14 looms respectively.[25]

Querétaro, of course, was *the* woolen textile center of the eighteenth century. As the data in Table 5.2 indicate, its progress to first rank began in the seventeenth century and was inversely proportional to the fortunes of the obrajes to the south. From small beginnings in the late 1580s, the obrajes grew to six in 1640, doubled by 1718, and reached a maximum of thirty in 1743.[26] By all appearances, the first half of the eighteenth century saw increased investment, a view shared by the owners there.[27] Numbers fluctuated sharply over the next few decades, but the maximum held steady as late as 1781. In other words, the century from 1640 to 1740 witnessed a period of growth, whereas the years 1740 to 1780 represented stasis. The period between 1790 and 1810 was more complex. Overall, numbers stabilized after falling sharply from the period 1740-80. But, given the number of working looms, output grew after 1790 and continued to do so until the rebellion in 1810, falling sharply in its aftermath.

What happened between the 1780s and early 1790s in Querétaro? We will consider the effects of *comercio libre* in more detail, but the recovery (and growth) of working looms in the decade following the new regime (1789) indicates that comercio libre did not undermine the obraje in the short run, particularly when warfare intervened.[28]

TABLE 5.2
Obrajes in Querétaro, 1580-1810

Decade	Number	Working Looms
1580	1	?
1640	6	?
1710	13	?
1740	30	?
1770	23-26	?
1790	16	150-180
1800	18	280
1810*	19	290

* Until the outbreak of the Hidalgo rebellion. The 290 working looms fell to 68 in 1812.

Sources: Super, *La vida en Querétaro*, pp. 86-87; Brading, "Noticias sobre la economía de Querétaro," passim; list of obrajes in 1777, AGNM, Aduanas, vol. 44; don Juan Antonio de Arce to the viceroy of New Spain, México, Jun. 12, 1773, AGI, México 2098; "Obrajes o fábricas de paños burdos que hay . . . ," AGNM, Alcabalas, vol. 37; memorial signed by Antonio de la Carcoba et al., Querétaro, Feb. 1, 1812, AGNM, Indiferente de Guerra, vol. 281-A, exp. 1.

The disastrous consequences of the frost and droughts of 1785 are well known, but they were essentially short-run.[29] The decade of the 1780s as a whole was difficult for ranchers, and this, perhaps, was of more lasting effect.[30] The movement of working looms in the two decades preceding the rebellion of 1810, however, suggests a caution. Capacity increased, and efficient producers benefited at the expense of marginal ones.

Moreover, as the data in Figure 5.1 indicate, the consumption of raw wool belies a simple pattern of decline. In the later 1760s, consumption ranged from 36,000 to 70,000 arrobas of wool. In 1798 and 1799, during the first period of the neutral trade, consumption reached 74,000 arrobas yearly, even though fewer obrajes operated than between 1740 and 1780. During the second neutral trade (1805-1808), consumption dropped sharply in response to an upswing in imports. But in 1808, consumption rose to levels beyond that of the 1760s, and demand continued strong to the eve of the rebellion. In short, a decline in the capital stock of the obrajes not-

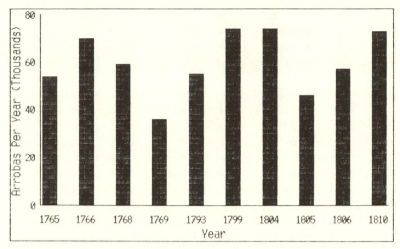

FIGURE 5.1
Wool Consumption in Querétaro, 1765-1810

Sources:
1765-67, 1768, 1769: Computed from tax collections on wool delivered for use in Querétaro and San Juan del Río. AGNM, Alcaldes Mayores, vol. 1.
1767-68: Diputados del comercio de Querétaro to the visitor-general of New Spain, Querétaro, Feb. 16, 1768, AGI, México 2098.
1793: Obrajes o fábricas de paños burdos que hay . . . , AGNM, Alcabalas, vol. 37.
1799: "Cuenta general de cargo y data," Querétaro, Jan. 7, 1800, AGNM, Indiferente de Guerra, vol. 35-A.
1804-1806: Gregorio Valleño and Pedro Russi to the corregidor of Querétaro, Querétaro, Sept. 10, 1807, AGNM, Civil, vol. 1871, exp. 10.
1810: Memorial signed by Antonio de la Carcoba and Manuel Samaniego del Castillo, Querétaro, Feb. 1, 1812, AGNM, Indiferente de Guerra, vol. 281-A, exp. 1.

withstanding, the demand for wool in Querétaro continued strong. If the obrajes grew from 1640 to 1740 and remained stable until the 1780s, their record was, at worst, mixed before 1810. Despite a litany of complaints about rising materials and labor costs, and despite competition from trapiches, the gross profits of the obrajes surpassed the 18 percent considered unsatisfactory when the industry stood in ruins in the early 1830s.[31]

There were, nevertheless, some grounds for discontent among the owners. The expansion of the trapiches in Querétaro and the competition they posed were not imaginary. Between 1693 and 1803, their numbers grew more than tenfold, from thirty to 340.[32] Since the increase paralleled a general decline in smaller obrajes, the upswing in the trapiches was all the more striking. Why should one class of small producers replace another, a development too persistent to be explained by chance alone?

The substitution was, above all, a matter of flexibility in labor supply. As the relative demand for woolens in Querétaro grew, its obrajes were chronically short-handed; they resorted to forced labor to cover the deficit. The trapiches, on the other hand, were family-based. "One [member] weaves, the others spin and card, and all efficiently contribute to finishing the work for sale. Although yielding little profit, it provides them with a modest, if humble subsistence."[33] The supply of such labor in Querétaro had increased during the eighteenth century, as a comparison of families counted there in 1740s and 1790s would suggest.[34] Consequently, the trapiches were well positioned to enlarge production at relatively lower cost. The comparative advantage of the obraje was its ability to expand output under significant labor constraints, particularly as commercial needs outpaced the ability of native labor to supply them. In the eighteenth century, and particularly in the Bajío, this condition was reversed, and the fundamental advantage of the obraje eroded.

Regional population growth and changing tastes enlarged the market for the trapiches. "All these weavings are sold in the same district . . . in roadside stands, small markets, and public places." The trapiches produced lighter woolens rather than broadcloth, an advantage in competing with increasingly popular cottons. Whereas some trapiches indeed specialized in cottons, others perhaps manufactured both and attained a flexible and profitable output mix. The obrajes, which specialized in denser weaves, were unable to compete, and some violated guild standards by thinning, stretching, or otherwise reducing the quality and weight of the product.

In this context, the "regulatory" theory of the decline of the obrajes makes some sense. The trapicheros were small fish. An 1803 Querétaro tax list (lists from other years are no different) makes the point clearly, for the majority of weavers that were surveyed owned but one loom and were liable for a use tax on it of 2 reales per year.[35] This was nothing in relation to the hundreds, and at times thousands, of pesos in fees and costs that a visita to a larger obraje could produce, and officials chose their targets accordingly.[36] In the meantime, smaller producers operated virtually without costly labor regulation or the threat of it, evaded guild standards of quality, and sometimes spoiled markets for their larger competitors.[37] In the long run, these advantages made a difference, particularly when there were hundreds of smaller weavers, for market supply was no more than the sum of the individuals' supply curves. The situation grew progressively worse over the eighteenth century, much to the dismay of the obrajeros.

Why were smaller obrajes particularly vulnerable? The answer is complex. But a partial explanation returns to the fundamentals of labor supply. Obrajes did possess economies in the use of power and influence, and forced labor was acquired at lower unit cost by larger operators. Two smaller operators might secure in the aggregate as many shanghaied workers as a large one, but the sum of their costs (bribes, favors, tips, and so forth) was probably larger, even more so if the smaller operators were nonentities with little chance to retaliate. As conditions tightened in the eighteenth century, the entry of titled nobility such as the Condes de Casa de Loja, Sierra Gorda, Torre Cosío, and Regla into the ranks of owners of obrajes brought considerable political power to bear in the competition for labor. These men could and did play a rough game, and their presence biased the distribution of resources. As a consequence, smaller obrajes tended to disappear.

Finally, it is worth repeating an earlier point. The obraje was a response to market imperfections, and the improvement or removal of these imperfections reduced the incentive to invest in a costly system. But most analyses of the Bajío in the late colonial period point to its demographic and economic transformation and the emergence of a mobile class of wage earners in agricultural, mining, and industrial enterprise.[38] This tendency—to the extent it existed—worked against the obrajes there, even as shifting patterns of regional economic advantage supported them. The resulting pattern of growth was easily disturbed, subject to considerable fluctuation, and was not irreversible. The ambiguity of Querétaro's fragile prosperity, visible in contradictory and sometimes paradoxical evidence, was an artifact of the economic forces at work.

MODELS OF REGIONAL ECONOMIC CHANGE

There are several ways to explain change in the geographical distribution of the obrajes. One explanation—essentially macroeconomic—focuses on factors peculiar to regional expansion or stagnation. The other is microeconomic and focuses on the relation between the geography and the technology of woolen textile manufacture. Both approaches are interesting, and elements of both are relevant.

A salient factor in the microeconomic approach is the cost of transporting finished woolens relative to the wool clip. During the eighteenth century, some wool for use in the Valley of Mexico came from the Valley of Toluca.[39] But more often, wool from the Bajío and the Tierra Adentro was shipped to Mexico City, and then reshipped to Puebla.[40] To send the grease weight of the wool clip from north of the Bajío to Mexico City and beyond was expensive relative to shipping woolens over an equal distance, and this helped determine long-run patterns of regional change. There was, of course, always mention of the *casas de trasquila*, shearing stations to which the sheep were run on their way to Mexico City prior to slaughter for mutton.[41] The *casas de trasquila* would reduce transportation costs but could not eliminate them. Moreover, losses from theft, death, and accident may have left the system no cheaper than mule train; not enough evidence of its operation, however, survives to merit serious consideration.

If one compares the hypothetical cost of purchasing paño de Querétaro and then shipping it to Mexico City with the cost of purchasing wool near Querétaro and shipping it to the capital for manufacture, an interesting result emerges. Although the method of computation in Table 5.3 is crude and sensitive to assumptions about costs and prices, it implies a 15 percent savings in purchasing woolens in Querétaro and shipping them to Mexico City, over purchasing fleece for an equivalent quantity of woolens and shipping it to the capital for manufacture. Fifteen percent may seem insignificant, but relative to the gross margins of obrajes in the Valley of Mexico or Acámbaro, it was not. Moreover, with demand being price-elastic—increasingly so during the eighteenth century as cotton substitutes for woolens became generally available—even a small advantage in purchasing woolens over wool would produce the shift from "importing" wool for manufacture to importing finished woolens for distribution. Furthermore, the argument is even more valid for the Puebla-Tlaxcala basin. It cost at least as much to reship wool from Mexico to Puebla as it did from the Tierra Adentro to the Valley of Mexico. If anything, the incentive to substitute woolens for fleece was stronger in Puebla.

Thus, in the early 1690s, several masters of obrajes in Mexico City complained that "newly founded" obrajes in Querétaro and Celaya had invaded their traditional markets in the Tierra Adentro and in the colder northern mining districts such as Parral, so "the business of this city [Mexico] had diminished much."[42] Humboldt also attributed the ruin of the obrajes of Texcoco in part to competition from Querétaro, and a contemporary *poblano* ascribed Puebla's ruin to "the great number of obrajes established in other cities of the King-

TABLE 5.3

Cost of Production in Mexico City and Environs Compared with
Cost of Purchase in Mexico City

Item	Cost of Production[a] (in reales)
35.7 arrobas (grease weight) wool @ 28 reales/arroba	1,000
Excise on purchase of wool (6 percent)	60
Freight (60 leagues' radius of Mexico)	143
Subtotal, wool delivered to Mexico City	1,203
Indigo, firewood, oil, etc.	578
Subtotal	1,781
Value-added in manufacture (factor payments)	1,325
Total (direct) cost of production	3,106
Unit cost of production	15.5

Item	Cost of Purchase[b] (in reales)
7.57 arrobas paño de Querétaro	1,000
Excise on purchase of woolens (6 percent)	60
Freight (60 leagues' radius of Mexico City)	30
Total paño de Querétaro delivered to Mexico	1,090
Unit cost of purchase	13

[a] *Method*: 1,000 reales could purchase 35.7 arrobas of wool in Querétaro in 1793. According to Ramón María Serrera, *Guadalajara ganadera. Estudio regional novo-hispano, 1760-1805* (Seville, 1977), p. 259, transport costs from any point 60 to 100 leagues' radius of Mexico City in 1792 were 4 reales per arroba. Cost of transport follows directly (35.7 × 4). Direct manufacturing costs are taken from Table 2.4 of this book and used for Mexico City for want of better data. In Querétaro, the ratio of these costs to wool costs was about 1.9 to 1, the ratio I employ. Since 7 arrobas of wool (grease weight) yielded a cuarterón of paño, 35.7 arrobas should have yielded a bit more than 5 cuarterones, or 200 varas. Unit costs follow directly.

[b] *Method*: 1,000 reales in 1793 could buy 7.5 arrobas of paño. Why 7.5? If 7 arrobas of wool (grease weight) made a cuarterón of paño (roughly 39.5 varas), then 39 varas could not have weighed much more than 3.5 arrobas, the weight of wool after washing. Thus, there were 11 varas of paño in an arroba's weight of cloth. In 1793 prices at Querétaro, 11 varas cost 132 reales. The excise assumed may not have been paid, and this would have lowered costs slightly. All other computations follow directly.

Note: All these calculations are arguable. For Puebla, a declaration of Miguel de Castillo in 1740, AJM, leg. 92, contends that it cost 16 pesos per carga of grease weight to transport wool from San Juan de los Ríos in Durango to Huehuetoca, at the northern edge of the Valley of Mexico, and that transportation to Puebla would cost an additional 15 to 24 reales. Tedious calculations suggest that this raised the incentive to bring woolens rather than wool into Puebla by a slight amount relative to Mexico City.

dom."[43] By the 1790s, the Royal Excise concluded that much Querétaro cloth (paño de Querétaro) was sold in the capital and had run its obrajes out of business.[44]

A sample of prices in Figures 5.2 through 5.5 supports this interpretation. The price of paño de Querétaro registered in Mexico City follows a negative trend after 1724. On the other hand, the price of cloth made by all other producers (including some in the Valley of Mexico) fell rapidly between 1727 and 1760, only to turn upward again between 1780 and 1805, just as did the prices of broadcloth and other bays.[45] In other words, a falling general level of prices eliminated marginal, high-cost producers, and the falling relative price of Querétaro cloth in particular undermined the position of its rivals. These trends are equally evident in the price of raw wool, itself 53 percent of the direct cost of cloth and hence, a major determinant of supply.[46] There is, in other words, no evidence of productivity change in the obrajes in the eighteenth century, a period for which we have usable quantitative evidence.

The macroeconomic approach focuses on changes in aggregate supply and total demand. Most historians follow the conventional emphasis on demand, whose proxies are easier to identify and to measure. David Brading, for example, has examined the demographic work of Sherburne Cook and Woodrow Borah in its implications for the late colonial demand. In his view, "the area of settlement north of the river Lerma, including the Bajío and Jalisco, prospered where central and southern Mexico may well have experienced an arrest in their fortunes, both economic and demographic. In comparative terms, Meso-America was in retreat whereas the frontier zones were on the march."[47] In the sense of the analysis here, the obrajes of the Bajío were best positioned to capitalize on this demographic sea change and the shift in regional demand that it implied. Moreover, as Guadalajara and its region prospered, the obrajes of Querétaro were the principal beneficiaries.[48]

To the south, Puebla and its hinterland underwent a complex pattern of transformation. The city suffered a series of random economic shocks in the early eighteenth century and lost population, even as its agricultural hinterland expanded. The woolen obrajes, as we know, were largely abandoned, their demise hastened by access to the seacoast and to contraband that competed for those finer lines of clothing to which good broadcloth had contributed.[49] Geography and proximate endowments, however, offered raw cotton drawn from Veracruz as a potential solution. In the one instance of protoindustrial growth that New Spain experienced, cottons provided em-

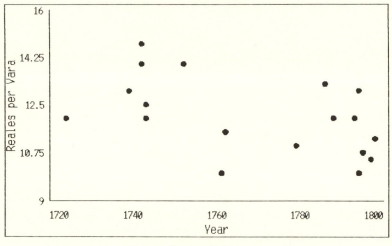

FIGURE 5.2

Price of Paño de Querétaro, Mexico City, 1724-1805

Sources: Prices here and in Figures 5.3, 5.4, and 5.5 are drawn from a variety of sources in AGNM, AJM, and ANM. As a consequence, they are neither homogeneous nor consistent. Most represent market quotations, but a significant number are drawn from decedents' inventories. There was a significant variety of grades of cloth within a given type, so it is difficult to interpret movements based on isolated instances. The strongest evidence that the overall trends are not misleadingly depicted is the similarity in the movement of raw and finished woolen prices. See the text for details.

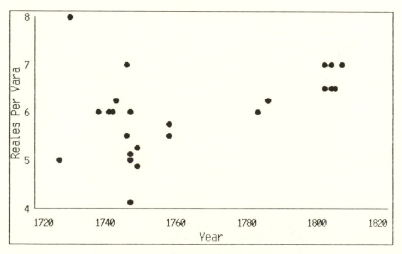

FIGURE 5.3

Price of Bayeta Ancha (Broadcloth)
Mexico City, 1727-1805

147

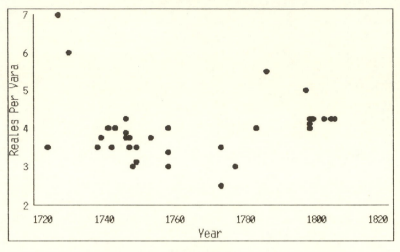

FIGURE 5.4
Price of Bayeta Angosta, Mexico City, 1727-1805

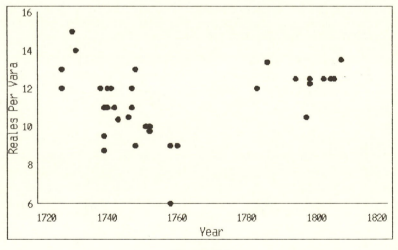

FIGURE 5.5
Price of Paño, Mexico City, 1727-1807

148

ployment to the rural population and supported the development of an urban commercial industry in Puebla after 1750.[50] Hence, while the demand for woolens from Puebla fell, the market for its cottons, the new basis of regional prosperity, increased. This was regional specialization at its most significant, based on new examples of comparative advantage, abetted by market forces, and evident in the emerging response to changing patterns of aggregate demand and supply.

TOTAL PRODUCT, CONTRABAND, AND TRADE

How, why, and when did the volume and value of woolens produced by the obrajes change over the colonial period? How were these fluctuations related to the volume of fair trade and contraband? Is it possible to model the demand for woolens in relation to other sources of textiles? These are major questions, but the data to answer them are distressingly thin. Industry, unlike shipping, mining, and other Crown-regulated activities, left no public registers. To provide answers, we must resort to estimation and outright guessing. No better way exists.

There are virtually no estimates of total woolen output at any moment during the colonial period. Yet drawing on figures provided earlier, Mexico City and Puebla could have reasonably and jointly produced a million pesos worth of woolens annually around 1600. There were also scattered obrajes in Texcoco, Cholula, Tepeaca, and Tlaxcala, but it is unlikely that they accounted for more than a third of the total product. Including the latter, then, woolen output by the obrajes in 1600 was about 1.5 million pesos, or 1.5 pesos per capita. Since José María Quirós estimated annual per capita expenditure on woolens at 3 pesos in 1817, we have a reasonable figure for 1600.[51]

What of the period before 1600? The first obrajes were not established until the late 1530s, and output could not have been much larger, say, in 1575 than it was in 1600. Logically, Indians accounted for little consumption at an early stage of market development; decimation in the epidemics of 1545-48 and 1576-81 radically reduced their effective demand. In other words, the non-Indian population, estimated by Cook and Borah at some 90,000 around 1580, had a disproportionate impact on demand.[52] Its growth perhaps accounts for the revival of the Atlantic trade between 1562 and 1592, and for the appearance of imports whose high prices drove the establishment of the obrajes.[53]

By the 1580s, Puebla's obrajes, which had exported much to Peru, were affected by the expansion of the Peruvian textile industry, but growth elsewhere continued unabated. The slowdown and stagnation of the Atlantic trade between 1593 and 1650 were paralleled by an expansion of obrajes in Querétaro and the Valley of Mexico. Indeed, the establishment of obrajes in Coyoacán between 1640 and 1679—the period of fewest sailings from Spain during the seventeenth century—suggests the competitive relation between colonial industry and maritime trade, and well into the 1690s the Indies market was surfeit with textiles.[54] What were the lines of cause and effect? There can be no definitive explanation, but logic suggests a fall in colonial demand as the obrajes substituted for imports. This entailed a reduction in transatlantic supply, one exacerbated by the terrible years of the 1640s and 1650s. There was consequently further scope for the replacement of scarce imports and for the growth of the woolen industry in Coyoacán and Querétaro. If losses in Puebla were replaced and commercial activity penetrated the countryside, late-seventeenth-century production could be estimated at 1.5 to 2 million pesos, allowing for the additional output of obrajes on rural estates.

The eighteenth century presents a complex set of issues. Existing estimates of woolen output are incomplete, and confused by the vicissitudes of war and peace, by altered commercial regimes, and by enlarged contraband activity. Let us consider these topics in the following sequence: the determinants of domestic production, contraband, estimates of total output, and the effect of trade.

Determinants of Eighteenth-Century Production

Although it would be disirable to focus on the Bajío, the serial evidence to do so is unavailable. As an alternative, we employ the alcabala *concertado* by the gremio de obrajería of Mexico City. For most of the century, the obrajes of Mexico City and its environs did not pay excise on finished goods. Instead, most (but not all) members of the guild made an annual lump-sum payment to the consulado (and later, to the Royal Excise). The records of the concertado payment have been preserved.[55] Although the payment apparently had no direct relation to the value of output, it may be conservatively interpreted as a function of real or perceived capacity to pay, and thus as a proxy for *relative* variations in output. Between 1739 and 1787, there are figures for all but a few years, here plotted in Figure 5.6.

The trend through 1780 is negative (the line falls from left to right), consistent with the decline of the Valley's obrajes. The discontinuity appearing in 1780-81 reflects a major modification in the administration of the alcabala. A decree of October 20, 1780 suspended the turnover tax (*reventa*) on woolens, raised the overall rate from 6 percent to 8 percent, and imposed an ad valorem of 2.67 percent on all textiles from the obrajes, sold or not.[56] Whether the policy was uniformly and consistently enforced is unclear, but the demanded payment jumped sharply.[57] Yet even at this new level, a negative trend continued. In other words, the *level* of payment was renegotiated, but its trend remained unchanged. Output continued to fall.

I incorporate three arguments to account for changes in output. One, the "Florescano hypothesis," relates variations in output to the price level of maize.[58] The second links output to the effects on transatlantic trade produced by the wars of the eighteenth century. The third, an income hypothesis, connects woolen production to silver output. The resulting model was tested through ordinary least squares regression.[59] If Florenscano is correct, a rising level of maize

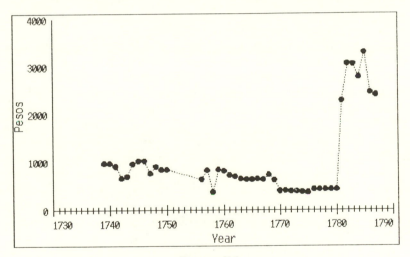

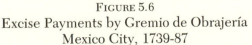

FIGURE 5.6
Excise Payments by Gremio de Obrajería
Mexico City, 1739-87

Source: for 1739 through 1750, "Razón individual de todo lo producido de Reales Alcabalas y demás derechos . . . con inclusión del dos por ciento . . . desde 15 de abril 1744," AGNM, Aduanas, vol. 7, f. 243; for 1756 through 1790, see Fonseca and Urrutia, *Historia general de real hacienda*, 2: [insert] "Productos que ha recibido la real aduana de México desde el año de 1754 hasta el de 90 en los ramos que se expresan."

prices reduced demand for all other goods and entailed a fall in textile output (why a fall in textile prices fails to clear the market in Florescano's work is a mystery). If the war hypothesis serves, warfare (primarily with England) blocked Spanish shipping and increased colonial output, as obrajes substituted woolens for scarce imports. If the final hypothesis is correct, increasing colonial income—here measured by the output of silver—led to greater production of woolens in the obrajes, assuming that woolens were a normal good.

Although I ran the regression in several forms (in first differences, with lags, and with prices in percentage deviations from a cyclical median), the connection between maize prices and textile output does not materialize. Indeed, it was difficult to produce the expected (negative) sign of the maize price coefficient. This reflects both the inadequacy of the output proxy and a flaw in Florescano's argument. He assumes that demand for maize was price-inelastic, at times completely so. The market power of the great hacendados of the Chalco naturally flows from the assumption.[60] But as prices rose, individuals surely purchased less maize and compensated, albeit unsuccessfully, by consuming other foodstuffs.[61] And with improvements in transportation, the market area for the Valley of Mexico grew and brought other sources of maize into supply. Thus, variations in maize prices did not necessarily reduce the demand for and output of other goods. Of course, the horrors of 1785-86 placed the economy *in extremis* and produced the effect hypothesized. But aside from periods of acute crisis, Florescano's model of internal demand appears incorrect. Why should an economy with otherwise flexible prices suffer large reductions in output as maize prices rose? Florescano sees the structural crisis of the 1930s in late-eighteenth-century Mexico, which is ingenious but wrong. Textile output fell only when high maize prices were associated with epidemic disease. The reason is simple. Diseases that killed the population killed the obraje workers and reduced textile supply and output.[62] This is very different from attributing the entire fall in output to a decrease in demand.

The war hypothesis fares much better. A dummy variable for warfare shows the correct sign, mostly a consequence of increased output during the War of the Austrian Succession (1739-48). May we generalize from this? Strictly speaking, no, because the t-statistic is small, the results for 1762-63 (Spain's entry into the Seven Years' War) are equivocal, and the regression line must be shifted radically during Spain's involvement in the War of American Independence (1779-83). Yet a similar phenomenon was reported after 1796, when

Spanish trade with the colonies virtually ceased, and the textile industry in Mexico once again quickened.[63] We can safely override statistical problems and generalize that warfare reduced trade and stimulated the output of the obrajes.

The final or income hypothesis produces the most interesting result. The sign of the coefficient is unexpectedly negative—woolen production fell as the output of silver rose. The sign of the income elasticity is negative, which indicates that woolens from the obrajes were, technically speaking, inferior goods. The result is not statistically significant and "leans" toward the conclusion rather than supporting it fully. Nevertheless, it has intuitive appeal: the consumption of woolens from obrajes fell with increasing socioeconomic status. As economic development proceeded, the obrajes did less well. They were an outgrowth of colonialism, and of relatively autarchic colonialism at that. Industry of this sort, in short words, did not presage higher levels of economic development.

Contraband: Estimates and Conjectures

Contraband textiles were imported outside legal channels. Although Spanish goods could be contraband, smuggling is usually identified with foreign merchandise. The reasons are well known. Even fair trade was based on foreign goods. As Henry Kamen puts it, "Evidence for the massive export of European textiles to America is unquestionable.[64] European penetration of the Spanish imperial market dates from around 1600, when French textiles, particularly Rouen linens (ruán), began to recover from the Wars of Religion. At the same time, the output of Dutch linens and says for export grew at Haarlem and Leiden.[65] By the late seventeenth century, the French controlled much of the legal textile trade through Seville, and considerable quantities of French textiles came to Veracruz during the War of the Spanish Succession (1700-15), a time of nearly unprecedented contraband trade with the Indies.[66] The English entered the Indies trade during the years following 1562, primarily through the export of fine woolen kerseys. By the 1660s, "Spanish" cloths constituted a significant share of English exports, and by 1750, southern Europe—and indirectly, Spanish America—had become the largest market for English woolens of all types.[67] In general, English activity in the Caribbean increased steadily at the expense of the Dutch after the seizure of Jamaica (1655), and the proportion of British domestic exports to the West Indies rose from 5 percent to 25 percent between 1700 and 1797.[68]

The creation of a base in the Caribbean and the right to supply slaves in the early eighteenth century gave England the opportunity for enlarged smuggling to the Spanish Empire. Nevertheless, how much took place, and did it affect the obrajes? The scattered estimates that exist cannot resolve the question. One could reconstruct the trade from Jamaica after the Freeport Act of 1766 from British records, but that is another project. Instead, we employ proxies to estimate contraband. The source is Elizabeth Schumpeter's compilation of English overseas trade statistics.[69]

The export of stuffs and printed cottons to the British West Indies (primarily Jamaica and Trinidad) are the proxies selected. Both were frequently mentioned in New Spain as items of contraband that damaged domestic industry; thus, an examination of their connection to the Mexican economy is logical.[70] The model here links the output of silver, warfare, and the production of woolens to the export of both stuffs and printed cottons and is tested through ordinary least squares regression. The Mexican silver variable is easily justified, since silver financed smuggling, created the capacity to import, and circulated as the principal hard currency of the Anglo-American colonies.[71] Warfare frequently interrupted commercial channels, and conflicts between Britain and Spain had a clear, if uncertain, impact on trade between the two. The cross-elasticity between Mexican and British woolens indicates their competition and potential substitutability. Because the data were not available for all years, it was necessary to run the regression in a variety of ways.[72]

Let us look first at the export of printed cottons in the two decades following the Freeport Act. The performance of the model is very good—too good, in fact. The problem with it is "overfitting," or having nearly as many regressors as observations, thereby producing a nearly deterministic result. It would ordinarily be unwise to rely on such a model, but the limited data offer little choice. For that reason, I report only the signs of the regressors. Silver output has a positive sign—the more that it was mined in Mexico, the more printed cottons were exported to the British West Indies. Obraje output has a negative sign—the less wool woven, the more British cottons exported, and vice versa. The hypothesized relation between silver and cottons is a logical one, the statistical problem notwithstanding. It suggests that British cottons exported to the Caribbean approximate those smuggled to Mexico. These figures are reproduced (in logarithmic transformation to accommodate their range) in Figure 5.7.

The results for obraje production indicate a tendency for British

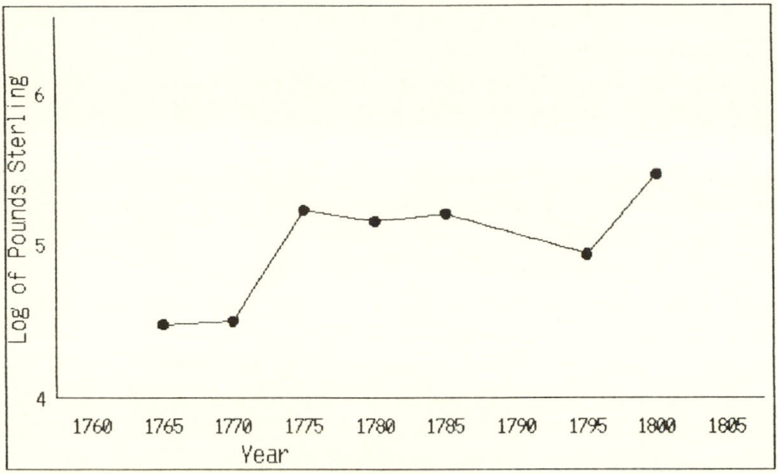

FIGURE 5.7
British Export of Printed Cottons
to British West Indies, 1765-1800

Source: Schumpeter, *English Overseas Trade*, Table 37.

cottons smuggled into Mexico to displace colonial woolens. This closely paralleled the unprecedented increase in productivity experienced by the British cotton textile industry in the years following the Treaty of Paris (1783). Indeed, between 1780 and 1812, the real cost of British cottons fell by nearly 70 percent, attributable to the mechanization of carding and spinning.[73] The obrajes were simply unable to compete, for productivity gains within them were limited to driving labor harder. As the economy of Spanish America was gradually opened after 1765, such differentials increasingly mattered. In other words, the growing integration of the Spanish Empire into the Atlantic economy coincided with the early stages of Britain's industrial revolution and rendered the obrajes increasingly obsolete.

The model also generates other results. Mining output, for instance, may be a good proxy for the demand for smuggled cottons, since silver financed the merchandise deficit that smuggling created. The war dummy, while not statistically significant, has a positive sign. It suggests that warfare between Britain and Spain disturbed normal trading patterns, restricted legal imports, and encouraged British cottons as contraband substitutes. This very problem was discussed in wartime cedulas dealing with English trade in 1779 and 1796, so its existence is hardly conjectural.[74]

Our series for the smuggling of woolens spans the entire eighteenth century. It relates the British export of woolen stuffs to the West Indies to Mexican silver output and to warfare. This model performs well; the silver and war variables are statistically significant. Their interpretation is analogous to the model for printed cottons. Mexican silver output (whose partial correlation with stuffs exported is .88) measures the demand for contraband, because silver was the primary means of paying for it. Moreover, a proxy for the production of domestic woolens (the concertado payment) again produces a negative sign: woolen stuffs sent to the British West Indies correlate negatively ($-.62$) with obraje production in the Valley of Mexico.[75] In other words, woolens smuggled from the British West Indies tended to displace those made in New Spain.

Estimating the demand for contraband in this way will displease those interested in the size of the bill. There are figures available, although most are variants on the same two or three sources. One places trade between Jamaica and the Spanish Main at £300,000 yearly between 1670 and 1700, and figures in the neighborhood of £200,000 also appear with a certain frequency.[76] After Jamaica had

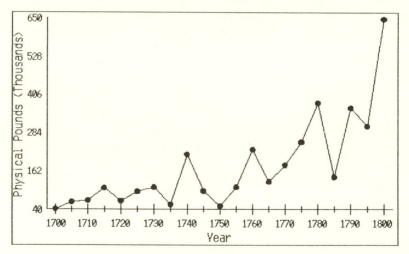

FIGURE 5.8
British Export of Stuffs to British West Indies
1700-1800

Source: Schumpeter, English Overseas Trade, Table 44.

been British for more than a century, a report of 1761 put the value of contraband with the Spanish Empire at the staggering sum of 6 million pesos per year.[77] In 1797, the syndic of the consulado of Veracruz figured the introduction of smuggled "ropa" into New Spain at 2 million pesos.[78] Finally, between September 1807 and April 1810, 2.7 million pesos of contraband were seized in Veracruz alone, with goods such as corduroy concealed in boxes marked "SUGAR."[79] When contemporaries spoke of "immense amounts" of contraband "inundating" markets and destroying native industry, they were not exaggerating.

Trade and Total Output

Clearly, then, whatever enlarged trade to Mexico undermined the prosperity of the obrajes. Although contemporaries were most impressed by contraband, Bourbon policy, with its emphasis on freer trade, exercised a similar influence. As John Fisher clearly demonstrates, Spanish America experienced "a substantial and sustained growth in the value of trade" between 1778 and 1796.[80] After 1789, New Spain shared in this expanding commerce as well.

Although this discussion has pointed principally to the impact of British cottons on Mexican industry, the Spaniards themselves were far from idle. In particular, calico production (*indianas* and *indianillas*) appeared in Catalonia in the 1730s and grew rapidly in the American market thereafter. By 1783, the Compañía de Hilados de Algodón, formed in 1772, was producing 250,000 pieces of printed calicoes a year for sale in America.[81] Moreover, the extension of "comercio libre" to New Spain in 1789 created falling prices born of "too much competition and abundance," according to a merchant schooled in the old system.[82] Comercio libre not only enlarged the quantity of Spanish cottons available but also brought added English competition to bear. Woolens called *paño de segunda* and *paño de tercera clase* were one example. In Mexico, some maintained that "we have nothing in the Peninsula equivalent to segunda inglés," which was "the miserable consumption of the poor."[83] López Cancelada, although hardly disinterested, thought woolens made in the Querétaro "suffer[ed] a great deal with the introduction of paño de segunda inglés and *bayetones*," whereas bays and serges made in Acámbaro suffered "more or less in proportion to imports from Europe of goods that substitute for them."[84] A crude measure shows that the price of segunda inglés fell from 21 reales per vara in the *arancel* of 1778 to 16 for distribution through Querétaro in 1791, to between 14 and 16 in 1796, and to a low of 10 reales per vara in 1818.[85] Not surprisingly, the consulado of Mexico complained that the obrajes of Mexico City and Querétaro, with costs at 18 reales per vara, could not withstand the competition.[86] Well could Father Melchor de Talamantes remark that "the only way to sustain those factories would be to close the port [of Veracruz] to European commerce."[87]

But in the decade after 1796, when Spain lost the carrying trade to its colonies, the port was hardly closed. Indeed, precisely the opposite occurred. Soon after the news of permission to trade with neutrals reached New Spain, one merchant wrote an obraje owner in Querétaro:

> The latest packet into Veracruz brought much news. . . . [The] King has granted foreigners permission to supply this colony with all sorts of goods—other than English—because the blockade of Cádiz has left America short of everything. Because of this . . . there will be much foreign cloth to be had more cheaply than what comes from those factories [in Querétaro].[88]

One indication of the problem appears in Figure 5.9, which measures imports of paño through Veracruz from 1806 through 1819. The total import figure is derived from several different categories in the commercial accounts but gives some indication of official woolen imports. From 1806 to 1812, imports fluctuated between 150,000 and 800,000 pesos per year (excluding 1809), a substantial sum. In 1809, they soared to nearly 1.5 million pesos. Quantities were smaller in the later 1810s, but they could still reach 350,000 pesos per year. These figures appear large, but they can be judged only in relation to domestic production. How large was obraje production during the eighteenth century?

Eighteenth-Century Production

There are a variety of estimates for the production of woolens by the obrajes in eighteenth-century Mexico. One analysis, probably based on data used for the enumeration of 1793, concluded that there were thirty-six obrajes in New Spain, each manufacturing a yearly average of 18,000 pesos in bays, druggets, palmilla, and common woolens for sale in the capital alone; this amounts to some 648,000 pesos.[89] Miguel Domínguez thought that the obrajes of Querétaro produced 7,000 pieces of woolens worth 500,000 pesos per year in the early 1800s.[90] In 1781, the obrajes of Acámbaro made nearly 65,000 pesos

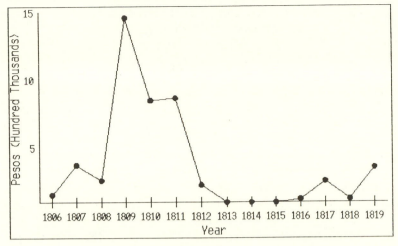

FIGURE 5.9

Import of Paño Through Veracruz, 1806-19

Source: Compiled from Inés Herrera Canales, *Estadística del comercio exterior de México (1821-75)* (México, 1980), pp. 96, 98, 102, 106, 108, 111, 113, 115, 118. A list of the categories aggregated is available on request. No values reported for 1813-15.

of woolens.[91] In a very rough way, these numbers support an output of 1 to 1.5 million pesos per year in the late 1700s, a figure much lower than Quirós' total of 7.4 million pesos.[92] Even a doubling of the estimate to account for woolens made in the telares sueltos and on rural estates yields no more than 3 million pesos yearly.

On the face of it, the estimates indicate that real output may have not been much larger in 1800 than in 1700. If the growth of Querétaro and Acámbaro simply offset decline elsewhere—consistent with the pattern identified—these results make sense. Yet there is the matter of population growth, for even constant per capita expenditures should have raised total demand after 1700. Here the effects of larger imports, contraband, and domestic cotton production are most evident. Catalonian calicoes, cheaper British prints and cloths, and progressively more cottons from Puebla combined to satisfy the demand that obrajes would otherwise have met. It is impossible to apportion responsibility more precisely, because the numbers are not there. No one factor was sufficient to undermine the obrajes, but the combined effect of all factors produced a long-term weakening. Centers such as Querétaro and Acámbaro were better positioned to weather the outcome, as were some larger obrajes elsewhere. Yet all were vulnerable to random shocks by the end of the eighteenth century. These shocks were not long in coming.

THE END OF THE OBRAJES

The first was the outbreak of the rebellion of 1810. In the Bajío, the result was disaster for the obrajes. The records of the town council of Querétaro offer striking proof of its effects. As raw materials became scarce by July of 1811, workers in the trapiches, obrajes, and telares sueltos of Querétaro were fired, and it was difficult to recruit and retain labor under such straitened circumstances.[93] The textile industry fell into a state of "absolute inaction," and some obrajes were coverted into prisons to hold rebels.[94] The skirmishing around Querétaro that broke out in the fall of 1810 was followed by continuing depredations. On the night of October 15, 1811, insurgents tried to carry off the paño 18no used for army uniforms from several fulling mills around Querétaro.[95] By late 1811, the situation had become very serious and turned disastrous in the opening months of 1812.[96] On the eve of the insurrection, there were nineteen obrajes operating 291 looms in Querétaro. Through December of 1811, the corregidor Domínguez reported that only eight were in operation.[97] By February of 1812, four obrajes had ceased operation altogether, and four more verged on closing down. Most of the remainder could hold out but a few months more.[98] Output had fallen sharply, from 10,372 pieces in 1810 to 2,448 pieces, and sales in 1811 had been practically nonexistent. The owners complained of an "almost absolute lack of necessary materials" because of the "present barbarous and destructive insurrection" that had "annihilated the ranchers that supplied the wool" and obstructed the roads for the transport of what little remained.[99] By 1812, the situation had hardly improved, and scant recovery was evident. Only five obrajes were in operation, and these with production sharply reduced.[100]

The woolen industry in Querétaro and its environs stagnated long after the rebellion had been quelled and, indeed, well into the 1830s. In a reply to a survey by the Banco de Avío, a group of owners of obrajes in Querétaro noted in 1831 that only 44 broad and 140 narrow looms operated, with the output of cloth, friezes, sarapes, and other woolens a dismal 1,200 pieces.[101] Consumption of raw wool was reduced to 13,000 arrobas, and employment had fallen to about a thousand operatives. The circulating capital of the industry—estimated in 1808 to be 800,000 pesos—had fallen to 100,000. What caused this stagnation? The owners answered without hesitation:

"This evil finds its origin in the war, and is not reparable without an improvement in our manufactures that will deprive the foreigner of the trade without prejudicing the consumer."[102]

How could civil war inflict a permanent change, rather than one whose effects were temporary, not to say beneficial, once the conflict ended? Was there no "pent-up" demand for cloth to be satisfied after hostilities ceased? The owners argued that the major market for the obrajes prior to the insurrection were the haciendas of the Tierra Adentro. When the war broke out, Querétaro was cut off from its markets, and the hacendados found it necessary to do with homespun. By erecting trapiches on their haciendas, estate owners found they could save money and even improve the quality of the cloth if they wished. "Today they have no need to order cloth from us, because they make it for their own profit, at a lower price, using the workers that consume it." The situation was lost. "Given that shipments of our cloth are diminished and their basis forever destroyed, we shall never again see our obrajes as they were before the insurrection, unless the cloth is improved so as to find markets throughout the republic, and even overseas."[103]

In other words, the owners believed that an economic involution had taken place during the insurgency and deprived them of important markets. On the one hand, isolation from Tierra Adentro reduced demand. On the other, violence in the Bajío—the region most affected by the insurgency—disturbed the source of supply.[104] It is not difficult to understand the result. Nevertheless, by 1817, most of the violence had ended. There were almost certainly unsatisfied demands from the war years and a need for rough woolens in rural recovery. Why did the industry fail to recover?

Several factors explain this failure. First, the collapse of silver mining during and after the war reduced direct demand for woolens in packing, clothing, saddles, and blankets at the mines themselves. Second, haciendas supplying fewer goods to mines were obliged to reduce expenditures and therefore purchased fewer woolens. And third, the overall decline in the mining economy of the Bajío produced a generalized fall in urban demand, which affected the obrajes. In other words, the multiplier effects of mining were not trivial, if only at a regional level.[105] Nevertheless, a reduction in the demand for woolens should not have reduced output in the long run. Prices were flexible and should have fallen to clear the market. Some obrajes—how many is impossible to say—could have absorbed the fall until demand recovered. That this did not occur suggests that still other forces were at work. These affected both supply and demand.

Supply was reduced; falling output in the face of shrinking demand was the result. Although the ranches on which the industry depended ultimately recovered, a major credit contraction accompanied and followed the rebellion. Its dimensions are impossible to estimate, but virtually every source confirms its presence. The collapse of mining and the export of capital deepened the contraction.[106] Since obrajes obtained their working capital through borrowing, their business was inevitably affected. The scale of their operations diminished as they reduced output. The persistence of this contraction was an important element in the persistent stagnation of the obrajes after the rebellion was defeated.

Nevertheless, both supply and demand determine output; something clearly reduced the real (versus money) value of demand after the war. Hence, it is necessary to revisit the role of foreign trade.

FOREIGN TRADE ONCE MORE

The economic recovery from the insurrection coincided with the opening of consumer demand in Mexico to even greater foreign trade. As a consequence, the demand for textiles that would have been supplied domestically was satisfied instead by foreign producers. The explanation is simple. Britain, which produced textiles at a lower cost in terms of other goods foregone, possessed comparative advantage over Mexico. As trade between the two nations grew, Britain specialized in textiles, for Britain did this best. Once Britain's specialization in textiles was complete, there would be room for Mexican production. Mexicans who could not produce textiles efficiently would find alternative uses for their capital and labor. End of story.

There is much to recommend the analysis, if only because it summarizes the economics succinctly. The liberalization of international trade under the Bourbons, the loss of the carrying trade to the colonies after 1796, and the emergence of successor states to the former Spanish colonies were played out against the background of the Industrial Revolution in Great Britain. As a result of productivity gains, the years between 1817 and 1850 were marked by falling prices, a deflation longer and sharper than the inflation that marked the Napoleonic wars.[107] It was Mexico's experience to enter the international market at precisely this time, and the results were predictable. A textile industry shaped and sheltered under colonial sta-

162

tus, but weakened by the forces described, was now almost wholly destroyed. The obrajes that produced woolens could not compete, and cottons suffered as well.

To be sure, anecdotal evidence supports this position. It would be hard to find a major weaving center during the 1820s that did not bemoan the effects of foreign competition. In 1824, a commission of the national congress concluded that "foreign goods currently cost but half or a third of what they did when a fixed number of Spanish vessels could put in to these shores," a statement that clearly referred to textiles.[108] In 1829, the governors of Jalisco and Zacatecas complained: "Hardly born, and reduced to crude cottons and woolens, we have seen [our industry] perish with the import of these same goods. Their cheapness permits our artisans no profit from their work."[109] The Ayuntamiento of Puebla contended that the Napoleonic Wars brought prosperity to Puebla, but peace was another matter. Markets had been opened to all goods; only protection offered a remedy to foreign competition.[110] The governor of the state of Puebla found its industries in the deepest depression. "Its products, as a natural result of their backwardness, cannot compete with foreign merchandise, whose free import has depressed their value in the extreme."[111] In 1824, the textile makers of Guadalajara asked for protection from various foreign goods.[112] Prisciliano Sánchez, then governor of the state, blamed English calicoes for the ruin of local cotton and chintz and for the destruction of printing and weaving shops. Local woolens—says, friezes, and sarapes—offered scant prospect for improvement, for they were sold among the poor, who had no interest in higher quality.[113] In Querétaro, one observer wrote in 1822 that "The import of ordinary and second-class cloths should not be permitted, because in their absence, consumers will necessarily purchase domestic ones."[114] Two years later, the governor of the state announced that import restrictions alone could save the textile industry in Querétaro.[115] The list of these pleas, and the liberal rebuttals offered them, could be extended indefinitely.[116]

How accurate were these complaints, and what policies were designed to deal with them? In late 1821, an ad valorem tariff of 25 percent was enacted, but it was modified in favor of an outright prohibition of cheap cottons and linens in 1822.[117] A decree of 1824 was to amend the tariff of 1821, and paño de segunda and tercera clase, sarapes, and friezes were prohibited. This was a protectionist victory and constituted a reversal of imports permitted since the application of the Regulation of 1778 to New Spain.[118] In 1827, a renewed tightening of imports was attempted. The Mexican government, over the objections of the American and British ministers, raised duties on cottons that could still be imported.[119] Late in the year, paño de primera clase was added to the list of prohibitions, and a decree of 1829 added bays to the list.[120] Thus, throughout the first decade of independence, the complaints of artisans and politicians brought progressively greater restrictions to the variety and number of textiles that could be legally imported. And yet the flood continued. Iturbide, Guadalupe Victoria, and Vicente Guerrero seemed powerless to halt the influx of British merchandise. Guerrero in particular came to power on the basis of popular discontent caused by the unemployment that accompanied larger imports. He fell when he was unable to stem the tide.[121]

Let us, for the moment, ignore the issues of economic welfare that the question of free trade presents and concentrate on the quantity of imports relative to national production. Did British—and to a much lesser extent—American imports swamp domestic production and produce wholesale unemployment? Is the anecdotal evidence correct? The answer, I believe, is yes.

In Figure 5.10, we consider the relation between the declared

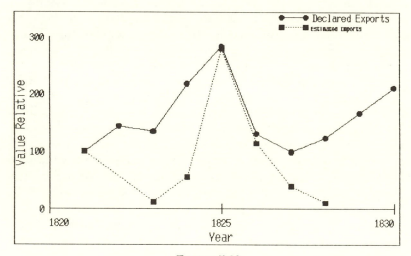

FIGURE 5.10
British Woolen Exports to Mexico and South America
Versus Mexican Imports, 1821-30

Source: Britain: Parliamentary Papers, 2: 71-82; Mexico: Herrera Canales, Estadística, pp. 118, 124, 127, 130, 135, 140, 145, 149. A list of the categories aggregated is available on request.

value of exports of British manufactured woolens to Mexico and South America and woolen imports into Mexico from all sources. Both series have been reduced to an index of relative values (1821 = 100) for comparative purposes. The correlation of the series in first differences is .82 for 1822-28, an indication of close correspondence in their rates of change. Both series peak in 1825, the year of British recognition of Mexico, when Mexican woolen imports amounted to nearly 1.3 million pesos. The latter figure is large; at the current rate of exchange it ranges between 50 percent and 100 percent of estimated woolen production in the early nineteenth century. The point is very simple. Even if, as some argue, British textile exports were small by British standards, they were nevertheless large in relation to the productive capacity of the recipient. Imports were cheaper and sturdier and possessed the cachet of foreign quality. They substituted for domestic woolens and satisfied a portion of demand that postwar recovery provided. Small wonder that the Querétaro owners wondered where their markets had gone!

The course of British cottons exported to Mexico follows a pattern that is, in some respects, the same. Cottons also rose to a peak of roughly 668,000 pounds sterling in 1825, followed by a lesser peak in 1827, and a high of 692,000 pounds sterling in 1830. Although the

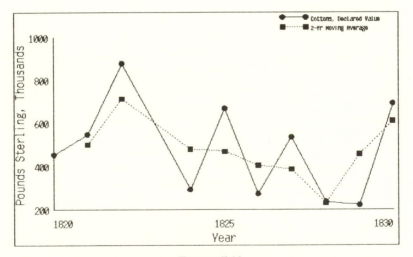

FIGURE 5.11
British Cotton Manufactures Exported to Mexico
Declared Value, 1820-30

Source: *Parliamentary Papers*, 2: 67-70.

Mexican market trended downward throughout the 1820s, one manufacturer from Glasgow observed that "for three or four years, there were considerable fortunes made in Mexico."[122] A small understatement. William Bullock, for instance, estimated Mexican textile output at 1.5 million pounds sterling after independence, which seems quite high.[123] If we take average British cotton exports to Mexico in the 1820s in relation to Bullock's estimate, we derive a lower-bound estimate of 30 percent. In other words, at minimum, at the current rate of exchange, British exports in the 1820s were 30 percent of national production, and other base estimates provide an upper-bound figure of as much as 60 percent.[124] It is easy to see why Mexican cotton producers complained so bitterly about British imports during the 1820s. As for American trade, it was still relatively small and overwhelmingly composed of reexports. It serves no purpose to detail its movements here.[125]

Conclusion: Good Grapes in Scotland?

Whether or not an industry should be protected is a question as old as Adam Smith's gibe about Scottish wines. There has been no end of debate to the matter, and it cannot be resolved here. What is clear is that Mexico's obrajes, weakened by structural changes in the late eighteenth century, were virtually destroyed by civil war and foreign trade in the 1810s and 1820s. Viewed from the standpoint of neoclassical theory, it was simply a case of comparative advantage. Nevertheless, Britain's former North American colonies took a rather different route. In the United States, the tariffs of 1816, 1824, and 1828 offered substantial protection to the New England cotton industry. By at least one account, removing protection would have devastated it. The lesson to be drawn from the American experience is clear. A sudden and radical liberalization of trade can have a drastic impact on the industrial sector of a developing economy.[126]

Nevertheless, Mexico most emphatically did not operate under a regime of free trade in the 1820s, pace artisans, governors, and others angered by *introducciones extranjeras*. Why, then, was its industry undermined?

If prohibited goods continued to be imported, prohibitions were evidently ineffective. There are two reasons for this. First, it was not impossible to "reclassify" goods so as to evade restrictions, for the schedules themselves were complex and ambiguous. Second, there was widespread admission that customs officials were corrupt and did not enforce prohibitions already on the books.[127] In other words, it was one thing to regulate, and another to enforce, a pattern of fiscal behavior established in the colonial period.

Another argument depends on supply and demand and is illustrated in Figure 5.12. In essence, a large difference in price between British imports and Mexican textiles reduces the Mexican share of the market. The Mexican producers cannot compete. In response, a tariff is levied to raise the domestic price of imports. How much of the market Mexican producers could then recover depends upon a host of factors, principally the elasticities of supply and demand, and the level of the tariff. Nevertheless, even a significant (or strictly enforced) tariff might lead to nothing more than a small recovery by Mexican producers and the continuing importation of significant quantities of British goods. This is apparently what happened. "Successful" protection would have required higher (or more rigorously enforced) levels of protection than were offered.

Yet successful protection, in reducing imports, would also reduce tariff revenues. This was a major dilemma. Between 1822 and 1832, tariff collections provided, on the average, 45 percent of total federal revenues.[128] For a government hard pressed to meet its expenses, such a reduction could be disastrous. As consequence, it is understandable why national politicians in the First Republic sought a balance between free trade and prohibition. By definition, either extreme yielded zero revenue. From the perspective of the federal government, the "optimal" tariff was necessarily lower than what manufacturers might have wished. The course that statesmen such as Alamán struck was therefore a wise, and indeed an inspired, one. The establishment of the Banco de Avío was to provide subsidies to industrialists, a response to the dilemma that tariff protection implied. The subsidy, to be realized through the creation of loans at negative real rates of interest, would allow domestic producers to maintain their competitiveness by reducing costs.[129] Whether the Banco could have succeeded in its purposes is moot. It lacked secure access to sufficient supplies of loanable funds and was a casualty of the political turmoil of the 1830s. The one possibility—and the model suggests it—is that the demand for imports was relatively inelastic. Under those circumstances, a higher (or more rigorously enforced) tariff would have produced more rather than less revenue. Had this revenue been channeled into Banco de Avío, the bank's fate might well have been different. With a larger, stable industrial sector, an alternative tax base—and room for maneuver on trade policy—would have been available. Yet all this is speculative: some problems simply lack solutions.

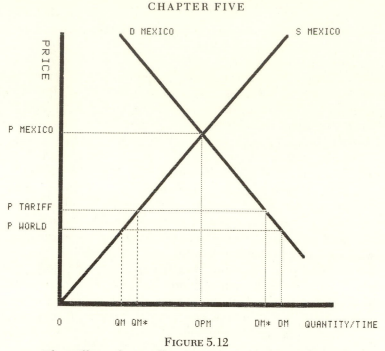

FIGURE 5.12

The Effect of a Tariff on Mexican Textile Production

The price of Mexican textiles before trade is "P MEXICO," and the quantity produced "OPM." Let trade begin with the outside world. The world price is "P WORLD," essentially the price of British imports delivered in Mexico. At this price, quantity demanded in Mexico is DM, but Mexican producers will supply only QM. The difference (QM − DM) is made up by British imports.

Next, let Mexico impose a tariff, which raises the price of textiles to "P TARIFF." At this price, Mexicans will supply QM*, but consumers will demand DM*. The difference, again, is supplied by imports.

What is the result? The posttariff price to Mexican consumers is higher than the free-trade price but lower than the price to Mexicans in a world without trade (given by the difference P MEXICO − P TARIFF). Mexicans demand more textiles than before trade (OPM) but less than in a world of free trade (DM* − DM).

Clearly, the magnitude of the various effects will depend on relative elasticities of supply (e.g., Mexico's supply is assumed unit elastic, whereas Britain's is assumed perfectly elastic) and demand, on differences in domestic and world prices, and on the level of the tariff. In this example, a substantial tariff would be necessary to reduce the share of imports in the market (here DM* − QM*/DM*). Thus, substantial imports could continue in the presence of a tariff, the apparent result in Mexico in the 1820s.

Source: After Charles P. Kindleberger and Peter H. Lindert, *International Economics*, 6th ed. (Homewood, IL, 1978), p. 109.

Benjamin Franklin wrote that no nation was ever ruined by trade.[130] Franklin, however, died in 1790, too soon to test the proposition on the successor states of the Spanish Empire in America. Whatever the merits of liberal economic thought, its preference for free trade and British tutelage did not serve early republican Latin America well. Where market imperfections were substantial, free trade did far more harm than good.

ALTHOUGH other passages of *The Wealth of Nations* are perhaps better known, Adam Smith's discussion of woolens, England's traditional staple industry for a long while, is likewise enlightening. The example, used to illustrate the principle of specialization, is worth quoting:

> The woollen coat, for example, which covers the day laborer, as coarse and rough as it may appear, is the produce of the joint labour of a great multitude of workmen. The shepherd, the sorter of the wool, the wool-comber or carder, the dyer, the scribbler, the spinner, the weaver, the fuller, the dresser, with many others, must all join their different arts in order to complete even this homely production. How many merchants and carriers, besides, must have been employed in transporting the materials from some of those workmen to others who often live in a very distant part of the country! . . . What a variety of labor too is necessary to order to produce the tools of the meanest of those workmen! To say nothing of such complicated machines . . . [as] the mill of the fuller, or even the loom of the weaver, let us consider only what a variety of labor is required in order to form that very simple machine, the shears with which the shepherd clips the wool. The miner, the builder of the furnace for smelting the ore, the feller of the timber, the burner of the charcoal to be made use of in the smelting-house, the brick-maker, the brick-layer, the workmen who attend the furnace, the mill-right, the forger, the smith, must all of them join their different arts in order to produce them.[1]

The number of people involved in producing just this one coat, concluded Smith, "exceeds all computation." But that, of course, is precisely the point. Whatever its organization and productivity, and whatever its reliance upon markets or command for factor supplies, the demands of traditional woolen manufacture were varied. This was as true in New Spain as in Britain. To render Smith less gracefully, the value added by woolens was large: more so than rough estimates indicate. Or so circumstances in the 1820s suggest.

What difference did the disappearance of the obrajes make? In neoclassical terms, Mexico was better off without inefficient industry, for it acquired textiles at lower cost in trade than through domestic manufacture. Nevertheless, doubts persist about such a model, if only because the economy could not easily absorb labor released by trade. The "factor proportions problem," the persistence of equilibrium unemployment, has long been controversial in development economics because it denies that the labor market must clear.[2] Yet persistent unemployment in Mexico in the 1820s was familiar and frequently tied to the crisis in textile production. When H. G. Ward visited Puebla in 1825, unemployment due to falling demand for local cottons and woolens was apparent. Ward, of course, represented British interests and believed the region's estates could absorb displaced artisans. But he held little hope for Mexico City, whose condition in late 1823 appalled him. Ward's description of the city's large underclass makes for grim reading.[3] His fears were justified, as the sack of the Parián (central market) in 1829 by a mob swelled by unemployed artisans amply demonstrated.[4] Although the history of the First Republic (1824–35) remains largely uncharted, its political instability was worsened by falling income and employment, in part a consequence of the crisis in textile production.

Nevertheless, some observers object that the crisis was purely commercial, and that subsistence production was unaffected. Accordingly, the market was divided into noncompeting groups, essentially imports and domestic goods, which were, at best, imperfect substitutes.[5]

This view is debatable. By the late eighteenth century, imports per se were no longer strictly luxury goods, as the falling price and widespread use of British printed cottons demonstrate. More important, trade *did* affect indigenous production. The dimensions of the market fluctuated with the demand for money income; Villa Alta and Sultepec, for instance, depended on commercial sale of textiles. Once manta and paño de rebozo became commercial items, they were subject to competition from imports as well. Moreover, peasant textile producers who avoided commercial opportunities were not necessarily better off. Some did so because of diminishing returns in agriculture, and accumulated little capital as a result.[6] The history of south-central Mexico—of Oaxaca, Guerrero, and southern Puebla, all centers of artisan textile manufacture—is a record of stagnation and progressive impoverishment rather than a triumph of peasant autarchy.[7]

The postimperial crisis was not limited to Mexico. Its effects were felt throughout the former textile centers of the Spanish Empire, as a brief review of their history shows. In frontier areas, such as Chile, the inability of the Spaniards to subdue the natives disrupted the settlement economy; in the south, the Araucanian revolt of 1599 destroyed the obrajes. Those in central Chile also disappeared between 1600 and 1630, casualties of growing specialization in ranching and of expanding penetration of woolens made in Quito.[8] Demand from the mines of the Peruvian Sierra, and the relatively high cost of reaching them, was a greater incentive for the growth of the textile industry. So, for example, between 1585 and 1610, obrajes in Córdoba supplied Potosí with woolens.[9] The obrajes of Vilcashuaman marketed woolens in Huamanga, itself linked to the mercury mines at Huancavelica and to the silver mines in Castrovirreyna.[10] Potosí also purchased woolens made in the Audiencia of Quito by obrajes in Otavalo, Ambato, Latacunga, and Riobamba, and from Cuzco as well.[11]

The obrajes of Peru first appeared in the 1560s, or within three decades of the Spaniards' arrival. They prospered throughout the seventeenth century and did well for much of the eighteenth.[12] The obrajes of Quito followed a comparable path, emerging in the 1560s, and expanding substantially during the seventeenth century, with export markets in Lima, New Granada, and elsewhere. But the eighteenth century witnessed a reversal, as English and French textiles deprived Quito of the Lima market.[13] Much the same happened to the obrajes of Cuzco in the late eighteenth century. The influx of British bays, the competition of the *chorrillos*, or smaller producers, in La Paz, and the inclusion of the intendancy of Potosí in the new viceroyalty of Río de la Plata in 1777 reduced the market for Peruvian woolens.[14] Imports of medium quality continued strong, and by 1814, the la Plata consumed 3 million yards of British calico and muslin, to the disadvantage of Peruvian manufactures, formerly staples of mass consumption.[15]

In Peru, the effects were equally apparent. As in New Spain, colonial contraband signaled the changing significance of trade, and by 1740, its volume was significant.[16] Independence brought substantial change to the commercial regime, with erratic, sometimes contradictory, policies regulating foreign trade. Again, British imports were of fundamental concern, and their competitiveness, even in the interior, was rapidly established. By 1826, Manchester cottons were in abundant supply, as were muslins from Preston and Bolton, whose "disastrously" low prices displaced Peruvian cottons or *tocuyos*.[17] The result, as in Mexico, was protectionist sentiment, whose political expression came in enactments of 1826, 1827, 1830, and 1833. But, just as in Mexico, prohibitions proved ineffective; the de-

mand for imports seemed price inelastic. Similar consequences ensued, as British textiles found their way into provincial society earlier and more deeply than in the Río de la Plata. By 1830, the obrajes
of Cuzco, like those of Querétaro, were ruined. Britain's comparative advantage was the cause, and Peruvian unemployment, the
consequence.[18]

The crisis of domestic industry in Mexico and Peru provided the
context and the cause of subsequent political instability. Rather than
benefitting from trade, both nations suffered falling income and employment and the loss of reinvestible earnings. Their experiences
exemplify the impact of the Industrial Revolution on colonial and
neocolonial areas and the ensuing "deindustrialization" that occurred. As Amiya Kumar Bagchi argues, the smooth redeployment
of resources characteristic of neoclassical technological change may
be largely illusory, if only because "a part of the adjustments . . . in
the advanced capitalist countries took place overseas . . . hidden
from the view of most economists."[19] The result, he maintains, was a
reduction in the extent and efficiency of the market and a general
predisposition to structural rigidities.[20] This does not imply that
trade was malevolent, or that Britain looted Mexico and Peru. It
does suggest that neither Mexico nor Peru could easily "endogen-
ize" market capitalism, modernization, or stable political institutions through trade, at least in the early nineteenth century.

Questions of political economy thus assumed peculiar urgency in
early republican Latin America. In Mexico, the debate echoed older
concerns and focused on trade, mining, and manufacturing. In an
address of 1825, Lucas Alamán, then secretary of domestic and foreign affairs, argued that

> The mines are the source of the real wealth of this nation, and
> all that some speculative economists have said against this prin-
> ciple has been vigorously rebutted by experience. So we have
> constantly seen agriculture, commerce, and industry follow the
> progress of the mines, advancing with these, and decaying in
> the same proportion.[21]

Alamán, of course, did more than tilt with the ghost of Adam
Smith, as his intelligent support for the Banco de Avío (1830–42)
shows. He spoke from personal experience and thought investment
in mining was an efficient stimulus to total demand. Others intui-
tively saw, however, that *total* and *domestic* demand were different.
In the words of one writer:

Mining is not wealth . . . [and] silver alone does not make a nation rich and happy. . . . [A] nation, although it has much silver, if it has not industry sufficient unto itself [is not wealthy] . . . What the Europeans want the Mexicans to be is the man rich with silver who depends on them, who uses silver to exchange for what they bring, which we cannot make. . . .[22]

This was a telling point, and it questioned whether mining promoted domestic growth. The course of trade in the nineteenth century did little to support Alamán's contention. For one example, the "leakage" of demand in the course of building the Mexican railways is well known.[23] For another, not *once* between 1825 and 1885 did Mexico register a merchandise surplus in trade with the United States. In relation to North America (and, very probably, to the world as a whole), Mexico was already behaving in typically "underdeveloped" fashion, consuming more than it produced and relying on imports to bridge the gap. The silver Mexico employed to finance the resulting deficit depreciated after 1865 and exacerbated balance-of-payments problems.[24] In short, there were immense disadvantages to mining as an "engine of growth," even if it offered apparent stability to public finance in the short run.

Not all the costs of mining were tangible or easily measured. For one thing, mining does not encourage a correct understanding of wealth. Unlike industry, which emphasizes planning, deferred consumption, and the accumulation of productive assets, mining values ownership of a wasting resource and the luck of the draw. The desperate financial straits of the First Republic offer an object lesson. Where the United States had a merchant marine, Mexico had flooded mines. What the United States earned from sales of foodstuffs and shipping services, Mexico perforce borrowed. Mexico had silver; the United States had Mexico. Which nation was richer in the long run? Perhaps God gave to the miner Borda, and Borda gave back to God, but neither divine providence nor beautiful churches provide a basis for economic development.[25] The collapse of the woolen industry in Mexico was not responsible for this outlook, but its demise did nothing to combat it.

Nevertheless, as we have seen, it would be incorrect to equate the development of obrajes and markets in Mexico, for the relationship was rather the reverse. Despite the obrajes' role in colonial supply, their potential for transformation into industrial enterprise was limited. Their technological obsolescence, meaningful in light of the Industrial Revolution, underscores the point. Yet the source of that obsolescence provides a way of thinking about the economy as a whole. In Mexico relative labor costs provided little incentive for innovation; they reflected the weakness of the labor market and a reliance upon coercion.

Nor was technological stagnation limited to industry. Although we know little of productivity change in Mexican agriculture, there was no sign of "improving landlords," which is odd in light of reputed levels of rural indebtedness. Why did rising debt service not drive estate owners to seek higher income and to innovate, as it did in England?[26] The answer may lie in the relationship of landlord to tenant, analyzed by Shane Hunt and David Brading. For Hunt, the relationship was a "bad bargain" in which workers' productivity on subsistence lands allowed the estate to pay low wages and reduce costs. The efficient minifundista, in other words, subsidized the inefficient hacendado.[27] Brading, in a commentary on the work of Andrés Molina Enríquez, concludes that the "hacienda . . . survived by reason of the low wages paid to its peons [contrasted with] the intensely cultivated plots of rancheros and Indian villages. . . ."[28] The ability of landlords to control the labor supply, and to pay less than its supply price, permitted an inefficient, technologically backward agrarian regime to survive.

Sixteenth-century transportation development was similarly distorted. Ross Hassig argues that early Spanish settlers used *tamemes*, or Indian bearers, "because the Indians could be forced to [carry] . . . as part of . . . encomienda obligations, and were thus 'cheaper' than mules or wagons to the *encomendero*, if not to society as a whole." The use of underpriced porters perpetuated Spanish reliance on them and reduced the apparent need to construct roads to accommodate mule trains and wagons.[29] In this, as in agriculture, coercion distorted prices and incentives and limited the opportunities for technical change.

The symmetry that these examples bear to the obraje is not coincidental. Taken together, they indicate that technological change in the Mexican economy was not independent of social relations; development was both a social and an economic process. Factor prices and relative scarcity were not determined independently of political power. Indeed, in the very long run, the history of preconquest Mesoamerica was a record of growing reliance on political responses to economic requirements rather than of recourse to market-price allocation. The militarization of postclassic society was, in this sense, a forced solution to constraints on supply, principally in agriculture and transport technology.[30] The expansion of tribute collection, the use of coercion in its enforcement, and a reliance on corvée labor suggest that trade—voluntary, market-based exchange—was inadequate to sustain the population under Aztec control. Moreover, this was true despite the relatively high productivity of lacustrine transportation and agriculture in the Valley of Mexico.[31] Admittedly it may be inaccurate to see these arrangements as an "Asiatic mode of production" in which most property was held by the state. Yet they do not support the view that resources, particularly labor, were allocated through the market.[32] The conflicting pattern of exchange and coercion that typified Spanish colonialism thus existed long before the Conquest. It simply assumed peculiar clarity under the demands of European commercial capitalism.[33]

Viewed in this way, there was no contradiction between the exercise of compulsion and the existence of capitalism in colonial Mexico. What neoclassical analysis terms market imperfections—particularly elevated transportation costs—were a functional part of the Mesoamerican landscape, the result of difficult terrain and limited technological options. Their consequences, such as ethnic fragmentation and difficulties in communication, were further barriers to economic integration. The history of attempts to extend and to unify regional and local markets in Mexico therefore has had social and political consequences as well. The weakness of political consensus, the persistence of regional power, the sense of nationalism without nation—central threads of nineteenth-century political history—reflected slow growth and the costs of building a national economy. So, too, did the search for unifying principles, both religious and secular, in the aftermath of the colonial regime. For Mexico, unification and the liquidation of the colonial regime began slowly, incompletely, and painfully in the nineteenth century. Their completion eludes the nation still.

APPENDIX

The Measurement of Cloth

As Manuel Carrera Stampa observed, units of measurement in New Spain were unsystematized. This is not surprising. Standardization of weights and measures did not generally begin until the late eighteenth century.[1] As a consequence, measures of cloth in colonial Mexico fluctuated from one place to another and from year to year. Even the standards employed by the same obraje frequently changed.

Measures of raw wool also varied widely. A *carga* might weigh from 10 to 16 arrobas and contain two *tercios* or *sacos* of raw wool.[2] Similarly, cloth measurements from Mexico City, Puebla, and León over nearly two centuries (1597, 1690, and the later 1770s) show significant variance.[3] In Puebla, a piece of cloth ranged from 35 to 40 varas, depending on whether it was "fine" or "18no." Bays ran 80 varas to the piece; says had 120 varas. In 1690, in the Valley of Mexico, a piece of cloth ran 53 or 54 varas. Palmilla ran 60 varas. A say ran to 100 varas per piece. "Paño 16no" ran 50 to 60 varas to the piece. "Paño 6no" had 60 varas per piece. On the hacienda "Santa Ana Pacueco" in León in the later 1770s, a say ran 70 to 90 varas per piece. A bay had about 40 varas. A serge ran 80 to 90 varas. And in 1800, a "tejido" in Acámbaro ran 100 to 115 varas to the piece. In other words, the variance among measurements was very high. Labels such as a "piece" of broadcloth or frieze could be nearly useless in judging quantities. It is not difficult to see why strong family ties were important in the textile trade. Without trustworthy agents, how else could one tell what he or she was buying or selling?

GLOSSARY OF TECHNICAL TERMS

All terms are defined by their use in the obrajes. Many are discussed in detail in Francisco J. Santamaría, *Diccionario de mejicanismos* (4th ed., México, 1983) and in Hugo A. Mejías, *Préstamos de lenguas indígenas en el español americano del siglo xvii* (México, 1980). Nora Fisher's *Spanish Textile Tradition of New Mexico and Colorado* (Santa Fe, 1979) offers a splendid guide to the varieties of Mexican woolens. Kax Wilson, *A History of Textiles* (Boulder, CO, 1979), offers an overview of tools and techniques.

administrador	manager or managing partner of an obraje
alcaparrosa	copperas: a fixative used in dyeing
alumbre	alum: a fixative used in dyeing
añil	indigo
aviador refaccionario	financial backer to an obraje
batán	fulling or felting mill
bayeta	bays or baize: half-worsted woolen, felt, or flannel
bayetón	blanket cloth: a heavier bayeta
canillas	bobbins
canillero	bobbin boy
cardador	carder
cardas	brushes used to strip, straighten, and align wool fibers
chiapaneco	Chiapas-style cotton skirt
composición de obraje	regularization of an obraje's license by payment of fee
corte de manga	woolen shawl commonly lined with cotton
cuadrilla	workers' housing provided by an obraje; a group or class of specific workers
encerrar	to retain or to lock up, frequently for debt
enredo	an Indian skirt
frizado	frieze: a coarse woolen with an uncut nap
fundidor de paños	cloth jobber or broker
grana	cochineal
gremio	guild or trade association
hilador	spinner or preparer of yarn
huipil	waist-length sleeveless cotton blouse worn by Indian women
iscapeso	carded wool
iscatel	combed wool

179

jerga	serge: a thick, coarse cloth
jerguetilla	thinner variety of jerga
lana puerca	unwashed wool
lana tinta	dyed wool
lanilla	thin woolen cloth, frequently of better quality
maestro examinado	master craftsman certified by guild license
manta	generic term for cotton cloth
manteca	tallow
mayordomo	foreman of an obraje
obrador	domestic weaving shop
obraje	textile manufactory, generally for woolens
obrajero	the owner of an obraje, or an employee in one
obrajuelo	smaller obraje or trapiche
palmilla	generic term for very cheap woolen
paño	heavier woolen or "old drapery" made from carded yarn
peine	a yarn comb
perchar	to examine a cloth for defects
pie	yarn for the warp
prensa	cloth press
prensa de fuego	hot press
prensa fria	cold press
quechquemitl	triangular shawl worn by Indian women
rebozo	generic term for shawl of any fabric
retacero	a cottage worker in cloth, especially in Acámbaro
sabanilla	handwoven sheeting
sayal	say: a coarse woolen yardage fabric
tejoleta	*see* tlacos
telar	generic term for treadle loom
telar suelto	"independent" or single loom not found in an obraje
tequesquite	weak, alkaline soponifying agent
tequio	assigned task or quota, in both obrajes and cottage industry
tienda de paños	cloth store, frequently attached to an obraje
tienda de raya	truck store of the obraje
tlacos	tokens, sometimes copper, or chits employed in a truck store
trama	yarn for the weft
trapiche	a small textile shop
trapichero	one who owned a trapiche, or worked in one
tundir	to shear the raised nap of the finished woolen
tundidor	the worker who sheared the raised nap of the finished woolen

ABBREVIATIONS IN NOTES

AGI   Archivo General de Indias, Seville
AGNM   Archivo General de la Nación, México, DF
AHINAH Archivo Histórico del Instituto Nacional de Antropología e Historia,
        México, DF
AJM   Archivo Judicial de Jurisdicciones y Distritos Federales, México, DF
AJP   Archivo Judicial, Puebla
AJQ   Archivo Judicial, Querétaro
ANM   Archivo de Notarías, México, DF

exp.   expediente
f.   foja
leg.   legajo

BAGN   *Boletín del Archivo General de la Nación* (México)
HAHR   *Hispanic American Historical Review*
HISLA   *Historia Económica y Social de América Latina*
Hist Mex *Historia Mexicana*
JEH   *Journal of Economic History*
T Am   *The Americas*

NOTES

CHAPTER ONE

1. Part One, Chapter One.

2. Conde de Revillagigedo, *Instrucción reservada* (México, 1966), pp. 190-91.

3. Domingo de Berengaña to the minister of the Indies, México, Feb. 14, 1783, AGI, México 2372.

4. Croix to the minister of the Indies, México, May 20, 1767, AGI, México 1366.

5. Charles III to the viceroy of New Spain, San Ildefonso, Sept. 12, 1783, AGI, México 2372.

6. Philip II to the viceroy of New Spain, San Lorenzo, Sept. 6, 1594, AGI, México 23; Lucas Alamán, "Memoria sobre el estado de la agricultura e industria de la república . . . en cumplimiento del artículo 26 del decreto orgánico de 2 de diciembre de 1842" (México, 1842) in Secretaría de Hacienda y Crédito Público and Nacional Financiera, S.A., *Documentos para el estudio de la industrialización en México, 1837-45* (México, 1977), p. 11.

7. One survey was made as the result of a circular order of Apr. 9, 1781, and the reports are found in AGNM, Alcabalas, vol. 571. A second survey, taken in 1793, may be found in AGNM, Alcabalas, vol. 37. The final survey, made in 1799, appears in AGNM, Historia, vol. 122.

8. José Joaquín Real Díaz and Antonia M. Heredia Herrera, "Martín de Mayorga (1779-1783)," in Antonio Calderón Quijano, ed., *Los virreyes de Nueva España en el reinado de Carlos III*, 2 vols. (Seville, 1967-68), 2: 157-59.

9. Mayorga to the joint directors of the Royal Excise, México, Jan. 8, 1781, AGNM, Alcabalas, vol. 521. A note on the translation of *alcabala* as "excise" rather than as "sales tax": The *OED* defines excise as "a duty charged on home goods, either in the process of their manufacture or before their sale to the home consumer." Although the regulations governing the alcabala on textiles were complex and frequently changed, a few points are clear. First, both raw materials and final product were subject to tax as *primera* and *segunda especie*. Second, the final product was to be taxed only once after the abolition of the *reventa*, or turnover tax, in 1756, rather than whenever the good changed hands. By a viceregal decree of 1780, however, a tax of 2.67 percent was deemed effective on all woolens produced by the obrajes, whether or not the goods were sold (2.67 percent was determined as one-third of the then-current levy of 8 percent on final sales). The alcabala was thus understood by its administrators to be not only a sales tax but an excise in the strict sense of the term. I have therefore translated alcabala accordingly, although a case can also be made for the phrase "sales tax." See AGNM, Impresos Oficiales, vol. 5, f. 212, and the

testimony accompanying the letter of the Audiencia to the minister of the Indies, Apr. 26, 1785, AGI, México 1416. A similar use of the term "excise" appears in David A. Brading, *Miners and Merchants in Bourbon Mexico, 1763-1810* (Cambridge, Eng., 1971), p. 29.

10. Letter from David Brading to the author, Cambridge, Eng., Nov. 8, 1983.

11. Miguel Páez and Juan Navarro to the viceroy of New Spain, México, Jan. 16, 1781, AGNM, Alcabalas, vol. 521.

12. Ibid.

13. Consulta written by don Alonso de Arriaga Agüero, México, Jan. 28, 1690, AGI, Contaduría 806, Ramo 3.

14. Comisión de visita de Simón de Padilla, México, Jun. 8, 1706, AGNM, Civil, vol. 1735, exp. 1.

15. Consulta written by don Alonso de Arriaga Agüero, México, Jan. 28, 1690, AGI, Contaduría 806, Ramo 3.

16. Eric van Young, *Hacienda and Market in Eighteenth-Century Mexico: The Rural Economy of the Guadalajara Region, 1675-1820* (Berkeley, 1981), pp. 108-9n.

17. Testimony of Domingo de Sandoval, México, May 16, 1747; petition of Gregorio de Aldama, México, May 6, 1747; and the notification to Sandoval, México, May 6, 1747, AJM, leg. 100.

18. To the intendant of México, Malinalco, Dec. 30, 1805, AGNM, Civil, vol. 1682.

19. José María Muriá, ed., *Historia de Jalisco*, 4 vols. (Guadalajara, 1980), 2: 155-56; Rodney D. Anderson, *Guadalajara a la consumación de la Independencia: Estudio de su población según los padrones de 1821-1822* (Guadalajara, 1983), pp. 104-5.

20. The date of the document on which these numbers rest should be a caution to economic historians about believing everything they read. Although the "Estado que manifiesta los obrajes formales y telares que hay . . ." carried the date Oct. 17, 1801, it relied on data collected in 1793. The "Estado" itself appears in two places: AGNM, Alcabalas, vol. 37, and AGNM, Historia, vol. 122. To check the date, compare the figures on the talley sheet with the numbers in the individual reports dated 1793. The talley sheet was composed later but was based on the figures reported in 1793. Therefore, it should *not* be used to document the effects of the trans-Atlantic trade blockade of 1799.

21. *Actas Constitucionales Mexicanas (1821-1824)*, 10 vols. (México, 1980), 9: 552.

22. Report of Vicente Domingo Lombardini, Tlaxcala, Nov. 24, 1793, AGNM, Alcabalas, vol. 37.

23. Real Orden of Nov. 28, 1808, San Lorenzo, AGI, México 2372.

24. Extracts of reports from Guadalajara, Monterrey, Guanajuato, Zacatecas, and Saltillo, all in AGNM, Alcabalas, vol. 521.

25. Vicente Domingo Lombardini to the joint directors of the Royal Excise, México, Dec. 10, 1779, AGNM, Aduanas, vol. 67, exp. 1.

26. Based on reports filed from Guadalajara, Monterrey, Guanajuato, Zacatecas, and Saltillo, all in AGNM, Alcabalas, vol. 521.

27. Computed from data supplied by Clemente de Apresa to the joint directors of the Royal Excise, Acámbaro, Apr. 30, 1781, AGNM, Alcabalas, vol. 521.

28. Report filed from San Luis Potosí, AGNM, Alcabalas, vol. 521.

29. To the viceroy of New Spain, San Pablo Apetatitlan, Nov. 20, 1807, AGNM, Civil, vol. 1682.

30. Petition of Manuel José Grijalva [Tlaxcala, 1772], Rosenbach Museum and Library, Philadelphia, Pennsylvania.

31. Vicente Domingo Lombardini to the joint directors of the Royal Excise, México, Dec. 10, 1779, AGNM, Aduanas, vol. 67, exp. 1.

32. Petition of Ignacio Covarrubias for the Gremio de Trapicheros de Acámbaro, México, Jun. 8, 1779, AGNM, Aduanas, vol. 44, par. 30.

33. AGNM, Padrones, vol. 105.

34. Forty-four out of seventy-two men surveyed.

35. Auto acordado, México, Apr. 17, 1690, AGI, Contaduría, 806, Ramo 3.

36. Ordinance dividing the city of Querétaro into cuarteles mayores, Querétaro, Mar. 5, 1796, AGNM, Bandos, vol. 18.

37. Cited in John C. Super, "Querétaro Obrajes: Industry and Society in Provincial Mexico, 1600-1810," HAHR 56 (1976): 213.

38. Juan Fuentes Murillo to the general accountant of the Media Anata, México, Jul. 20, 1773, AGNM, Media Anata, vol. 19.

39. "Obrajes o fábricas de paños que hay actualmente en esta ciudad de Querétaro y su jurisdicción," AGNM, Alcabalas, vol. 37.

40. Juan Fuentes Murillo to the general accountant of the Media Anata, México, Jul. 20, 1773, AGNM, Media Anata, vol. 19.

41. Extract of the report of the excise officer of Querétaro, AGNM, Alcabalas, vol. 521; list of trapicheros who presented themselves for payment of the excise, AGNM, Media Anata, vol. 19.

42. José Pérez Becerra to the director of the Royal Excise, Querétaro, Oct. 2, 1778, AGNM, Aduanas, vol. 44.

43. Vicente Fuentes Murillo to Lázaro de Aroceto y Garra, Querétaro, Aug. 20, 1773, AGNM, Media Anata, vol. 19.

44. Woodrow Borah, "Race and Class in Mexico," *Pacific Historical Review* 23 (1954): 331-42.

45. J. R. Poinsett, *Notes on Mexico Made in the Autumn of 1822 . . .* (London, 1822), p. 185.

46. "Memoria de Estatuto . . . ," in Enrique Florescano and Isabel Gil Sánchez, eds., *Descripciones económicas generales de Nueva España, 1784-1817* (México, 1973), p. 224. The estimate of a market of approximately 1 million consumers for imports is given in "Consecuencias que tendría, según el Consulado de Veracruz, el establecimiento del comercio libre en la Nueva España," in Luis Chávez Orozco, ed., *La libertad del comercio en la Nueva España en la segunda década del siglo XIX* (México, 1943), p. 103.

47. Ruth D. Lechuga, *La indumentaria en el México indígena* (México, 1982),

pp. 17-19; Donald and Dorothy Cordry, *Mexican Indian Costumes* (Austin, 1968), pp. 50-171.

48. "Consecuencias que tendría, según el Consulado de Veracruz, el establecimiento del comercio libre en la Nueva España," in Chávez Orozco, ed., *La libertad del comercio en la Nueva España*, p. 103.

49. "Notable carta reservada," BAGN, 1st ser., 2 (1931): 198.

50. Revillagigedo, *Instrucción reservada*, p. 191.

51. Conde de Revillagigedo, "Notable carta reservada," BAGN, 1st ser., 1 (1930): 202.

52. M. Hernández Sánchez-Barba, "Las Indias en el siglo XVIII," in Jaime Vicens Vives, ed., *Historia de España y América social y económica*, 5 vols., 2 ed. (Barcelona, 1971), 4: 382.

53. Demetrio Galán to the director of the Royal Excise, Zacamulpa, Jan. 22, 1802, AGNM, Alcabalas, vol. 165; Fernando Rosenzweig Hernández, "La economía Nova-Hispana al comenzar el siglo XIX," *Ciencias políticas y sociales* 9 (1965): 473.

54. Domingo Casadorino to the joint directors of the Royal Excise, Temascaltepec, Apr. 26, 1781 (copy produced in 1803), AGNM, Alcabalas, vol. 165.

55. Circular order of Mar. 22, 1793, AGNM, Alcabalas, vol. 165.

56. Revillagigedo, "Notable carta reservada," BAGN, 1st ser., 1 (1930): 203.

57. Report of Juan Domingo de Urriza from Teotitlán del Camino, AGNM, Alcabalas, vol. 37; Manuel de Flon, "Notas estadísticas de la Intendencia de Puebla (1804)," in Enrique Florescano and Isabel Gil Sánchez, eds., *Descripciones económicas regionales de Nueva España. Provincias del centro, sudeste, y sur, 1765-1827* (México, 1976), p. 166.

58. Petition of don Salvador Gueraveo, Zinapécuaro, AGNM, Mercedes, vol. 81, 141v-143.

59. Carta reservada of José Pérez Becerra to the director of the Royal Excise, Querétaro, Jan. 25, 1782, AGNM, Alcabalas, vol. 105, exp. 3, title 14.

60. Reports from Charcas and Huajuapa, AGNM, Alcabalas, vol. 37.

61. See the descriptions in Table 1.2 for this.

62. Reports from Toluca, Salamanca, Zitácuaro, and Valladolid, AGNM, Alcabalas, vol. 37.

63. Report from Zacatecas, AGNM, Alcabalas, vol. 37.

64. Report from Valladolid, AGNM, Alcabalas, vol. 37.

65. David A. Brading, *Haciendas and Ranchos in the Mexican Bajío: León, 1700-1860* (Cambridge, Eng., 1978), p. 196.

66. Report from Ixtlahuaca, AGNM, Alcabalas, vol. 37.

67. Reports from Saltillo and Durango, AGNM, Alcabalas, vol. 37.

68. Reports from Taxco and Tochimilco, AGNM, Alcabalas, vol. 37.

69. Report from Toluca, AGNM, Alcabalas, vol. 37.

70. Report from Metepec, AGNM, Alcabalas, vol. 37.

71. Muriá, *Historia de Jalisco*, 2: 154; Ronald Spores, *The Mixtecs in Ancient and Colonial Times* (Norman, OK, 1984), pp. 134-35; Alejandra Moreno Toscano, *Geografía económica de México (siglo XVI)* (México, 1968), p. 92; José

Rodríguez Vallejo, *Ixcatl, el algodón mexicano* (México, 1976), pp. 58-60, 66-85; "Sobre si convendrá perpetuar la gracia que exime de todos derechos al algodón, café y añil de la isla de Cuba" [1806], Archivo Histórico de Hacienda, leg. 664-26.

72. Eduardo Arcila Farías, *Reformas económicas del siglo XVIII en Nueva España*, 2 vols. (México, 1974), 2: 37-38; bando of Mar. 10, 1767, AGNM, Inpresos Oficiales, vol. 7; AHH, leg. 664-26, as above; Luis Chávez Orozco and Enrique Florescano, eds., *Agricultura e industria textil de Veracruz. Siglo XIX* (Jalapa, 1965), pp. 71-78.

73. G.P.C. Thomson, "The Cotton Textile Industry in Puebla During the 18th and 19th Centuries." Paper presented to the Conference on the Economic History of Spanish America at the End of the Colonial Period: Mexico and Peru, 1760-1810 (Bielefeld, Germany, 1982); and his "Economy and Society in Puebla de los Angeles 1800-50" (Ph.D. diss., Oxford Univ., 1978).

74. Consulado of Veracruz, "Noticias políticas económicas de su distrito," [1798], and report of the syndic of the consulado of Veracruz, Veracruz, Nov. 24, 1798, both in AGI, Indiferente General, leg. 2466; "Sobre si debe cobrar alcabala de aquellas pequeñas siembras de algodón," (1795) AGNM, Aduanas, vol. 149.

75. *Actas Constitucionales Mexicanas*, 9: 560; Quirós, "Memoria de Estatuto," in Florescano and Gil Sánchez, eds., *Descripciones económicas generales*, p. 244.

76. Jacques Soustelle, *Daily Life of the Aztecs on the Eve of the Spanish Conquest* (Stanford, 1961), p. 137; Moreno Toscano, *Geografía económica*, p. 60; Cordry and Cordry, *Mexican Indian Costumes*, pp. 7-8; Rodríguez Vallejo, *Ixcatl*, pp. 25-26; Patricia Anawalt, "Costume and Control: Aztec Sumptuary Laws," *Archaeology* 33 (1980): 42-43.

77. David S. Landes, *The Unbound Prometheus. Technological Change and Industrial Development in Western Europe from 1750 to the Present* (Cambridge, Eng., 1969), p. 83.

Chapter Two

1. Luis Chávez Orozco, *Historia económica y social de México* (México, 1938), chap. 2.

2. Petition of Jacinto Romeo, México, Apr. 26, 1690, AGNM, Civil, vol. 1435, exp. 1.

3. AGNM, Mercedes, vol. 81, f. 141v-43.

4. Cited in Manuel Carrera Stampa, "El obraje novo-hispano," *Memorias de la Academia Mexicana de la Historia* 20 (1961): 149.

5. Herman Freudenberger and Fritz Redlich, "The Industrial Development of Europe: Reality, Symbols, Images," *Kyklos* 26 (1964): 372-403.

6. Abbott Payson Usher, *The Industrial History of England* (Boston and New York, 1920), p. 347.

7. George Kubler, *Mexican Architecture of the Sixteenth Century*, 2 vols. (New Haven, 1948), 1: 189. Fernand Braudel perceives incipient architectural

specialization in the eighteenth century. See his *Capitalism and Material Life, 1400-1800* (New York, 1973), pp. 201-2.

8. See Plate 24 of Francisco Fernández del Castillo, *Apuntes para la historia de San Angel (San Jacinto Tenanitla) y sus alrededores* (México, 1913), for an early-twentieth-century view of this structure, since demolished.

9. Diligencias prepared by the corregidor of Coyoacán, Mar. 30, 1737, AGNM, Tierras, vol. 578, exp. 2.

10. Petition [1749?], San Miguel el Grande, AGNM, Civil, vol. 2296, exp. 1.

11. Apr. 15, 1806.

12. Appraisal made by don José Antonio de la Roca and don Manuel Alvarez, México, Sept. 12, 1748, AJM, leg. 101.

13. Appraisal made by don Joaquín García de Torres, México, Oct. 17, 1752, AGNM, Tierras, vol. 856, exp. 2.

14. Cf. the appraisal made by José de Medinas of a Puebla obraje, Mar. 27, 1736, AJP.

15. Primer auto de visita to the obraje of don Balthasar de Sauto, San Miguel, Aug. 14, 1758, AGI, México 1047.

16. The passage describing the obraje of José Pimentel is taken from an entrega dated Mar. 15, 1757, AGNM, Civil, vol. 188, exp. 4.

17. Freudenberger and Redlich, "Industrial Development of Europe," p. 385.

18. V. Vázquez de Prada, *Historia económica y social de España*, 3 vols. (Madrid, 1978–), 3: 420-36, 576-83; Carmen Viqueira Landa, "Los orígenes de la industria textil en México," *Ingeniería* [UNAM], new ser., 53 (1983): 99; Lyle N. McAlister, *Spain and Portugal in the New World*, 1492-1700 (Minneapolis, 1984), pp. 21-23; Pierre Chaunu, *La España de Carlos V*, 2 vols. (Barcelona, 1976), 1: 85-91.

19. Viqueira Landa, "La industria textil," pp. 99-100; Eufemio Lorenzo Sanz, *Comercio de España con América en la época de Felipe II*, 2 vols. (Valladolid, 1979), 1: 435-436.

20. Lorenzo Sanz, *Comercio de España con América*, 1: 427, 430; Blanca Lara Tenorio, *Algunas mercancías que llegaron de España a Puebla en 1549* (México, 1978).

21. Henry Kamen, *Spain, 1469-1714. A Society of Conflict* (London, 1983), p. 158; Lorenzo Sanz, *Comercio de España con América*, 1: 34.

22. David Szewczyk, "New Elements in the Society of Tlaxcala, 1519-1618," in Ida Altman and James Lockhart, eds., *Provinces of Early Mexico* (Los Angeles, 1976), pp. 145-46; Woodrow Borah, *Justice by Insurance. The General Indian Court of Colonial Mexico and the Legal Aides of the Half-Real* (Berkeley, 1983), p. 26.

23. Philip Curtin, *Cross-Cultural Trade in World History* (Cambridge, Eng., 1984), pp. 81-89.

24. John Hicks, *A Theory of Economic History* (Oxford, 1969), p. 101.

25. Enrique Florescano, "La formación de los trabajadores en la época colonial, 1521-1750," in Enrique Florescano et al., *La clase obrera en la historia de México: De la colonia al imperio*, 2d ed. (México, 1981), pp. 19, 26, 32, 59;

Pedro Carrasco, "The Political Economy of the Aztec and Inca States," in George A. Collier, Renato I. Rosaldo, and John D. Wirth, eds., *The Inca and Aztec States, 1400-1800. Anthropology and History* (New York, 1982), pp. 25, 27, 34.

26. Viqueira Landa, "La industria textil," p. 97.

27. James William Taylor, "Socio-economic instability and the Revolution for Mexican Independence in the Province of Guanajuato" (Ph.D. diss., Univ. of New Mexico, 1976), p. 162; Eric R. Wolf, "The Mexican Bajío in the Eighteenth Century. An Analysis of Cultural Integration," in Middle American Research Institute, *Synoptic Studies of Mexican Culture* (New Orleans, 1957), p. 186.

28. Ronald Coase, "The Nature of the Firm," in George J. Stigler and Kenneth E. Boulding, eds., *Readings in Price Theory* (Chicago, 1952), pp. 331-58.

29. Alfred D. Chandler, Jr., *The Visible Hand. The Managerial Revolution in American Business* (Cambridge, MA, 1977).

30. Indeed, there are numerous instances of disintegrated or uncentralized weaving establishments that existed in better organized markets. The most famous eighteenth-century example was the Royal Factory of Guadalajara in Spain. Here, the entire process of making woolens, from washing to finishing, was put out to the artisans of the region. See Rafael Aracil, "El treball tèxtil. Per una história de la societat pagesa tradicional: Les formes de trebell (XI)," *L'Avenç* (Barcelona) 41 (1981): 579-80. I am grateful to James S. Amelang for this reference. Another good example is the Kensington district of Philadelphia in the 1850s, where spinning, weaving, and dyeing took place in separate establishments and permitted small shops with little capital to specialize. See Philip Scranton, *Proprietary Capitalism. The Textile Manufacture of Philadelphia, 1800-1885* (New York, 1983), pp. 208, 318, 334.

31. Peter Rees, "Transporation," in Brian W. Blouet and Olwyn M. Blouet, eds., *Latin America. An Introductory Survey* (New York, 1982), pp. 116-17.

32. Woodrow Borah, "Inflation in Nueva Galicia, 1557-1598: Auctions of Tribute Maize" (unpub. ms., 1985).

33. "Cuenta que presenta Don Antonio Gutiérrez de Linares como apoderado de Doña María Teresa Montes de Oca . . . ," México, Jun. 14, 1740, AJM, leg. 92.

34. Fernand Braudel, *The Mediterranean and the Mediterranean World in the Age of Philip II*, 2 vols. (New York, 1972), 1: 438; Landes, *Unbound Prometheus*, p. 127.

35. Computed from data supplied by Clemente de Apresa to the joint directors of the Royal Excise, Acámbaro, Apr. 30, 1781, AGNM, Alcabalas, vol. 521.

36. The data for the estimate are taken from AGI, Contaduría 806, Ramo 3. The ordinary least squares regression yields, with standard errors in parentheses:

$$\log Q = 2.94 + .45 \log \text{LOOMS} + .38 \log \text{LABOR}$$
$$(.21) \qquad\qquad (.22)$$
$$R^2 = .49 \quad F(2/28) = 15.61$$

The equation is a log-linear transformation of the Cobb-Douglas production function, i.e., $Q = A\, K^\alpha\, L^\beta$, with K set at the number of working looms reported, and L equal to the number of workers. The estimate is collinear in K and L and not in reduced form. For the theoretical problems involved, see Mark Blaug, *Economic Theory in Retrospect*, 3d ed. (Cambridge, Eng., 1978), pp. 473-76, 487-89. Statistical problems are treated in Michael Intriligator, *Econometric Models, Techniques, and Applications* (Englewood Cliffs, NJ, 1978), pp. 262-84.

37. Richard N. Clarke, "Scale Economies, Entry, and Welfare," *Journal of Economics and Business* 36 (1984): 161.

38. Chandler, *Visible Hand*, p. 244.

39. Carlo M. Cipolla, *Before the Industrial Revolution. European Society and Economy, 1000-1700* (New York, 1976), pp. 95-108. For the data on which these ratios are based, see the following: summary inventories for the obraje "Panzacola" in the concurso de acreedores of the merchant house of Vértiz y Oteyza, AJM, Seccion Concursos; inventory of the obraje of Juan Pérez Cota y Madera, AGNM, Tierras, vol. 697; similarly, for a Jesuit obraje, see AGNM, Tierras, vol. 680.

40. Cipolla, *Before the Industrial Revolution*, pp. 100-3, 106.

41. William P. Glade, "Obrajes and the Industrialization of Colonial Latin America," in Charles P. Kindleberger and Guido di Tella, eds., *Economics in the Long View*, 3 vols. (London, 1982), 2: 25.

42. David A. Brading and Harry E. Cross, "Colonial Silver Mining: Mexico and Peru," HAHR 52 (1972): 558; Brading, *Miners and Merchants*, pp. 146-49; Peter J. Bakewell, *Silver Mining and Society in Colonial Mexico, Zacatecas 1546-1700* (Cambridge, Eng., 1971), pp. 124-28; María Guadalupe Ordóñez y Chávez, "Lineamientos generales del trabajo libre asalariado de los indios en la Nueva España," in José Luis Soberanes Fernández, coord., *Memoria del II Congreso de Historia del Derecho Mexicano* (México, 1981), p. 314.

43. Cf. Stephen Marglin, "What Do Bosses Do? The Origins and Function of Hierarchy in Capitalist Production," *The Review of Radical Political Economics* 6 (1974): 60-112.

44. Landes, *Unbound Prometheus*, pp. 117-19; Thomson, "Cotton Textile Industry in Puebla."

45. Florescano, "La formación de los trabajadores," in Florescano et al., *La clase obrera*, p. 94.

46. Moreno Toscano, *Geografía económica*, p. 68; Spores, *Mixtecs*, pp. 124-25, 160; Joseph W. Whitecotton, *The Zapotecs. Princes, Priests, and Peasants* (Norman, OK, 1977), p. 178.

47. Alfred W. Crosby, Jr., *The Columbian Exchange. Biological and Cultural Consequences of* 1942 (Westport, CT, 1972), p. 92.

48. Braudel, *The Mediterranean*, 1: 85-99; P. Lamartine Yates, *Mexico's Agricultural Dilemma* (Tucson, AZ, 1981), p. 102.

49. François Chevalier, *Land and Society in Colonial Mexico. The Great Hacienda* (Berkeley, 1963), p. 95.

50. Muriá, *Historia de Jalisco*, 1: 417, 422.

51. Chevalier, *Land and Society*, p. 95.

52. Woodrow Borah, "Latin America, 1610-60," in J. P. Cooper, ed., *The Decline of Spain and the Thirty Years' War, 1609-48/59* [Volume 4 of *The New Cambridge Modern History*] (Cambridge, Eng., 1970), p. 721; Ramón María Serrera, *Guadalajara ganadera: estudio regional novohispano, 1760-1805* (Seville, 1977), pp. 299-318.

53. Dorothy Boyd Bowen, "A Brief History of Spanish Textile Production in the Southwest," in Nora Fisher, ed., *Spanish Textile Tradition of New Mexico and Colorado* (Santa Fe, NM, 1979), pp. 5-6.

54. John C. Super, *La vida en Querétaro durante la colonia, 1531-1810* (México, 1983), p. 50.

55. For example, see Herman W. Konrad, *A Jesuit Hacienda in Colonial Mexico. Santa Lucía, 1576-1767* (Stanford, 1980), pp. 175-84; Charles H. Harris, III, *A Mexican Family Empire. The Latifundio of the Sánchez Navarros, 1765-1867* (Austin, 1975), pp. 79-93.

56. A statement based on guías and facturas of the Royal Excise in AGNM, Aduanas, vol. 133. Also see Juan López Cancelada, *Ruina de la Nueva España si se declara el comercio libre* (Cádiz, 1811), p. 14; Super, *La vida en Querétaro*, pp. 125-26.

For Jaral's share of the trade, I have constructed an estimate based on several sources. According to the excise officer in Querétaro, Jaral was sending 14,000 arrobas of wool there in the later 1770s. From tax receipts (discussed later), I would estimate that about 36,000 arrobas of wool entered the excise district of Querétaro and San Juan del Río in 1769. With margins for error and fraud, one might plausibly figure Jaral's share at 30 percent to 40 percent of the total.

57. Harris, *Mexican Family Empire*, pp. 82, 86.

58. Harris, *Mexican Family Empire*, pp. 88-89; Konrad, *Santa Lucía*, pp. 176-77.

59. John H. Coatsworth, "The Limits of Colonial Absolutism: The State in Eighteenth-Century Mexico," in Karen Spalding, ed., *Essays in the Political, Economic and Social History of Colonial Latin America* (Newark, DE, 1982), pp. 30-31, 34, 37.

60. Or so thought Adam Smith, *The Wealth of Nations* (Cannan ed.), bk. 4. chap. 1.

61. José Pérez Becerra to the director of the Royal Excise, Querétaro, Jan. 25, 1782, AGNM, Alcabalas, vol. 105, exp. 3; letter of Martín de Bernabé to the director of the Royal Excise, Acámbaro, May 10, 1785, AGNM, Alcabalas, vol. 103.

62. "Balance que se hace en este obraje perteneciente a . . . Don José Antonio Negrete . . . ," México, Jul. 1, 1746, AGNM, Tierras, vol. 680.

63. Landes, *Unbound Prometheus*, p. 80.

64. Ramón Sánchez Flores, *Historia de la tecnología y la invención en México* (México, 1980), pp. 73-74, 129, 143; Nora Fisher, "The Treadle Loom," in

Fisher, ed., *Spanish Textile Tradition*, pp. 192-93; Landes, *Unbound Prometheus*, p. 84.

65. The general basis for this description is the statement by the owner of an obraje, don José Mariano Loreto de la Canal, San Miguel el Grande, Sept. 1, 1759, AGNM, Civil, vol. 880. Also helpful were Usher, *Industrial History*, pp. 195-224; Paulino Iradiel Murrugarren, *Evolución de la industria textil castellana en los siglos XIII-XVI* (Salamanca, 1974), pp. 167-208; Herbert Heaton, *The Yorkshire Woolen and Worsted Industries*, 2d ed. (Oxford, 1965); J. Geraint Jenkins, *The Wool Textile Industry in Great Britain* (London, 1972); J. Bronson, *The Domestic Manufacturer's Assistant . . . in the Arts of Weaving and Dyeing . . . in the Manufacture of Cotton and Woolen Goods* (Utica, NY, 1817); Aracil, "El treball tèxtil," pp. 579-81; Kax Wilson, *A History of Textiles* (Boulder, CO, 1979).

66. David A. Brading, "Notas sobre la economía de Querétaro y de su corregidor don Miguel Domínguez, 1802-1811," BAGN, 2d ser., 11 (1970), first documents; Pendleton Woolen Mills, *The Wool Story*, 5th ed. (Pendleton, OR, 1980), p. 7; *Memoria de la Secretaría de Estado y del despacho de Relaciones Interiores y Exteriores* (México, 1832), p. 18; William H. Dusenberry, *The Mexican Mesta. The Administration of Ranching in Colonial Mexico* (Urbana, IL, 1963), p. 32.

67. Nora Fisher and Joe Ben Wheat, "The Materials of Southwestern Weaving," in Fisher, ed., *Spanish Textile Tradition*, pp. 197-98.

68. *Actas Constitucionales Mexicanas*, 9: 561.

69. *Registro Oficial*, May 24, 1831.

70. Bronson, *Domestic Manufacturer's Assistant*, pp. 40-43.

71. Brading, "Notas sobre la economía de Querétaro," p. 281.

72. Ibid.

73. I infer this from the words of an entry in the "Balance que se hace en este obraje . . . [de] don José Negrete," México, Jul. 1, 1746, AGNM, Tierras, vol. 680: "por 36 arrobas 16 libras de lana lavada que regulada por puerca hacen 73 arrobas 7 libras a 2 pesos monta 192 pesos 3 reales"; Aracil, "El treball tèxtil," p. 579.

74. Declaration of don Ignacio de Urizar y Arrom, Tlaxcala, Nov. 6, 1722, AGI, México, 663A; Dorothy Boyd Bowen and Trish Spillman, "Natural and Synthetic Dyes," in Fisher, ed., *Spanish Textile Tradition*, p. 208.

75. Declaration of don Francisco Jiménez, Cholula, Nov. 9, 1722, AGI, México, 663A.

76. Brading, "Notas sobre la economía de Querétaro," pp. 281-82.

77. In general, see AGI, México, 663A.

78. Bronson, *Domestic Manufacturer's Assistant*, pp. 43-44.

79. Brading, "Notas sobre la economía de Querétaro," pp. 281-82; Bustamante, *Actas Constitucionales Mexicanas*, 9 : 561.

80. Usher, *Industrial History*, pp. 197-98.

81. F. C. Spooner, "The European Economy, 1609-50," in Cooper, ed., *Decline of Spain and the Thirty Years' War*, pp. 94-96.

82. AGNM, Historia, vol. 74, f. 431, and vol. 122, "Muestras de los tejidos del obraje de Tacuba . . . 23 de Noviembre de 1799." Both volumes contain snippets of the cloth, and my descriptions are based on them. For the width of the loom, see "Obrajes o fábricas que hay actualmente en esta ciudad de Querétaro y su jurisdicción," AGNM, Alcabalas, vol. 37.

83. In general, see the reports in AGI, Contaduría 806, Ramo 3.

84. Cerralvo ordinances, México, May 10, 1633, Title 4, AGI, México 75.

85. I infer this from the following line of the inventory appearing in "Cuenta y relación jurada que doña Manuela de Rivera . . . ," AGNM, Tierras, vol. 686: "la blanca cardada o yscapeso."

86. Title 4 of the Cerralvo ordinances, cited above in note 84. For the term "tequio" and a description of it, see "Obrajes o fábricas que hay actualmente en esta ciudad de Querétaro y su jurisdicción," AGNM, Alcabalas, vol. 37.

87. Auto of the corregidor of Coyoacán, Mar. 30, 1737, AGNM, Tierras, vol. 578, exp. 6; statement of don Sancho de Posadas y Agurto, México, Jan. 5, 1690, AGI, Contaduría 806, Ramo 3.

88. Pedro Telmo Primo, *Querétaro en 1822. Informe* (México, 1944), p. 40; see "Obrajes o fábricas que hay actualmente en esta ciudad de Querétaro y su jurisdicción," AGNM, Alcabalas, vol. 37; the statement of don José Mariano Loreto de la Canal, San Miguel el Grande, Sept. 1, 1759, AGNM, Civil, vol. 880; and the citation of Balthasar de Sauto, San Miguel, Jul. 27, 1761, AGI, Mexico 1047.

89. Usher, *Industrial History*, pp. 202, 207; statement of don Diego de Contreras, México, Jan. 27, 1690, AGI, Contaduría 806, Ramo 3.

90. Statement of don Diego de Contreras, México, Jan. 27, 1690, AGI, Contaduría 806, Ramo 3.

91. Usher, *Industrial History*, pp. 205-6; Louis C. Hunter, *A History of Industrial Power in the United States* (Charlottesville, VA, 1979), pp. 22-23.

92. Luis Romero to the intendant of Guanajuato, Acámbaro, Sept. 23, 1808, AGNM, Civil, vol. 1682, exp. 3.

93. Computed from summary inventories for the obraje "Panzacola" in the concurso de acreedores of the merchant house of Vértiz y Oteyza, AJM, Seccion Concursos.

94. Stefano Fenoaltea, "Slavery and Supervision in Comparative Perspective: A Model," JEH 44 (1984): 635-68.

95. "Indicacciones económicas-políticas," in Luis Córdova, ed., *Protección y libre cambio: el debate entre 1821 y 1836* (México, 1971), pp. 92-93.

96. Harris, *Mexican Family Empire*, pp. 32-33.

97. Luis Romero to the intendant of Guanajuato, Acámbaro, Sept. 23, 1808, AGNM, Civil, vol. 1682, exp. 3.

98. José Martínez Moreno et al. to the joint directors of the Royal Excise, Querétaro, Sept. 29, 1780, AGNM, Aduanas, vol. 76, exp. 2.

99. Hunter, *Industrial Power*, p. 25.

100. Miguel Domínguez to the viceroy of New Spain, Querétaro, Nov. 17, 1804, AGNM, Subdelegados, vol. 5.

101. Juan Fernández del Vivero to the Crown [Tlaxcala, 1633], AGI, México 75.

102. Luis Romero to the intendant of Guanajuato, Acámbaro, Sept. 23, 1808, AGNM, Civil, vol. 1682, exp. 3.

103. José Jesús Hernández Palomo, *La renta del pulque en la Nueva España, 1663-1810* (Seville, 1979), pp. 207-10.

104. Enrique Florescano, *Precios del maíz y crisis agrícolas en México (1708-1810)* (México, 1969), p. 91.

105. Peter Mathias, *The First Industrial Nation. An Economic History of Britain, 1700-1914* (London, 1969), pp. 61-62, 186.

106. Cf. Brian Hamnett, *Politics and Trade in Southern Mexico, 1750-1821* (Cambridge, Eng., 1971), pp. 2, 119, 140, Appendix 12; report of the excise officer in Oaxaca, AGNM, Alcabalas, vol. 37.

107. Francisco Antonio Navarrete, *Relación peregrina de la aqua corriente . . . de Santiago de Querétaro* (México, 1739), p. 34.

108. Detailed in a map of San Miguel in AGNM, Tierras, vol. 813, exp. 3.

109. Antonio Villaseñor y Sánchez, *Theatro Americano*, 2 vols. (México, 1746-48), bk. 1, chap. 11; a map of the jurisdiction of Coyoacán in AGNM, Padrones, vol. 6.

110. The Salto del Agua district and its adjacent aqueduct are clearly shown in a perspective drawing of Mexico City from 1749, reproduced as "Planta y Descripción de la Imperial Ciudad de México," available in the Biblioteca Nacional in the Sala de Manuscritos. Numerous references are found to obrajes on the Calzada de la Piedad during the eighteenth century (and earlier, if one examines the titles of the properties run at the time of sale). See, for example, the rental contract signed by don Pascual de Alos y Vidal, México, May 6, 1763, AJM, leg. 124; depósito irregular en don Nícolas García de la Mora, México, Apr. 15, 1735, AGNM, Tierras vol. 676; there are also references in AGI, Contaduría 806, Ramo 3.

111. Hans Pohl et al., "Aspectos sociales del desarrollo de los obrajes textiles en Puebla colonial," *Comunicaciones. Proyecto Puebla-Tlaxcala* 15 (1978): 41.

112. *Historia general de México*, 4 vols. (México, 1976), 2: 242-45; Robert C. West and John P. Augelli, *Middle America: Its Lands and Peoples*, 2d ed. (Englewood Cliffs, NJ, 1976), pp. 242-45; Rees, "Transportation," in Blouet and Blouet, eds., *Latin America*, pp. 118-19.

113. Woodrow Borah and Sherburne F. Cook, "The Urban Center as a Focus of Migration in the Colonial Period: New Spain," in Richard P. Schaedel et al. eds., *Urbanization in the Americas from Its Beginning to the Present* (La Hague, 1978), pp. 383-97.

114. Thomas E. Borcherding and Eugene Silberberg, "Shipping the Good Apples Out: The Alchian and Allen Theorem Reconsidered," *Journal of Political Economy* 86 (1978): 131-38.

115. "Memoria de las cuentas le tengo entregado Don José Riaño" [1762], Spanish Archives of New Mexico [Santa Fe, NM], TW 559. I am grateful to Ross Frank for this information.

116. The principle of entry was nevertheless operative, and after 1750, high prices for imported woolens from New Spain encouraged the production of substitutes in New Mexico. Ward Alan Minge, "*Efectos del País*: A History of Weaving Along the Río Grande," in Fisher, ed., *Spanish Textile Tradition*, pp. 8-28.

117. Antonio Ulloa, "Noticia o descripción de los paises que median entre la ciudad y puerto de Veracruz en el Reino de Nueva España hasta los asientos de minas de Guanajuato, Pachuca, y Real del Norte, sus territorios, climas, y producciones," n.p., n.d., Obadiah Rich collection, no. 9, 359r, New York Public Library.

118. A document of c. 1777, *San Miguel el Grande* (México, 1950), p. 106.

119. Mark Beaufoy, *Mexican Illustrations* (London, 1828), pp. 178, 237-38.

120. Carrera Stampa, "Obraje novohispano," pp. 149, 165; Oscar Alatriste, *Desarrollo de la industria y la comunidad minera de Hidalgo del Parral durante la segunda mitad del siglo XVIII* (México, 1983), p. 122.

121. Information of Bachiller Francisco Crisóstomo de la Mata et al., San Miguel el Grande, Nov. 18, 1758, AGI, México 1047; Joaquín Sánchez de Tagle to the viceroy of New Spain, San Miguel el Grande, Jan. 7, 1754, AGNM, Subdelegados, vol. 34.

122. Testimony of Tomás Luengo, México, Jan. 9, 1690, AGI, Contaduría 806, Ramo 3.

123. Wolf, "Mexican Bajío in the Eighteenth Century," in Middle American Research Institute, *Synoptic Studies*, p. 184.

124. Report of the excise officer of León, AGNM, Alcabalas, vol. 521.

125. José Antonio Alegre to the director of the Royal Excise, León, Oct. 5, 1779, AGNM, Aduanas, vol. 44.

126. AGNM, Mercedes, vol. 81, f. 140-40v.

127. Wolf, "Mexican Bajío in the Eighteenth Century," in Middle American Research Institute, *Synoptic Studies*, p. 184.

128. Konrad, *Santa Lucía*, pp. 208-12.

129. Report of Miguel Páez de la Cadena, México, Nov. 2, 1784, AGI, México 1416.

130. Testimony of José de Paz, México, Jan. 7, 1690, AGI, Contaduría 806, Ramo 3.

131. Testimony of José de los Santos, México, Jan. 10, 1690, AGI, Contaduría 806, Ramo 3; Nora Fisher, "Yardage," in Fisher, ed., *Spanish Textile Tradition*, p. 144.

132. Peter James Lampros, "Merchant–Planter Cooperation and Conflict: The Havana Consulado, 1794-1832" (Ph.D. diss., Tulane Univ., 1980), p. 300; letterbook of don Francisco Sáenz de Escobosa, AJM, leg. 192; letters dated Aug. 11, Sept. 13, and Dec. 23, 1797; Jan. 20 and Jan. 27, 1798 (all to don Pedro Garza, Querétaro); Colin Palmer, *Slaves of the White God. Blacks in Mexico 1570-1650* (Cambridge, MA, 1976), p. 51.

133. Testimony of don Diego García Castro, México, Jan. 10, 1690, AGI, Contaduría 806, Ramo 3.

134. Testimony of Capt. Pedro Albarrán Carrillo, México, Jan. 10, 1690, AGI, Contaduría 806, Ramo 3.

135. Petition of don Juan José Pérez Cano, México, Sept. 14, 1767, AGNM, Civil, vol. 76, exp. 26; Clemente Apresa to the joint directors of the Royal Excise, Acámbaro, Apr. 30, 1781, AGNM, Alcabalas, vol. 521; Christon Archer, *The Army in Bourbon Mexico, 1760-1810* (Albuquerque, 1977), pp. 171, 173, 176.

136. "Cuenta de lo gastado en el vestuario y medio vestuario en la Real Brigada de Artilleros . . . ," found in "Diligencias . . . [del] Señor don José Casasola," AJM, leg. 167.

137. Decree of the Marqués de Croix, México, Mar. 20, 1770, AGNM, Aduanas, vol. 23.

138. Comments of the subinspector during a junta de guerra, Havana, Nov. 13, 1797, AGI, Cuba 1506B.

139. "Estado que manifiesta los efectos recibidos en el Nuevo Establecimiento de los talleres del vestuario del Ejército . . . ," *Gaceta del Gobierno Supremo de México*, Feb. 22, 1825.

140. Karl Polanyi, *The Great Transformation. The Political and Economic Origins of Our Time* (Boston, 1957), esp. chaps. 4-6.

141. Small quantities of Mexican bays and paño were sent to Venezuela. See Eduardo Arcila Farías, *Comercio entre Venezuela y México en los siglos XVII y XVIII* (México, 1950), pp. 99-101; for shipments to Central America, see Victor H. Acuña-Ortega, "Le commerce extérieur de Royaume de Guatemala au XVIII siècle, 1700-1821: Une étude structurelle" (Thèse du doctorat, Université de Paris-Sorbonne, 1978), p. 23.

142. John H. Coatsworth, *Growth Against Development. The Economic Impact of Railroads in Porfirian Mexico* (DeKalb, IL, 1981), chap. 4.

143. Guadalupe Nava Oteo, "La minería bajo el Porfiriato," p. 342, and Ciro Cardoso and Carmen Reyna, "Las industrias de transformación (1880-1910), pp. 397, 400, in Ciro Cardoso, ed., *México en el siglo XIX (1821-1910). Historia económica y de la estructura social* (México, 1983).

144. Robert A. Potash, *Mexican Government and Industrial Development in the Early Republic: The Banco de Avío* (Amherst, MA, 1983), pp. 149, 153.

CHAPTER THREE

1. For Mexico City, see the petition of Juan de Alva and Lucas de Acuña, Madrid, Jun. 14, 1729, AGI, México 644; for Acámbaro, see Vicente Domingo Lombardini to the directors of the Royal Excise, Sayula, Sept. 14, 1781, AGNM, Alcabalas, vol. 183; for Querétaro, see José Martínez Moreno et al. to the directors of the Royal Excise, Querétaro, Sept. 29, 1780, AGNM, Aduanas, vol. 76, exp. 2; for Puebla, see the petition of don Pedro de la Sota et al., Puebla [February 1800], AGNM, Industria, vol. 8, exp. 12.

2. Copies of both ordinances are found in AGI, México 644.

3. Petition of don Juan de la Peña, México, Sept. 18, 1728, AGI, México 644.

4. Archivo del Antiguo Ayuntamiento [Mexico City], Real Audiencia, Fiel Ejectoría, Inventario de Causas, vol. 3786, ff. 170v-174.

5. "Cuenta y relación que yo Antonio Loria doy como administrador que fui del obraje . . . de . . . Negrete," data general, entry 39, AGNM, Tierras, vol. 680.

6. Consulta of Gaspar Madrazo Escalera [México], March 9, 1724, AGNM, Civil, vol. 1712, exps. 4-5.

7. Ibid.

8. Ordinances 8 and 11 of 1676.

9. Usher, *Industrial History*, pp. 190-91.

10. Petition of don Juan de Ávila and don Juan de Alva, México, Jan. 24, 1738, AGNM, Civil, vol. 1435, exp. 4; Borah, *Justice By Insurance*, p. 13.

11. Decree of Apr. 26, 1750, AGI, México, 1809.

12. Testimony of Juan de Ávila, México, Dec. 14, 1718, AGI, Escribanía de Cámara 196-A.

13. Petition of don Felipe Novajas, México, Mar. 3, 1757, AGI, México 1809.

14. Vicente Domingo Lombardini to the directors of the Royal Excise, Sayula, Sept. 14, 1781, AGNM, Alcabalas, vol. 183.

15. This story is related in minute detail in AGNM, Aduanas, vols. 44 and 67, passim; see also Plácido Miguel Velázquez Gastelú to the director of the Royal Excise, Acámbaro, May 20, 1777, AGNM, Alcabalas, vol. 183.

16. Opinion of the fiscal, Manuel Merino, México, Jan. 5, 1781, AGNM, Aduanas, vol. 44.

17. José Pérez Becerra to the Royal Excise, Querétaro, Dec. 15, 1780, AGNM, Aduanas, vol. 76, exp. 2.

18. Certification by Pedro Russi and Gregorio Ballesteros, Querétaro, Sept. 9, 1791, AGNM, Aduanas, vol. 134.

19. Richard B. Lindley, *Haciendas and Economic Development. Guadalajara, Mexico, at Independence* (Austin, 1983), p. 81; Florescano, *Precios del maíz*, pp. 182-89.

20. Declaration of Francisco de Salazar, México, Apr. 19, 1746, AGNM, Tierras, vol. 676.

21. Contract dated Feb. 2, 1735, AGNM, Civil, vol. 1795, exp. 2.

22. Estimated from an obligation signed by José Andonegui and Juan Maldonado Zapata, Tacuba, Jul. 22, 1737, AGNM, Civil, vol. 1795, exp. 2. Total profits: 6,728 ps. = "x"/3, where "x" equals total profits. Pimentel's estimated average daily allowance is the difference between his gross and net share of the profits averaged over three years, i.e. (6,728 ps. − 3,291 ps.)/ (3 × 365 days) = 3 ps./day. The allowance does not include the cash value of his lodging at the obraje.

23. Petition of Juan Buenaventura Núñez de Villavicencio, México, Apr. 30, 1798, AGNM, Tierras, vol. 677.

24. Title history done by the notary García Mendieta Rebollo, AGNM, Tierras, vol. 676.

25. Contract and bill of sale, México [Jan. 1738], AGNM, Tierras, vol. 677.

26. Ibid.

27. Petition of the convent of San José de Gracia, México, Sept. 19, 1745, AGNM, Tierras, vol. 676.

28. Obligation of Teresa Alvarez de Quiñones, México, Jul. 9, 1695, AGNM, Tierras, vol. 676.

29. Arnold J. Bauer, "The Church and the Economy of Spanish America: Censos and Depósitos in the Eighteenth and Nineteenth Centuries," *HAHR* 63 (1983): 707-33, and "The Church and Spanish American Agrarian Structure, 1765-1865," *T Am* 28 (1971): 78-98.

30. Escritura signed by María Francisca de Estrada, México, Nov. 26, 1745, AGNM, Tierras, vol. 676. Brisas is identified as Pimentel's compadre in the account books of the manufactory in Tierras, vol. 677.

31. "Cuenta y relación jurada que doy yo Caetano López como . . . administrador que soy del obraje de don José Pimentel," AGNM, Tierras, vol. 677.

32. Petition of don Francisco de la Dehesa, México, Oct. 9, 1746, AGNM, Tierras, vol. 676. A capital market is based on the exchange of paper claims on future streams of income. Such a market was incipient in Western Europe in the last years of the seventeenth and early years of the eighteenth centuries. There was none in Mexico. The money market existed only in the rudimentary form defined by Stanley Jevons in *The Theory of Political Economy*, ed. R. D. Collison Black (Middlesex, Eng., 1970), chap. 4.

33. Petition of Antonio García, place and date illegible, AGNM, Tierras, vol. 1181.

34. Testimony of Juan de Ortega, México, Oct. 21, 1746, AGNM, Tierras, vol. 676.

35. Petition of don Manuel Peredo, México, Dec. 2, 1746, AGNM, Tierras, vol. 676; Eduardo Báez Macías, "Planos y censos de la ciudad de México, 1753," *BAGN*, 2d ser., 8 (1967): 1077.

36. Petition of Macario Vetancourt, México, Oct. 19, 1746, AGNM, Tierras, vol. 676.

37. Testimony of Juan Jacobo de Grosio, México, Oct. 21, 1746, AGNM, Tierras, vol. 676.

38. Ibid.

39. The distinction recognizes that the transactions costs of borrowing from pious funds were higher than those of borrowing from merchants. The formalities, requirements, and costs of executing a censo—the presence of a notary, witnesses, guarantors—were substantial, amortized over the long term, and not apt to be repeated weekly. Agreements with private aviadores were often ad hoc, less formal, and less costly to execute. Their frequency was correspondingly greater.

40. Van Young, *Hacienda and Market*, p. 182; Lindley, *Haciendas and Economic Development*, p. 37.

41. Entrega del obraje de Ansaldo, México, June 23, 1742, AGNM, Tierras, vol. 1181; certification by José de Arteaga y Pedroso, México, Jul. 3, 1747, and declaration of Juan de Malpica et al., México, Apr. 29, 1746, both in AGNM, Tierras, vol. 676.

42. Statement of José Pimentel, México, May 23, 1745, AGNM, Tierras, vol. 676.

43. Obligation of Juan Francisco de la Dehesa, México, Sept. 22, 1745, AGNM, Tierras, vol. 676.

44. AGNM, Civil, vol. 1742, exp. 12; petition of José Pimentel, Oct. 19, 1746, and obligation of Pedro Maltrana, México, Mar. 9, 1745, AGNM, Tierras, vol. 676.

45. Petition by the heirs of Juan de Brisas, México, Jan. 12, 1748, and petition of Cayetano López, México, Jan. 20, 1755, AGNM, Tierras, vol. 677.

46. Petition of José Marzo Calderón et al., México, Apr. 29, 1755, AGNM, Aduanas, vol. 11.

47. "Cuenta y relación jurada que doy yo Caetano López como . . . administrador que soy del obraje de don José Pimentel," AGNM, Tierras, vol. 677.

48. Inventory in proceedings dated May 9, 1755, AGNM, Aduanas, vol. 11; petition of Juan Antonio de la Paz, Mexico, Jan. 20, 1750, AGNM, Tierras, vol. 677.

49. "Sobre recaudar de don José Pimentel, dueño de obraje en Mixcoac," AGNM, Aduanas, vol. 11.

50. Ibid.

51. Petition of Antonia de Echendía, México, Mar. 9, 1759; contract between Echendía and Pascual de Alos y Vidal, México, Jan. 26, 1759; statements of account for Alos y Vidal and Pimentel, undated; petition of Pimentel, México, Dec. 5, 1758, all in AGNM, Tierras, vol. 2015, exp. 7; petition of Alos y Vidal, México, Dec. 7, 1758, AGNM, Tierras, vol. 2016, exp. 2.

52. Receipt signed by José Pimentel, Sept. 29, 1765, AJM, leg. 179.

53. Dec. 30, 1776, Libro de Difuntos Españoles, 24, Archivo Parroquial del Sagrario, México.

54. Testament of José Antonio Negrete, Sept. 16, 1747, AGNM, Tierras, vol. 680.

55. Petition of Juan de Noriega, México, Dec. 23, 1749; testimony of José Antonio Cortés, México, Oct. 23, 1749, both in AGNM, Tierras, vol. 680; petition of José Rafael de Molina, México, Feb. 13, 1751, AGNM, Tierras, vol. 681, exp. 1; poder of Manuel Herrera Puente, México, Aug. 21, 1754, ante Manuel Agustín López, ANM.

56. Inventory of accounts payable, México, Jun. 7, 1724, AGNM, Civil, vol. 2046, exp. 4.

57. Obligation of Juan de Noriega, México, Feb. 4, 1755, AGNM, Tierras, vol. 681.

58. Testament of Juan de Bocarrando, México, Apr. 16, 1747, ante Manuel Agustín López, ANM.

59. Petition of Juan de Noreiga, México, Dec. 23, 1749, AGNM, Tierras, vol. 686.

60. Testimony of Juan José Ruíz, México, Oct. 23, 1749, AGNM, Tierras, vol. 686; testament of Juan de Bocarrando, México, Apr. 16, 1747, ante Manuel Agustín López, ANM.

61. Petition of doña Francisca Sarmiento de Valladares et al., México, Sept. 30, 1748, AGNM, Tierras, vol. 680; "Recaudos de comproba . . . ," AGNM, Tierras, vol. 681.

62. Testimony of Santiago del Arenal, México, Nov. 22, 1751, AGNM, Tierras, vol. 856, exp. 2.

63. To arrive at this figure, I averaged half the profits over a twelve-year period, i.e., 17,000 pesos / 12 years = 1,416 pesos / year. To find the discounted rate of return, solve for "r.":

$$3,000 = (1,416 / 1 + r) + [1,416 / (1 + r)^2] + \ldots + [1,416 / (1 + r).^{12}].$$

The resulting rate of return is deceptively high. It assumes, for instance, that there were no costs to operating the obraje after the initial investment, which is obviously incorrect. The equation, in other words, does not solve for net present value.

64. Testimony of Santiago del Arenal, México, Nov. 22, 1751, AGNM, Tierras, vol. 856, exp. 2.

65. Depósito irregular, Jul. 12, 1745, AGNM, Tierras, vol. 856, exp. 2.

66. Power given by Juan Pérez Cota y Madera, Puebla, Jul. 24, 1747, AGNM, Tierras, vol. 697.

67. Testimony of Juan de Castañiza, Apr. 29, 1749, AGNM, Tierras, vol. 687; Brading, *Miners and Merchants*, p. 124; Richard J. Salvucci, "Aspectos de un conflicto empresarial: El obraje de Balthasar de Sauto y la historia social de San Miguel el Grande, 1756-1771," *Anuario de Estudios Americanos* 36 (1979): 419-20.

68. Petition of Jacinto Romeo, México, Apr. 26, 1690, AGNM, Civil, vol. 1435, exp. 1.

69. Memorial by Miguel de Blancas Belén, México, Apr. 28, 1690, AGNM, Civil, vol. 1435, exp. 1.

70. Inventory [1716], AGNM, Civil, vol. 223, exp. 1; Emma Pérez-Rocha, *La tierra y el hombre en la villa de Tacuba durante la época colonial* (México, 1982), p. 59.

71. Statement of the goods of Úrsula del Pozo, México, Apr. 3, 1723, AGNM, Civil, vol. 220, exp. 2; testament of Úrsula del Pozo, México, Feb. 15, 1716, AGNM, Civil, vol. 223.

72. Auto of Jan. 28, 1722, AGNM, Civil, vol. 223; a requerimiento dated México, Oct. 16, 1721, and the petition of Bartolomé de Angulo, México, Dec. 23, 1720, both in AGNM, Civil, vol. 234, exp. 1.

73. Letter of credit signed by Bartolomé de Angulo, México, Apr. 28, 1722, AGNM, Civil, vol. 223.

74. Letter of credit signed by Gil Lelo de Larrea, México, May 13, 1722, AGNM, Civil, vol. 223; there is more on Rebequi's possession of the obraje in AGNM, Civil, vol. 87, 2da parte, "El pedimento de don Vicente Rebequi"; Cayetano Cabrera y Quintero, *Escudo de armas de México* (México, 1746), bk. 4, chap. 7, par. 868; Charles F. Nunn, *Foreign Immigrants in Early Bourbon Mexico, 1700-1760* (Cambridge, Eng., 1979), pp. 141, 216n.

75. Neither Romeo nor Alvarez appears in J. Ignacio Rubio Mañé, "Gente de España en la ciudad de México. Año de 1689," *BAGN*, 2d ser., 7 (1966): 5-406.

76. Testament of Sebastián Alvarez, México, Sept. 30, 1682, AGNM, Tierras, vol. 260, exp. 1.

77. See the liquidation of the goods of Alvarez in favor of creditors, AGNM, Tierras, vol. 261, exp. 1.

78. Obligations signed by Alvarez in México, Mar. 1, 1711, and Jul. 11, 1711, AGNM, Tierras, vol. 260, exp. 1.

79. Inventory. Dec. 7, 1696, AGNM, Tierras, vol. 260, exp. 1.

80. Richard E. Greenleaf, "Viceregal Powers and the Obrajes of the Cortés Estate, 1595-1708," *HAHR* 48 (1968): 365-79.

81. Reconocimiento by Ana Covarrubias, May 23, 1692, AGNM, Civil, vol. 355; report of don Pedro de la Bastida, México, Apr. 1, 1690, AGI, Contaduría 806, Ramo 3.

82. Title history, México, Apr. 11, 1693, AGNM, Civil, vol. 355.

83. Obligation of Ana Covarrubias, México, Feb. 9, 1679, AGNM, Civil, vol. 355.

84. Rental agreement signed by Francisco de Ansaldo, México, Jan. 27, 1689, AGNM, Civil, vol. 355; escritura de cesión and escritura de espera, signed by Diego de Contreras, México, Dec. 29, 1687, AGNM, Civil, vol. 355; declaration of doña Clara María Salaeta y Escalante, México, Feb. 24, 1708, AGNM, Registro de Fianzas, vol. 4.

85. Inspection of the obraje "Ansaldo," Coyoacán, Jan. 25, 1690, AGI, Contaduría 806, Ramo 3.

86. Statement of Francisco de Ansaldo, Coyoacán, Jan. 25, 1690, AGI, Contaduría 806, Ramo 3.

87. Agreement signed by María Teresa Montes de Oca, México, Jan. 27, 1689, AGNM, Civil, vol. 355.

88. Petition of don Antonio García, México, Nov. 9, 1737, AGNM, Tierras, vol. 1181; "Cuenta que presenta don Antonio Gutiérrez de Linares como apoderado de doña María Teresa Montes de Oca," México, Jun. 14, 1740, AJM, leg. 92.

89. Ibid.

90. Agreement signed by María Teresa Montes de Oca, México, Jan. 27, 1689, AGNM, Civil, vol. 355; petition of José Antonio Ocharte, manager of "Ansaldo," calling García "owner," but a petition by Montes de Oca from about the same period reserves that title to herself. AJM, leg. 92.

91. AJM, leg. 92.

92. Petition of Pedro Lucio de Batantula [Coyoacán, 1739], AJM, leg. 92.

93. See the concurso listed in Figure 3.5 for this point.

94. See Iturralde's bid with a letter of credit signed by Juan Francisco de Lostre, México, Jan. 17, 1805, and documentation on the "Hacienda del Ojo," also in the concurso.

95. Return on capital [(income/assets) x 100 percent] would be lower than return on equity. In AGNM, Aduanas, vol. 134, José Castañares estimated that "Panzacola" 's profits were at least 5 pesos per piece. Taking the lower range of

a "standard" piece as a cuarterón of 30 varas, and using the current price for paño in Mexico City in the early 1790s, about 12 reales per vara, we calculate:

$$(5 \text{ pesos/piece} \times 8 \text{ reales/peso}) /$$
$$(30 \text{ varas/piece} \times 12 \text{ reales/vara}) = .11$$

96. The cuadrilla is discussed in the concurso. Other obrajes in Tlaxcala and San Miguel el Grande also had workers' housing.

97. Richard A. Posner, *The Economics of Justice* (Cambridge, MA, 1981), pp. 155-56.

98. Dowry of doña María Rosa Yáñez, Tlaxcala, Jan. 5, 1704, AGNM, Civil, vol. 178, 2da parte. The procedure used above can be applied, but the discounted rate of return is subject to the same limitations. The estimated return to the company (as opposed to either individual) would be around 35 percent.

99. "Memorial de los autos de concurso formados a bienes de don Pedro Mendoza y Escalante . . . ," México, Mar. 5, 1792, AGNM, Civil, vol. 178, 4a parte.

100. A copy of the title appears in AGNM, Civil, vol. 178, 2da parte; Reinhard Liehr, *Ayuntamiento y oligarquía en Puebla, 1787-1810*, 2 vols. (México, 1976), 1: 98.

101. Testament of Apresa y Gándara, Puebla, Jan. 30, 1703, ante Diego de Viera, found in the protocols of Francisco Valdéz (April 1706), ANM.

102. Draft of a cédula dated Nov. 14, 1719, AGI, México 412.

103. Auction of the estate of Pedro de Mendoza y Escalante, Puebla, Oct. 6, 1746, AGNM, Civil, vol. 178, 4a parte; Liehr, *Ayuntamiento y oligarquía*, 1: 151.

104. Petition of Diego Martín, Cholula, Dec. 6, 1718, AGNM, Civil, vol. 1628, exp. 2.

105. Testament of Juan Pérez Cota y Madera, Puebla, Sept. 12, 1748, AGNM, Tierras, vol. 697; also see AGNM, Tierras, vol. 698, f. 216.

106. Ibid.

107. Ibid., and dowry of Margarita Teresa Núñez de Molina, Puebla, Nov. 7, 1715, AGNM, Tierras, vol. 697.

108. According to his testament, Pérez Cota had 13,000 pesos in personal estate at the time of his marriage. A dowry of 12,000 pesos roughly doubled this.

109. Testimony of Juan de Castañiza, Puebla, Apr. 29, 1749; and bill of sale, México, Nov. 13, 1747, AGNM, Tierras, vol. 697.

110. Testimony of Juan de Castañiza, Puebla, Apr. 29, 1749; petition of Margarita Teresa Núñez de Molina, Puebla, Oct. 22, 1750, both in AGNM, Tierras, vol. 697; on Herrera Puente, see AGNM, Tierras, vol. 1034, exp. 3; for profits, see "Cuenta de albaceazgo dada por doña Margarita Núñez," Puebla, Dec. 31, 1751, AGNM, Tierras, vol. 698.

111. Petition of Margarita Teresa Núñez de Molina, Puebla, Oct. 22, 1750, AGNM, Tierras, vol. 697

112. Ibid.

113. José María Remontería to the directors of the Royal Excise, Tlaxcala, May 26, 1781, AGNM, Alcabalas, vol. 521.

114. Juan Villa Sánchez, *Puebla sagrada y profana. Informe dado a su muy ilustre ayuntamiento en el año de 1746* (Puebla, 1835), p. 112.

115. Contract for the farm of the excise, Tomás Díaz Varela and Antonio Lucas de Pineda, Santa Ana Chiautempan, Mar. 10, 1772, AGNM, Alcabalas, vol. 177, exp. 1.

116. Inventory of his wife's possessions in the unión de sumas y afeciones pasivas of Tomás Díaz Varela, Tlaxcala, May 22, 1783, AJM, leg. 148; Joaquín de Cosío to the viceroy, Puebla, Jul. 26, 1777, AGNM, Alcabalas, vol. 177, exp. 1.

117. Inventory of his wife's possessions in the unión de sumas y afeciones pasivas of Tomás Díaz Varela, Tlaxcala, May 22, 1783, AJM, leg. 148; and petition of Tomás Díaz Varela, Tlaxcala, May 16, 1783, AJM, leg. 148.

118. Villa Sánchez, *Puebla sagrada*, p. 112.

119. Ibid., pp. 112-13.

120. Testimony of José María Gutiérrez, México, May 26, 1777, AGNM, Alcabalas, vol. 177, exp. 1.

121. The counting of obrajes in San Miguel is drawn from the following sources: decree of the Conde de Fuenclara, Aug. 19, 1744, AGNM, Civil, vol. 820, exp. 10; and "Mapa de los obrajes . . . ," AGNM, Civil, vol. 1628. In 1744, there were two obrajes in San Miguel, and one was not in operation. By 1755, there were four or five operating between sixty-five and seventy-five looms. For competition for labor, see the testimony of Balthasar de los Reyes, San Miguel, Oct. 1, 1758, AGI, Mexico, 1047. For resource competition, see the petition of Balthasar de Sauto, [Puebla, n.d.], AGI, México 1047. For competition for managers, see the information of Bachiller Francisco Crisóstomo de la Mata et al., San Miguel, Nov. 18, 1758, AGI, México 1047, and AGNM, Civil, vol. 919, exp. 12.

122. Flor de María Hurtado López, *Dolores Hidalgo: Estudio económico, 1740-1790* (México, 1974), p. 67.

123. Petition of Manuel de la Canal, San Miguel [1749], AGNM, Civil, vol. 2296, exp. 1; statement of José Mariano Loreto de la Canal, San Miguel, Sept. 1, 1759, AGNM, Civil, vol. 880. exp. 2; Joaquín Sánchez de Tagle to the viceroy, Jan. 7, 1754, AGNM, Subdelegados, vol. 34; J. Ignacio Rubio Mañé, "Informes del estado económico y social de la villa de San Miguel el Grande, año de 1754," *BAGN*, 2d ser., 2 (1961): 355-74; information of Bachiller Francisco Crisóstomo de la Mata et al., San Miguel, Nov. 18, 1758, AGI, México 1047, and AGNM, Civil, vol. 919, exp. 12.

124. Petition of Balthasar de Sauto, San Miguel, Nov. 18, 1758, AGNM, Tierras, vol. 813, exp. 1; confession of Balthasar de Sauto, México, 1759, AGI, México, 1047.

125. Testimony of Bachiller Nícolas Alejandro Aguado, San Miguel, Dec. 14, 1767, AGI, México 1047; petition of Francisco Nícolas Lartundo, San Miguel, Sept. 26, 1755, AGNM, Tierras, vol. 813, exp. 1; Francisco de la Maza, *San Miguel Allende*, 2d ed. (México, 1972), pp. 17, 48; Esteban Sánchez de Tagle, *Por un regimento, el régimen* (México, 1982), pp. 86-90.

126. Inspection of the hacienda "Mexquito," San Miguel, Oct. 6, 1759,

AGNM, Civil, vol. 918, exp. 7; petition of Balthasar de Sauto, México [April 1759]; "Memoria y lista de todos los que . . . viven en tierra de Balthasar de Sauto extramuros de esta villa"; second inspection of the obraje of Balthasar de Sauto, San Miguel, Aug. 23, 1758, all in AGI, México, 1047; certification of sale by Balthasar de Sauto, México, Sept. 11, 1759, AGNM, Aduanas, vol. 13; statement of account given by Juan Eusebio González, San Miguel [1747], AGNM, Civil, vol. 218.

127. Inspection of the hacienda "Mexquito," San Miguel, Oct. 6, 1759, AGNM, Civil, vol. 918, exp. 7; "Mapa de los obrajes . . . ," AGNM, Civil, vol. 1628.

128. Petition of Balthasar de Sauto, México, Feb. 1, 1762, AGNM, Civil, vol. 872, exp. 7; information of Bachiller Francisco Crisóstomo de la Mata et al., San Miguel, Nov. 18, 1758, AGI, México 1047, and AGNM, Civil, vol. 919, exp. 12.

129. Lohman Villena, *Los americanos*, 2: 57-58, 223.

130. Rubio Mañé, "Gente de España," pp. 136, 217; Lohman Villena, *Los americanos*, 2: 323-24; Miguel Lerdo de Tejada, *El comercio exterior de México* (México, 1853), Documentos, no. 1.

131. J. Ignacio Rubio Mañé, "Alcaldes ordinarios y procuradores de la villa de San Miguel el Grande, 1700-1785," *BAGN*, 2d ser., 2 (1961): 375-92; Juan Agustín de Morfi, *Viaje de indios y diario de Nuevo México*, 2 vols. (México, 1935), 1: 45-49; Maza, *San Miguel Allende*, p. 19. I have computed the share of looms from "Mapa de los obrajes . . . ," AGNM, Civil, vol. 1628.

132. Morfi, *Diario de indios*, 1: 48-49; Harris, *Mexican Family Empire*, pp. 82-83; petition of Balthasar de Sauto, [Puebla, n.d.], AGI, México 1047.

133. "Extracto de los excesos . . . cometidos por el capitán reformado don Balthasar de Sauto . . . ," AGI, México 1047.

134. Mark A. Burkholder and D. S. Chandler, *From Impotence to Authority. The Spanish Crown and the American Audiencias, 1687-1808* (Columbia, MO, 1977), p. 32n.

135. Cédula, Feb. 9, 1761, AGI, México 1047; the Marqués de Cruillas to the minister of the Indies, México, Aug. 2, 1762, AGNM, Correspondencia de Virreyes, 2d ser., vol. 7; citation of Balthasar de Sauto, San Miguel, Jul. 27, 1761, AGI, México 1047; consulta of the corregidor of Querétaro, Querétaro, Aug. 4, 1761, AGI, México 1047. The cédula was suspended by a voto consultivo of the Audiencia of Aug. 2, 1761.

136. See note 121 above.

137. Posner, *Economics of Justice*, p. 194.

138. Clemente de Apresa to the directors of the Royal Excise, Acámbaro, Apr. 30, 1781, AGNM, Alcabalas, vol. 521.

139. "Valor de la ropa que han despachado . . . ," and Vicente Domingo Lombardini to the directors of the Royal Excise, México, Dec. 10, 1779, AGNM, Aduanas, vol. 67, exp. 1; Lombardini to the directors of the Royal Excise, May 15, 1779, AGNM, Alcabalas, vol. 205; contract for the excise tax, Acámbaro, Jun. 11, 1777, AGNM, Alcabalas, vol. 205.

140. Production and account books of the obraje of Mateo Mauricio García, AGNM, Civil, vol. 893, exp. 9.

141. "Noticias de fábricas, molinos, ingenios, lagunas, ríos, y puentes" (1794) in Florescano and Gil Sánchez, eds., *Descripciones económicas generales*, pp. 64-66.

142. Lieut. R. W. Hardy, R.N., *Travels in the Interior of Mexico in 1825, 1826, 1827, and 1828* (London, 1829), p. 503.

143. Statistics on Querétaro's population by no means agree. Alexander von Humboldt, *Political Essay on the Kingdom of New Spain*, 4 vols. (London, 1811-14, 1: 192, gives a late-eighteenth-century estimate of 27,000, which seems low. Using the Bucareli census, AGNM, Padrones, vol. 12, the city's population was 20,000, with a growth rate of near 4 percent. This implies a population of about 40,000 at the turn of the century. This is the figure given by Manuel Septién y Septién, *Historia de Querétaro desde los tiempos prehistóricos hasta el año de 1800* (Querétaro, 1967), p. 201. Pedro Antonio Septién, "Noticia sucinta de la ciudad de Querétaro (1791) . . . ," in Florescano and Gil Sánchez, eds., *Descripciones económicas regionales*, p. 46, puts the statistic at 36,000. The *Registro Oficial* of May 24, 1831, set Querétaro's population at 65,000 on the eve of the insurrection, saying it "had diminished considerably" by 1831. This is disputed by "Apuntes estadísticos que escribió el Sr. D. J. Francisco Bustamante relativo al departamento de Querétaro," *Boletín de la sociedad mexicana de geografía y estadística* 7 (1859): 539, citing an 1828 publication of a "society of literati in . . . Paris . . . to the effect that [Querétaro] lacked the [50,000 inhabitants] that it was said to have had in 1802." To end on a confusing note, Pedro Telmo Primo in *Querétaro en 1822* maintained that the city's population was 40,000 at the beginning of the nineteenth century.

144. Miguel José Solórzano to the director of the Royal Excise, Feb. 7, 1800, AGNM, Alcabalas, vol. 382. Antonio Pérez Velasco, *Elogio histórico del señor don Juan Antonio del Castillo y Llata* (México, 1818), p. 11.

145. Obligation of Diego Domínguez Rodríguez, México, Dec. 23, 1721, AGNM, Civil, vol. 601.

146. An account book documenting these transactions from 1703 to 1721 appears in AGNM, Civil, vol. 601.

147. Accounts of Andrés Rodríguez de Porras and Joaquín Valiño, in AJQ, leg. "Civiles, 1730."

148. This is based on the letterbook of Fernando Sáenz de Escobosa from 1795 through 1799, AJM, leg. 192, various dates.

149. Depósito irregular en Juan Manuel Primo, México, Mar. 20, 1758, ante José Pérez Cancio, ANM; cesión de bienes, and list of debts of don Antonio Camaño, AJQ, leg. "Civiles, 1722."

150. Index of testimony, Querétaro, 1757, AGNM, Tierras, vol. 2738, exp. 10; assessment made by José Antonio de la Peña, Querétaro, Sept. 10, 1760, AGNM, Civil, vol. 4, exp. 4; statement of accounts by Félix Malo, México, Jul. 24, 1766, AGNM, Civil, vol. 4, exp. 4.

151. Poder para testar, Querétaro, Apr. 4, 1750, ante Félix Antonio de

Araujo, in the protocols of José Pérez Cancio for March 1758, ANM; petition of Pedro Bernardino y Jordán to the Council of the Indies (ca. 1742), AGI, México 644.

152. Ibid.

153. Testament of Pedro Bernardino de Primo y Jordán, Querétaro, Mar. 12, 1755, ante Félix Antonio de Araujo, in the protocols of José Pérez Cancio, ANM.

154. Lohman Villena, *Los americanos*, 2: 57-58, 223.

155. AGNM, Aduanas, vol. 76, exp. 2., in which don José Martínez Moreno, a deputy of the guild, appears as "substituto por el Conde de Regla," an allusion to Regla's membership in the gremio de obrajería.

156. Information given by Tomás López de Ecala, Querétaro, Jun. 30, 1783, AGI, México 2098.

157. Census of Querétaro (1791), AGNM, Padrones, vol. 39; list of owners cited in "Obrajes o fábricas que hay . . . ," AGNM, Alcabalas, vol. 37.

158. López Cancelada, *Ruina de la Nueva España*, p. 27.

159. Archivo del Ayuntamiento de Querétaro, bk. 3, entry for Jan. 3, 1791.

160. Pedro Russi to the director of the Royal Excise, Querétaro, May 17, 1806, AGNM, Alcabalas, vol. 383.

161. John Super, "Querétaro obrajes," p. 56, and *La vida en Querétaro*, pp. 108, 132-33.

162. Report of don Esteban Gómez de Acosta, Querétaro, Jul. 15, 1743, AGI, Indiferente 107, Tomo 1.

163. David A. Brading, "Los españoles en México hacia 1792," *Hist Mex* 23 (1973): 126-44; Super, *La vida en Querétaro*, p. 103.

164. AGNM, Padrones, vol. 39, for Llata's position of alcalde; López Cancelada, *Ruina de la Nueva España*, p. 27; Pérez Velasco, *Elogio histórico*, p. 13.

165. "Padrón de Españoles de Esta Ciudad de Santiago de Querétaro," AGNM, Civil, vol. 2085, exp. 4. Compare, for instance, the residents of the Plaza Mayor with those on the Calle de los Infantes, Manzanas 43, 45, 114. Similar results have been obtained for Durango. See Michael Swann, *Tierra Adentro. Settlement and Society in Colonial Durango* (Boulder, 1982), pp. 277-301. Using different evidence, Super concludes the same in *La vida en Querétaro*, p. 105.

166. Mexico was not unlike other developing economies in this regard. See Peter Temin, *Causal Factors in American Economic Growth in the Nineteenth Century* (London, 1975), p. 50.

167. Lindley, *Haciendas and Economic Development*, pp. 41-42; Burton Benedict, "Family Firms in Economic Development," *Southwestern Journal of Anthropology* 24 (1968): 1-19.

168. Potash, *Banco de Avío*, pp. 77, 113, 118, 119; Enrique Cárdenas, "Algunas cuestiones sobre la depresión mexicana del XIX," *HISLA* 3 (1984): 3-22.

169. Philip Wayne Powell, "North America's First Frontier, 1546-1603," in George Wolfskill and Stanley Palmer, eds., *Essays on Frontiers in World History* (Austin, 1981), p. 18; Paul Vanderwood, *Disorder and Progress. Bandits, Police, and Mexican Development* (Lincoln, NE, 1981), p. 18.

170. Cf. S. D. Chapman, *The Cotton Industry in the Industrial Revolution* (London, 1972), p. 35; and his "Industrial Capital Before the Industrial Revolution: An Analysis of the Assets of a Thousand Textile Entrepreneurs c. 1730-50," in N. B. Harte and K. G. Ponting, eds., *Textile History and Economic History. Essays in Honor of Miss Julia de Lacey Mann* (Manchester, 1973), p. 136.

171. Armen Alchian, "Uncertainty, Evolution, and Economic Theory," in *Economic Forces at Work. Selected Works by Armen A. Alchian* (Indianapolis, 1977), p. 31.

CHAPTER FOUR

1. "Informe del Exmo. Señor Duque de Linares al Señor Marqués de Valero en el año 1716 . . . ," copy in AHINAH.

2. Albert O. Hirschman, "Rival Interpretations of Market Society: Civilizing, Destructive, or Feeble," *Journal of Economic Literature* 20 (1982): 1473.

3. Borah, *Justice by Insurance*, pp. 58-59.

4. This description is drawn from the statement of José Mariano Loreto de la Canal, San Miguel, Sept. 1, 1759, AGNM, Civil, vol. 880.

5. Statement of Joaquín Antonio Guerrero y Tagle, May 28, 1768, AGNM, Criminal, vol. 230, exp. 5. Owners who capitalized labor costs by payments in advance had strong incentive to regard indebted labor as fixed capital and to maximize its employment in industrial and nonindustrial activities. Thus the appearance of multiple tasks in the obraje. See Richard L. Rudolph, "Agricultural Structure and Proto-Industrialization in Russia: Economic Development with Unfree Labor," *JEH* 45 (1985): 54, 62.

6. As one owner put it, "there is a greater or smaller number of workers depending on what needs to be done in the obraje." Testimony of Antonio de Sierra, AGI, Contaduría 806, Ramo 3.

7. "Relación de los obrajes de paños que hay en este Reino . . . ," México, May 10, 1604, AGI, México 25.

8. Calculated from data on a composición de obrajes in AGI, Contaduría 806, Ramo 3.

9. Super, "Querétaro obrajes," pp. 206, 208.

10. Testimony of Francisco Quacho, Querétaro, Mar. 30, 1770, AGI, México 693B.

11. Testimony of José Manuel Ulloa, Querétaro, Mar. 30, 1770, AGI, México 693B.

12. López Cancelada, *Ruina de la Nueva España*, p. 27.

13. Calculated from a report of Santiago Riego to the Crown, México, Dec. 10, 1588, AGI, México 71.

14. Hans Pohl et al., "Aspectos sociales . . . de los obrajes textiles en Puebla," p. 42. The variance is not reported.

15. "Relación de los obrajes de paños que hay en este Reino . . . ," México, May 10, 1604, AGI, México 25.

16. David M. Szewczyk, "New Elements in the Society of Tlaxcala," in Altman and Lockhart, eds., *Provinces of Early Mexico*, p. 146.

17. On the Díaz Varela, see Chapter Three.

18. Diego Antonio Fernández de la Madrid to the viceroy, México, Apr. 7, 1759, AGI, México 1047.

19. Borah, "Race and Class," p. 344.

20. Ibid., p. 340. See also the parallel texts in Castilian and Nahuatl of a decree of May 9, 1740, AGNM, Hospital de Jesús, leg. 302, exp. 15.

21. Fernández del Castillo, *Apuntes para la historia de San Angel*, p. 138.

22. Frances Karttunen, "Nahuatl Literacy," in Collier et al., eds., *The Inca and Aztec States*, p. 407; Borah, *Justice by Insurance*, pp. 64, 83.

23. "Relación de los obrajes de paños que hay en este Reino . . . ," México, May 10, 1604, AGI, México 25; Szewczyk, "New Elements in the Society of Tlaxcala," in Altman and Lockhart, eds., *Provinces of Early Mexico*, p. 146; Hans Pohl et al., "Aspectos sociales . . . de los obrajes textiles en Puebla," p. 42.

24. Edmundo O'Gorman, "Visita de los obrajes y haciendas de la jurisdicción de la villa de Coyoacán (1660)," *BAGN*, 1st ser., 11 (1940): 81, 84.

25. Szewczyk, "New Elements in the Society of Tlaxcala," in Altman and Lockhart, eds., *Provinces of Early Mexico*, p. 147; Hans Pohl et al., "Aspectos sociales . . . de los obrajes textiles en Puebla," p. 42.

26. For all three obrajes see AGNM, Padrones, vol. 6. For "Panzacola" see also the concurso de acreedores of the firm of Oteyza y Vértiz, cited in Chapter Three.

27. Consulta of Esteban Gómez de Acosta, Querétaro, Aug. 4, 1761, AGI, México 1047.

28. "Padrón general . . . de Querétaro, 1778," AGNM, Padrones, vol. 12.

29. David A. Brading, "The Historical Demography of Eighteenth-Century Mexico: A Review," *Bulletin of the Society of Latin American Studies*, no. 25 (1976): 9, 13-15.

30. Diego Antonio Fernández de la Madrid to the viceroy, México, Apr. 7, 1759, AGI, México 1047; Greenleaf, "Viceregal Power and the Obrajes," p. 365; Alicia Skinner Cook, "India's Working Children," *Horizons* [Agency for International Development] 3 (1984): 26.

31. The full age distributions are based on the 1792 census of Coyoacán in AGNM, Padrones, vol. 6. They are tabulated in Richard J. Salvucci, "Enterprise and Economic Development in Eighteenth-Century Mexico: The Case of the Obrajes" (Ph.D. diss., Princeton Univ., 1982), pp. 221, 224.

32. Census of the barrio of San Juan, AGNM, Padrones, vol. 105; the age distribution appears in Salvucci, "Enterprise and Economic Development," p. 227.

33. O'Gorman, "Visita de los obrajes y haciendas . . . de Coyoacán," pp. 45, 56; see also Szewczyk, "New Elements in the Society of Tlaxcala," in Altman and Lockhart, eds., *Provinces of Early Mexico*, p. 147.

34. Visita to the obraje of Francisco de Briuega, Nov. 26, 1583, Archivo de la Secretaría Municipal de Puebla, vol. 221: "Expediente sobre visitas de obrajes, 1588-1621."

35. AGNM, Tierras, vol. 440, for a list of workers and indebtedness; Szewczyk, "New Elements in the Society of Tlaxcala," in Altman and Lockhart, eds., *Provinces of Early Mexico*, p. 147.

36. Indenture to the obraje of José Pimentel, México, Jun. 10, Oct. 4, and Oct. 5, 1746, ante Manuel López de la Palma, ANM; indentures to the obraje of Juan Bautista Salvares, Coyoacán, 1703, AJM, leg. 62; concurso de acreedores of the firm of Oteyza y Vértiz, cited in Chapter Three.

37. Liquidation of the accounts of the workers of "Mixcoac," Jul. 5, 1757, AGNM, Tierras, vol. 2016.

38. Petition of María Cecilia Rivera, México, Oct. 11, 1802, AGNM, Civil, vol. 1674, exp. 14.

39. AGNM, Civil, vol. 1359, exp. 3.

40. O'Gorman, "Visita de los obrajes y haciendas . . . de Coyoacán," p. 56.

41. Diego Antonio Fernández de la Madrid to the viceroy, México, Apr. 7, 1759, AGI, México 1047.

42. Assume an apprentice receives 30 pesos for a three-year indenture. If the owner pays the sum at the time of indenture, its present value is 30 pesos. Discounting at 5 percent shows that the present value falls to 27 pesos if paid over a three-year interval in three equal installments. If the owner pays the entire sum at the end of three years, its present value falls to 26 pesos, that is, simply $(30/1.05^3) = 26$ pesos. The owner does best by deferring payment as long as possible.

43. "Ocurso a Su Magestad por la Compañía de las Cinco Gracias," para. 3, Guadalajara, Dec. 11, 1777, reproduced by Carmen Castañeda, "Sobre una fábrica textil u obraje establecido en Guadalajara en el siglo XVIII," *Boletín del Archivo Histórico de Jalisco* 4 (1980): 15.

44. Borah, *Justice by Insurance*, p. 50.

45. The confusion is evident in the petition of Balthasar de Soto Noguera, who called don José Velázquez Lorea lieutenant colonel of the Real Sala del Crimen. José Velázquez Lorea, son of the legendary bandit hunter Miguel Velázquez Lorea, succeeded his father as proprietary judge of the Acordada in 1732 and was not an officer in the rival Sala del Crimen. See Colin MacLachlan, *Criminal Justice in Eighteenth-Century Mexico. A Study of the Tribunal of the Acordada* (Berkeley, 1974), pp. 32-34. Soto Noguera's petition appears in AGNM, Civil, vol. 820, exp. 11.

46. Undated petition to the viceroy; certification of the escribano de cámara, Vicente Sanfranco, México, Jul. 22, 1767, AGNM, Civil, vol. 1531, exp. 4.

47. Rebellious Indians from the Sierra Gorda and convicts from Guadalajara were sometimes found in Querétaro's obrajes. See "Autos de la tropa que fue a México para obrajes el año pasado de 1722 . . . ," Biblioteca Pública del Estado de Jalisco, Fondos Especiales, Audiencia de Guadalajara, Ramo Judicial, Civil; and the testimony of Antonio de la Cruz de Salas, Querétaro, Apr. 3, 1770, AGI, México, 693B.

48. Petitions of Nícolas de Panagos, Querétaro, May 25, 1733, and petitions

of José de Arteaga et al., Querétaro, May 27, 1733; notification of José de Arteaga, Querétaro, Jun. 2, 1733, all in AGNM, Civil, vol. 1531, exp. 4.

49. AGI, México 644.

50. Ibid.

51. Petition of the Conde de Casa de Loja [1756], AGNM, Civil, vol. 2296, exp. 1.

52. As in note 45 above.

53. For the tariff, see AGNM, Inquisición, vol. 912, exp. 24.

54. Diego Antonio Fernández de la Madrid et al. to the Crown, México, Jun. 26, 1767, AGI, México 1130.

55. Petition of Juan de Villalva y Velázquez and Martín de Oyarzábal [Querétaro 1781], AGI, México 1809.

56. Petition of [?] de Llanos y Valle, México, Mar. 3, 1717, AGNM, Civil, vol. 1628, exp. 1.

57. Report of Esteban Gómez de Acosta, Querétaro, Jul. 15, 1743, AGI, Indiferente, 107, tomo 1.

58. Assume that a peon and a convict are equally unsuited to textile work and are equally productive. The productivity of the criminal and the peon must be discounted by the probability that they will escape. Chances are, an experienced criminal will be more likely to make a successful escape.

59. Marqués de Croix to the minister of Marine and Indies, México, Aug. 26, 1768, AGNM, Correspondencia de Virreyes, 2d ser., vol. 12.

60. Riego to the Crown, México, Aug. 2, 1588, AGI, México 71.

61. Ibid.

62. Riego to the Crown, México, Dec. 10, 1588, AGI, México 71.

63. Lorenzo Sanz, *Comercio de España con América*, 1: 439.

64. Conde de Monterrey to the Council of the Indies, March, 1603, AGI, México 25.

65. Conde de Monterrey to the Crown, Nov. 18, 1603, AGI, México 25.

66. Francis Edward Pratt, "The Obraje in New Spain: A Case Study in the Failure of Royal Authority to Impose its Will" (M.A. thesis, Univ. of the Americas, 1965), pp. 63-64.

67. Conde de Monterrey to the Crown, México, Dec. 1602, AGI, México 25.

68. Ibid.

69. Pratt, "The Obraje in New Spain," pp. 66-67. There is also the suggestion in the "Relación de los obrajes que hay en este Reino . . ." [1603], AGI, México 26, that Indian labor was retired from the obrajes in Mexico City as a consequence of the measure of 1601.

70. Hans Pohl et al., "Aspectos sociales . . . de los obrajes textiles en Puebla," pp. 41-42.

71. Szewczyk, "New Elements in the Society of Tlaxcala," in Altman and Lockhart, eds., *Provinces of Early Mexico*, pp. 145-46.

72. O'Gorman, "Visita de los obrajes y haciendas . . . de Coyoacán," pp. 81, 84.

73. Super, *La vida en Querétaro*, pp. 96, 222.

74. Colin Palmer, *Slaves of the White God*, pp. 16-17; Borah, *Justice By Insurance*, p. 26.

75. Charles Gibson, *The Aztecs Under Spanish Rule. A History of the Indians of the Valley of Mexico, 1519-1810* (Stanford, 1964), p. 294.

76. A formal model might include the productivity of slave and free labor relative to their costs and might indicate the range over which either would be preferred. There is some evidence on what seem to be hire rates (or their equivalent) in Gonzalo Aguirre Beltrán, "El trabajo del indio comparado con el del negro en Nueva España," *México Agrario* 4 (1942): 204-7. It perversely indicates, however, that the relative price of black slaves (that is, their price in terms of Indians) fell rather than rose between the sixteenth and seventeenth centuries. The relation between the demand for slaves and the relative decline of the indigenous population is similarly unclear. Using statistics calculated by Borah, Cook, and Palmer, one can easily produce a perfectly (trivial) negative correlation between the two, since their combined figures yield only two points, 1595-1605 and 1605-22.

77. AGI, Contaduría 806, Ramo 3.

78. Inventory of slaves in "Apresa," Puebla, Apr. 9, 1706, ante Diego de Viera, inserted in a record of slave sales, Mixcoac, Apr. 28, 1706, ante Francisco Valdés, ANM.

79. Super, *La vida en Querétaro*, pp. 120, 222.

80. AGNM, Padrones, vol. 6.

81. Dennis Nodín Valdés, "The Decline of the *Sociedad de Castas* in Mexico City," (Ph.D. diss., Univ. of Michigan, 1978), chap. 5.

82. Valdés, "Sociedad de Castas," p. 165; Stanley L. Engerman, "Some Considerations Relating to Property Rights in Man," *JEH* 33 (1973): 47.

83. Valdés, "Sociedad de Castas," p. 156; James F. King, "Negro History in Continental Spanish America," in Howard F. Cline, ed., *Latin American History. Essays on Its Study and Teaching, 1898-1965*, 2 vols. (Austin, 1967), 1: 384n.

84. London, May 3, 1736, in Elizabeth Donnan, ed., *Documents Illustrative of the History of the Slave Trade to America*, 4 vols. (Washington, D.C., 1930-35), 4: 458.

85. Liquidation of the accounts of Agustín de la Rosa, Manuel Esteban, and Juan Luis, all in Coyoacán, Jul. 5, 1757, AGNM, Tierras, vol. 2016, exp. 2.

86. Diego Antonio Fernández de la Madrid to the viceroy, México, Apr. 7, 1759, AGI, México 1047.

87. Liquidation of the account of Miguel Santos, as in note 85 above.

88. Liquidation of the account of Juan Gregorio, as in note 85 above.

89. Statement of Antonio de Sierra, [Jan. 1690]; statement of Sancho de Posadas, México, Jan. 5, 1690, both in AGI, Contaduría 806, Ramo 3.

90. AGNM, Civil, vol. 1435, exp. 7.

91. Herbert Nickel, "Reclutamiento y peonaje de los gañanes indígenas de la época colonial en el altiplano de Puebla-Tlaxcala," *Ibero-Amerikanisches Archiv*, new ser., 5 (1979): 75.

92. George McCutchen McBride, "Peonage," *Encyclopaedia of the Social Sciences* (New York, 1937); "Peonage," unsigned article, *Encyclopaedia Britannica*, 11th ed.

93. Humboldt, *Political Essay*, 3: 464-65.

94. Sections 2-5, 9, 11, 16, and 28 on indebtedness, Juan Francisco de Montemayor y Córdova de Cuenca, *Recopilación de algunos mandamientos y ordenanzas del gobierno de esta Nueva España* (México, 1677), pp. 75-90, contained in Eusebio Ventura Beleña, *Recopilación sumaria de todos los autos acordados de la Real Audiencia . . .* , 2 vols. (México, 1787), vol. 1.

95. Both are reproduced in Richard Konetzke, *Colección de documentos para la historia de la formación social de Hispanoamérica, 1493-1810*, 3 vols. in 5 parts (Madrid, 1953-62), 2 (1): 71-85, 297-300.

96. Sections 1 and 2, in Juan Francisco de Montemayor y Córdova y Cuenca, *Recopilación sumaria de algunos autos acordados de la Real Audiencia . . .* (México, 1677), pp. 53-60, contained in Ventura Beleña, *Recopilación sumaria*, vol. 1.

97. A copy of this ordinance appears in Ventura Beleña, *Recopilación sumaria*, 2: 298-306.

98. Decree of Viceroy Linares, México, May 7, 1714, AGI, México 487.

99. The cédula is noted in Don Juan de Miranda et al. to the Crown, México, Jul. 8, 1638, AGI, México 75.

100. Diego Antonio Fernández de la Madrid to the viceroy, México, Apr. 7, 1759, AGI, México 1047.

101. Pedimento fiscal, México, Jun. 22, 1804, AGI, México 1809.

102. Petition of María Bonifacia [México, 1752], AJM, leg. 106; petition of Miguel Escalma, México, Mar. 4, 1757, AJM, leg. 115; petition of Luis Flores, México, Jan. 26, 1757, AJM, leg. 115.

103. Calculated from "Cuenta memoria y relación jurada que di don Cayetano López . . . ," México, Dec. 31, 1749, AGNM, Tierras, vol. 667.

104. Calculated from "Balance del obraje de Batán y de la Hacienda de San Francisco Paula, 1804," in Super, *La vida en Querétaro*, p. 243.

105. Petition of the owners of obrajes of Querétaro [August 1802], AGI, México 1809.

106. Miguel Domínguez estimated that 6,000 workers were employed in the obrajes while he was corregidor. Since women spun yarn at home, something less than 6,000 must represent the labor force of the obrajes strictly defined. If we assume that 1,000 women were spinners—in 1777-78 there were about 900 married men in the obrajes; it is reasonable to assume that their wives worked at cottage spinning—we may divide 1,500 and 2,000 by 5,000 to arrive at the statistic. See Brading, "Notas sobre la economía de Querétaro," p. 281.

107. Petition of the owners of obrajes of Querétaro, México, Sept. 9, 1801, AGI, México 1809. Italics mine.

108. Petition of the owners of obrajes of Querétaro [August 1802], AGI, México 1809. Cf. Brading, "Noticias sobre la economía de Querétaro," p. 287,

wherein Domínguez paints a very different and more familiar picture of peonage.

109. Super, "Querétaro obrajes," pp. 210-11n. The difference between working looms and looms installed is a measure of capacity utilization, which was around 50 percent in the fourteen obrajes Super examined in 1789.

110. Cerralvo ordinances, Title 4, México, May 10, 1633, AGI, México 75.

111. Calculated from "Cuenta memoria y relación jurada que di don Cayetano López . . . ," México, Dec. 31, 1749, AGNM, Tierras, vol. 667, and from "Balance del obraje de Batán y de la Hacienda de San Francisco Paula, 1804," in Super, *La vida en Querétaro*, p. 243.

112. Petition of the owners of obrajes of Querétaro, Querétaro, Aug. 31, 1807, AGNM, Civil, vol. 1871, exp. 10.

113. Humboldt, *Political Essay*, 3: 464.

114. Miguel Domínguez to the viceroy, Querétaro, Dec. 4, 1811, AGNM, Subdelegados, vol. 5.

115. First act of inspection, Aug. 14, 1758, AGI, México 1047.

116. See the concurso de acreedores of the firm of Oteyza y Vértiz, cited in Chapter Three.

117. List of debts, Querétaro, Jun. 8, 1725, AGNM, Tierras, vol. 440.

118. Visitas to various Puebla obrajes in early 1700, Archivo de la Secretaría Municipal de Puebla, vol. 224: "Expediente sobre obrajes y talleres."

119. Auto de providencia, San Miguel, Oct. 30, 1758, AGI, México 1047. Emphasis mine.

120. "Memorial y lista de todos los que . . . viven en tierras de Balthasar de Sauto," San Miguel, Mar. 2, 1768, AGNM, Tierras, vol. 932.

121. The regression, with standard error in parentheses, is:

$$\ln \text{Laborers} = 3.58 + .45 \ln \text{Average Debt}$$
$$(.0034)$$

$R^2 = .38$

$N = 4$

122. Dictamen of Lic. José Mariano Balderas Urteaga, Jul. 19, 1808 [México], AGI, México 1809.

123. Account of Juan Matías, 1745-46, AGNM, Civil, vol. 1689.

124. Petition of the owners of obrajes of Querétaro, México, Sept. 9, 1801, AGI, México 1809.

125. Article 4 of the ordinances: "Some in the obrajes are found to owe 40 and 50 pesos."

126. Brading, "Noticias sobre la economía de Querétaro," p. 297; report of don Esteban Gómez de Acosta, Querétaro, Jul. 15, 1743, AGI, Indiferente 107, Tomo 1.

127. Robert Evans, "Some Notes on Coerced Labor," *JEH* 30 (1970): 861-66.

128. Hans Pohl et al., "Aspectos sociales . . . de los obrajes textiles en Puebla," pp. 41-42.

129. Evans, "Coerced Labor," p. 861.

130. Petition of the owners of obrajes of Querétaro [August 1802], AGI, México 1809.

131. Super, *La vida en Querétaro*, pp. 182-84; Brading, *Miners and Merchants*, p. 228.

132. Milton Friedman, *Price Theory* (Chicago, 1976), p. 206; Peter Mathias, "Leisure and Wages in Theory and Practice" in his *Transformation of England. Essays in the Economic and Social History of England in the Eighteenth Century* (New York, 1979), p. 153, and more generally pp. 148-67.

133. Petition of Domingo de Sandoval, México, Jun. 2, 1747, AJM, leg. 100.

134. Marqués de Valero to the Crown, México, Dec. 13, 1721, AGI, México, 1328.

135. AGNM, Civil, vol. 1519, exp. 3.

136. Petition of Miguel de los Santos, México, Oct. 22, 1722, AGNM, Indios, vol. 45, no. 179, fs. 232-34.

137. Petition of José de Iturralde [Coyoacán, Jun. 8, 1768], AJM, leg. 124.

138. Diego Antonio Fernández de la Madrid to the viceroy, México, Apr. 7, 1759, AGI, México 1047.

139. Report of Diego Cornide Saavedra, May 24, 1766, AGI, México 1366.

140. Report of Diego Cornide Saavedra, May 6, 1767, AGI, México 1366. This was precisely the time at which convict labor was shifted from obrajes to presidios. The comparison, therefore, was hardly disinterested.

141. The lengthy record of this visita is in AGI, México 75.

142. William Bullock, *Six Months' Residence and Travels in Mexico . . .* , 2 vols. (London, 1825), 1: 217-18.

143. Declaration of Francisco Romero, Coyoacán, Oct. 1741, AJM, leg. 92.

144. Auto of Jul. 19, 1759, AGI, México 1047.

145. Cabrera y Quintero, *Escudo de armas de México* (Mexico, 1746), bk. 1, chap. 6, par. 73; bk. 4, chap. 1, par. 786; quotation from bk. 1, chap. 6, par. 76.

146. Questionnaire and various testimonies dated 1739, AGI, México 663A.

147. Conde de Monterrey to the Council of the Indies, March, 1603, AGI, México 25.

148. Petition of the owners of obrajes of Querétaro [August 1802], AGI, México 1809.

149. Super, *La vida en Querétaro*, p. 77.

150. Inspection of the obraje of José Escandón, AGNM, Civil, vol. 1435, exp. 7.

151. I owe these data to Gabriel Haslip Viera. For the assumption of a minimum wage of 3 reales per day as the opportunity cost of labor, see the consulta written by Balthasar Ladrón de Guevara, México, Oct. 14, 1778, AGI, México 1387; report of José Mecía de la Cerda y Vargas et al., México, Apr. 19, 1752, AGI, México 1130.

152. Weavers probably made about 4 reales per day and were thought to be the best paid, according to José Martínez Moreno, AGNM, Civil, vol. 1418, exp. 19. The same opinion was offered in the report of Francisco Javier Gamboa et al., Cap. 87, México, May 31, 1765, AGI, México 1130. According to Michael

Scardaville, "Crime and the Urban Poor: Mexico City in the Late Colonial Period" (Ph.D. diss., Univ. of Florida, 1977), p. 66, unskilled and semiskilled workers in late colonial Mexico City could expect to earn between 2 and 4 reales per day. In essence, a skilled laborer, the weaver, made what a semiskilled worker did, the difference being the apparent cost of coercion.

153. Report of Francisco Javier Gamboa et al., Cap. 95, México, May 31, 1765, AGI, México 1130.

154. "Relación de los obrajes de paños que hay en este Reino . . . ," México, May 10, 1604, AGI, México 25.

155. O'Gorman, "Visita de los obrajes y haciendas . . . de Coyoacán," p. 57; report of Francisco Javier Gamboa et al., Cap. 87, México, May 31, 1765, AGI, México 1130.

156. AGNM, Hospital de Jesús, leg. 319, exp. 65.

157. Diego Antonio Fernández de la Madrid to the viceroy, México, Apr. 7, 1759, AGI, México 1047.

158. Petition of Pedro Lucio de Bantantula [Coyoacán 1739], AJM, leg. 92; petition of Antonio de Arvieto, México, Oct. 7, 1746, AJM, leg. 99; confession of Manuel de Candía, México, Jun. 14, 1757, AGNM, Tierras, vol. 2016.

159. Report of Francisco Javier Gamboa et al., Cap. 87, México, May 31, 1765, AGI, México 1130.

160. Diego Antonio Fernández de la Madrid to the viceroy, México, Apr. 7, 1759, AGI, México 1047.

161. Testimony of Antonio de Marmolejo, San Miguel el Grande, Oct. 18, 1758, AGI, México 1047.

162. Hans Pohl et al., "Aspectos sociales . . . de los obrajes textiles en Puebla," p. 44.

163. Petition of the owners of obrajes of Querétaro [August 1802], AGI, México 1809.

164. George W. Hilton, "The British Truck System in the Nineteenth Century," *Journal of Political Economy* 55 (1957): 237-56, provides a valuable discussion.

165. Alfred Marshall, *Principles of Economics*, 7th ed. (London, 1916), pp. 552-53.

166. Diego Antonio Fernández de la Madrid to the viceroy, México, Apr. 7, 1759, AGI, México 1047; petition of Balthasar de Sauto, México, Jul. 17, 1759, AGNM, Civil, vol. 880, exp. 2.

167. Humberto F. Burzio, *Diccionario de la moneda hispanoamericana*, 3 vols. (Santiago de Chile, 1958), 1: 70-71; Braudel, *Capitalism and Material Life*, p. 334.

168. Declaration of Juan Fernández de Albarea, Coyoacán, Feb. 9, 1690; and declaration of don Francisco Pereyra de Silva, Feb. 11, 1690, AGI, Contaduría 806, Ramo 3.

169. AGNM, Hospital de Jesús, leg. 308, exp. 4.

170. Consulta of Pedro Carlos de la [?], Coyoacán, Apr. 24, 1751, AGNM, Hospital de Jesús, leg. 308, exp. 4.

171. Auto of Jun. 26, 1756, AGNM, Tierras, vol. 2016, exp. 2.

172. Cf. Sherburne Cooke and Woodrow Borah, "Indian Food Production and Consumption in Central Mexico Before and After the Conquest (1500-1650), in their *Population History*, 3: 129-76.

173. Petition of the owners of obrajes of Querétaro, México, Sept. 9, 1801, AGI, México 1809; Brading, "Noticias sobre la economía de Querétaro," p. 285.

174. Hans Pohl et al., "Aspectos sociales . . . de los obrajes textiles en Puebla," p. 44.

175. Visitas to various Puebla obrajes in early 1700, Archivo de la Secretaría Municipal de Puebla, vol. 224: "Expediente sobre obrajes y talleres."

176. Diego Antonio Fernández de la Madrid to the viceroy, México, Apr. 7, 1759, AGI, México 1047.

177. Ibid.

178. Declaration of Antonio de la Torre, México, Jun. 11, 1757, AGNM, Tierras, vol. 2016, exp. 2.

179. Reconocimiento de José Márquez, México, Apr. 27, 1757, AGNM, Tierras, vol. 2016, exp. 2.

180. Hilton, "British Truck System," p. 251.

181. Representation of the deputies of the merchants of Querétaro to the visitor-general of New Spain, Querétaro, Feb. 16, 1768, AGI, México 2098.

182. A strong statement of the mobility thesis appears in Enrique Florescano, "Antecedents of the Mexican Independence Movement: Social Instability and Political Discord," in Robert Detweiler and Ramón Ruíz, eds., *Liberation in the Americas. Comparative Aspects of the Independence Movements in Mexico and the United States* (San Diego, 1978), pp. 73-74.

183. Borah, *Justice by Insurance*, pp. 109-19.

184. Severo Martínez Pelayo, *La patria del criollo. Ensayo de interpretación de la realidad colonial guatemalteca*, 8th ed. (San José, Costa Rica, 1981), p. 487.

185. The following discussion is drawn from Blas Brazil, "A History of the Obrajes of New Spain, 1535-1630" (M.A. thesis, Univ. of New Mexico, 1962), chaps. 4-6.

186. Don Juan de Miranda et al. to the Crown, México, Jul. 8, 1638, AGI, México 75; Konetzke, *Colección de documentos*, 2 (1): 335-36.

187. Report of Francisco Javier Gamboa et al., Cap. 27, México, May 31, 1765, AGI, México 1130.

188. "Extracto del expediente formado sobre lo ocurrido de resultas de una Real Cédula expedida el año de 1754 . . . ," AGI, México 1257.

189. In general, see AGI, México 1047.

190. Ventura Beleña, *Recopilación sumaria*, 2: 298-306.

191. The course of the ordinances of 1767 may be traced in the index to AGNM, Bandos, vols. 6, 11, 20. Iturrigaray's version is found in AGI, México 1809. Also see Iturrigaray to the Crown, México, Jan. 27, 1806, AGNM, Correspondencia de Virreyes, 2d ser., vol. 48.

192. John H. Parry, *The Spanish Seaborne Empire* (New York, 1966), p. 175.

A fine discussion of the legal dimension of this issue appears in Ordóñez y Chávez, "Lineamientos generales," in Soberanes Fernández, coord., *Memoria del II Congreso de Historia del Derecho Mexicano*, pp. 309-35.

193. Borah, *Justice by Insurance*, pp. 245-46.

194. Hipólito Villaroel, *México por dentro y fuera* (México, 1831), p. 135. In general, see the following: AGNM, Civil, vols. 1813, and 1871, exp. 6; AGI, México 1809, passim.

195. Petition of Andrés Martín, AGNM, Civil, vol. 1519, exp. 13.

196. Petition of the owners of obrajes of Querétaro [August 1802], AGI, México 1809.

197. Brading, "Notas sobre la economía de Querétaro," 287.

198. Septién y Septién, *Historia de Querétaro*, p. 205.

199. Salvucci, "Aspectos de un conflicto empresarial," 425.

200. Gilberto Miguel Hinojosa, *A Borderlands Town in Transition, Laredo, 1755-1870* (College Station, TX, 1983), pp. 4-5; G. Michael Riley, *Fernando Cortés and the Marquesado in Morelos, 1522-1547. A Case Study in the Socioeconomic Development of Sixteenth-Century Mexico* (Albuquerque, 1973), p. 50.

201. Parry, *Spanish Seaborne Empire*, p. 192.

CHAPTER FIVE

1. Bullock, *Six Months' Residence*, 1: 105.

2. H. G. Ward, *Mexico*, 2d ed., 2 vols. (London, 1829), 2: 183.

3. Hardy, *Travels in the Interior of Mexico*, p. 503.

4. W. Taylor to the secretary of state, Alvarado, Mar. 29, 1824, U.S. Dept of State, Consular Dispatches from Veracruz, Record Group 59, National Archives, Washington, D.C.

5. Brian Hamnett, "The Economic and Social Dimensions of the Revolution of Independence in Mexico, 1800-1824," *Ibero-Amerikanisches Archiv*, new ser., 6 (1980): 12.

6. Jan Bazant, "Evolution of the Textile Industry in Mexico, 1544-1845," *Comparative Studies in Society and History* 7 (1964/65): 59.

7. Diego Antonio Bermúdez de Castro, *Theatro Anglopolitano* (Puebla, 1764), pp. 69-70.

8. Woodrow Borah, *Early Colonial Trade and Navigation Between Mexico and Peru* (Berkeley, 1954), pp. 80-88.

9. For Puebla's output, I used "Relación de los obrajes que se hallaron en la ciudad de los Ángeles por el mes de Junio de [1597]," AGI, México 23. I converted pieces to varas using equivalences given in the "Relación" and produced estimates using current prices. I derived estimates of production in a similar manner.

10. Manuel Flon to the viceroy, Puebla, May 12, 1790, AGNM, Intendencias, vol. 48, exp. 2.

11. Cayetano Reyes G., "Hilanderos y tejedores de Santa Ana Chiautempan, Tlaxcala, 1674," *BAGN*, 3d ser., 1 (1977): 11-12.

12. "Relación de los obrajes de paños que hay en este Reino . . . ," México, May 10, 1604, AGI, México 26.

13. Calculated from the report of Pedro de la Bastida, México, Apr. 1, 1690, AGI, Contaduriá 806, Ramo 3.

14. "Relacíon de los paños que de ordinario se hacen en México . . . [1597]," AGI, México 1366.

15. José Castañares to the general administrator of the aduana of México, May 8, 1793, AGNM, Aduanas, vol. 134; Juan Navarro to the viceroy, Oct. 17, 1801, AGNM, Historia, vol. 122.

16. Petition of don Miguel González Calderón, México, Nov. 5, 1781, AGI, México 1283.

17. AGNM, Padrones, unnumbered volume, ms. census for cuartel no. 30, fs. 10v-11 (1811); AGNM, Civil, vol. 987, exp. 11.

18. For the estimate and its sources, see note 9 above. Since output was estimated on data from six obrajes when roughly twenty-five existed, doubling to estimate the total is conservative.

19. Francisco Pérez Navas to the council of the Indies, México, 1711, AGI, México 644.

20. "Relación de los obrajes de paños que hay en este Reino . . . ," México, May 10, 1604, AGI, México 26.

21. José León Peñarrojas to the general administrator of the aduana of México, Mar. 20, 1793, AGNM, Aduanas, vol. 134.

22. "Plan que manifiesta los obrajes que hay en los suelos del alcabalatorio de Acámbaro" (1793), AGNM, Alcabalas, vol. 37.

23. I computed these statistics using "profits" reported by the obrajes of Antonio de Sierra, Sancho de Posada, Juan Gómez de Castrejón, Antonia de Arce, Francisco de Ansaldo y Peralta, Pedro de Ávila, and Manuel Martínez. Profits were expressed in reales, divided by the price of paño (reported to be 14 to 16 reales per vara) and multiplied by a reported 60 varas per piece. See AGI, Contaduría 806, Ramo 3.

24. See Chapter Three, section on San Miguel.

25. Report of Julián Dávila, AGNM, Alcabalas, vol. 37.

26. Super, *La vida en Querétaro*, pp. 86-8; Septién, "Noticia sucincta de la ciudad de Querétaro," in Florescano and Gil Sánchez, eds., *Descripciones económicas regionales*, p. 47.

27. See the list of licenses for expansion of existing obrajes and the establishment of new ones between 1723 and 1749, produced by José de Gorraéz and Antonio Messa, both in 1759, AGNM, Civil, vol. 2296. Copies of these documents are also found in AGI, México 1275; Brian Hamnett, *Revolución y contrarevolución en México y el Perú. Liberalismo, realeza y separatismo (1800-1824)* (México, 1978), p. 153.

28. Cf. D.C.M. Platt, *Latin America and British Trade, 1806-1914* (New York, 1972), pp. 11-12.

29. Florescano, *Precios del maíz*, pp. 149-50.

30. Luis Chávez Orozco, *Cuadro de la situación económica novo-hispana en 1786* (México, 1934), pp. 67-68.

31. *Registro Oficial*, May 24, 1831.

32. Super, *La vida en Querétaro*, p. 89.

33. "Obrajes o fábricas de paño que hay . . . ," AGNM, Alcabalas, vol. 37. Subsequent descriptions of the trapiches are drawn from this source.

34. Peter Gerhard, *A Guide to the Historical Geography of New Spain* (Cambridge, Eng., 1971), p. 225; Septién, "Noticia sucincta de la ciudad de Querétaro," in Florescano and Gil Sánchez, eds., *Descripciones económicas regionales*, p. 61.

35. See, for example, "Lista de telares de angosto que cobró el Guarda don Agustín Lobato en todo Julio de 1803," Querétaro, Jul. 23, 1803, AGNM, Alcabalas, vol. 98; and "Lista de los telares de angosto que cobró el guarda don Juan Antonio Herrera en todo Agosto 1791," Querétaro, Aug. 31, 1971, AGNM, Aduanas, vol. 133.

36. Petition, "Tomás Magado Polanco [Puebla, n.d.], AGNM, Civil, vol. 477, exp. 5.

37. "Obrajes o fábricas que hay . . . ," AGNM, Alcabalas, vol. 37.

38. For example, Brading, *Miners and Merchants*, pp. 223-33.

39. Petition of Manuel de Ibarra, México, Mar. 10, 1753, AGNM, Tierras, vol. 677.

40. Testimony of Juan de Castañiza, Puebla, Apr. 29, 1749, AGNM, Tierras, vol. 697; Juan Pérez Cota y Madera to Bernabé Alcalde Romero, Puebla, Oct. 19, 1740, AJM, leg. 92.

41. López Cancelada, *Ruina de la Nueva España*, pp. 15-16.

42. Statement of Alonso Ruíz del Rey, México, Jan. 11, 1690, AGI, Contaduría 806, Ramo 3; memorials of Juan Pérez de Mata, Diego Muñoz, and Francisco Díaz de Posada, México, Apr. 29, 1690, AGNM, Civil, vol. 1435, exp. 1.

43. "Tablas Económicas" in Florescano and Gil Sánchez, eds., *Descripciones económicas generales*, p. 158; Mariano Fernández de Echeverría y Veytia, *Historia de la fundación de la ciudad de Puebla de los Ángeles . . .* , 2 vols., 2d ed. (1962), p. 301.

44. Juan Navarro to the viceroy, Oct. 17, 1801, AGNM, Historia, vol. 122.

45. The scattergrams are based on market prices collected from various documents in AGI, AGNM, AJM, and AJQ. The sources, too numerous to list, are available on request.

46. In their trends, the scattergrams closely parallel the movement of raw wool prices. The best series, which is unpublished and not available for reproduction, appears in Cecilia Andrea Rabell Romero, "Los diezmos de San Luis de la Paz. Economía de una región del Bajío en el siglo XVIII" (unpub. ms., 1984), p. 88.

47. Brading, "Historical Demography of Eighteenth-Century Mexico," p. 16.

48. Ramón María Serrera, "La ciudad de Santiago de Querétaro a finales del siglo XVIII: Apuntes para su historia," *Anuario de Estudios Americanos* 30 (1973): 497.

49. Villa Sánchez, *Puebla sagrada*, pp. 49-51, 54, 56-57. For distance from the sea and protection of industry, see Braudel, *The Mediterranean*, 1: 322.

50. Thomson, "Cotton Textile Industry in Puebla," pp. 7-8.

51. Quirós, "Memoria de Estatuto," in Florescano and Gil Sánchez, eds., *Descripciones económicas generales*, p. 244.

52. Sherburne F. Cook and Woodrow Borah, "Racial Groups in the Mexican Population Since 1519," in their *Essays in Population History*, 3 vols. (Berkeley, 1971-79), 2: 197.

53. Tenorio, *Algunas Mercancías*.

54. Lutgardo García Fuentes, *El comercio español con América, 1650-1700* (Seville, 1980), pp. 294-95; Henry Kamen, *Spain in the Later Seventeenth Century* (London, 1980), pp. 116-19, and *The War of the Succession in Spain, 1700-15* (Bloomington, IN, 1969), p. 146.

55. For 1739 through 1750, see "Razón individual de todo lo producido de Reales Alcabalas y demás derechos . . . con inclusión del dos por ciento . . . desde 15 de abril 1744," AGNM, Aduanas, vol. 7, f. 243; for 1756 through 1790, see Fabián de Fonseca and Carlos de Urrutia, *Historia general de real hacienda*, 5 vols. (México, 1845), vol. 2: "Productos que ha recibido la real aduana de México desde el año de 1754 hasta el de 90 en los ramos que se expresan."

56. For changes in the administration of the excise, see the memorial signed by Pedro de Vértiz et al., México, Jun. 15, 1781, AGNM, Alcabalas, vol. 401; more on the change and its effects on the obrajes appears in a letter of the audiencia gobernadora to the minister of the Indies, México, Apr. 26, 1785, AGI, México 1416.

57. The difficulties of enforcement appear in a letter of Felipe Cleere to the director of the Royal Excise, México, Dec. 10, 1792, AGNM, Aduanas, vol. 134.

58. Florescano, *Precios del maíz*, pp. 153-54.

59. The regression results (with t-statistics in parentheses) for 1739-80:

$$P = 461.71 + 21.19M - 3.25T + 86.8W - .0034S$$
$$(1.55) \quad (-.31) \quad (.63) \quad (-.12)$$

where
P = annual concertado payment
M = median yearly maize price
T = time index set to 0 in 1739
W = dummy variable for declared war
S = physical output of silver

$\bar{R}^2 = .035$
$D\text{-}W = 1.26$
$F(4,30) = 1.31$

The results for 1781 and after, allowing for the change in the excise:

$$P = 82932 + 8.25M - 1726.8T - 5893.5W - .7S$$
$$(.17) \quad (-.74) \quad (-.69) \quad (-.70)$$

$\bar{R}^2 = -1.35$
$D\text{-}W = 2.7$
$F(4,1) = .28$

Sources: M: Florescano, *Precios del maíz*, pp. 115-17; S: Coatsworth, "Colonial Absolutism," in Spalding, ed., *Colonial Latin America*, Appendix 2.

60. Florescano, *Precios del maíz*, pp. 187-88.

61. Cook and Borah, "Indian Food Production," in their *Essays in Population History*, p. 140, for possible short-term substitutes.

62. In 1737, for example, the owner Cayetano López in Mexico City asked a baker to whom he owed money to forestall collection of a debt, because thirty-five workers in his obraje had died and another forty-eight were in the hospital. The effect on output is obvious. See López to don José de la Barrera, México, Apr. 24, 1754, AJM, leg. 105.

63. Andrés Cavo, *Los tres siglos de México durante el gobierno español*, ed. Carlos María Bustamante (México, 1836), pp. 179-80, pars. 186, 188.

64. Kamen, *Spain in the Later Seventeenth Century*, p. 137.

65. Jonathan I. Israel, *The Dutch Republic and the Hispanic World, 1606-1661* (Oxford, 1982), pp. 38, 54-55; Philip Benedict, "Rouen's Foreign Trade During the Era of the Religious Wars (1560-1600)," *The Journal of European Economic History* 13 (1984): 33-34.

66. Kamen, *War of Succession*, p. 146; Antonio García-Baquero González, *Cádiz y el Atlántico (1717-1778)*, 2 vols. (Seville, 1976), 1: 121.

67. G. D. Ramsay, *The English Woollen Industry, 1500-1750* (London, 1982), pp. 36-38; D. C. Coleman, *The Economy of England 1450-1750* (Oxford, 1977), p. 141.

68. R. P. Thomas and D. N. McCloskey, "Overseas Trade and Empire, 1700-1860," in Roderick Floud and Donald McCloskey, eds., *The Economic History of Britain Since 1760*, 2 vols. (Cambridge, Eng., 1981), 1: 91; Stephen Alexander Fortune, *Merchants and Jews: The Struggle for British West Indian Commerce, 1650-1750* (Gainesville, 1984), p. 124.

69. Elizabeth Boody Schumpeter, *English Overseas Trade Statistics, 1697-1808* (Oxford, 1960). Printed cottons are given in Table 37 and stuffs in Table 44, which are the series employed here.

70. Director of the Aduana to Lucas de Palacio, México, Sept. 9, 1820; and consulado of Veracruz to the viceroy of New Spain, Veracruz, Sept. 17, 1819, both in AGNM, Consulado, vol. 2, exp. 1; representation of José Bernardo Baz et al. to the consulado of México, Aug. 25, 1819 [copy of a document of 1815]; and representation of the consulado of México to the viceroy, México, Aug. 21, 1815, both in AGNM, Alcabalas, vol. 364.

71. Harry E. Cross, "South American Bullion Production and Export, 1550-1750," in J. F. Richards, ed., *Precious Metals in the Later Medieval and Early Modern World* (Durham, NC, 1983), p. 420; John J. McCusker, *Money and Exchange in Europe and America, 1600-1775. A Handbook* (Chapel Hill, 1978), p. 7.

72. I will report only the final results. The regression for 1765-85, with t-statistics in parentheses, is:

$$C = -352636 + 34.07S + 8624.74W - 51.29P$$
$$(18.93) \qquad (1.16) \qquad (-9.36)$$

Where

    C = printed cottons exported to British West Indies
    S = physical output of silver
    W = dummy variable for declared war
    P = paño output measured by concertado payment

$F(3,1) = 171.81$
$\bar{R}^2 = .99$
$D\text{-}W = 2.5$

73. D. N. McCloskey, "The Industrial Revolution 1780-1860: A Survey," in Floud and McCloskey, eds., *Economic History of Britain*, pp. 110-11.

74. For these cédulas, see AGNM, Historia, vol. 44, exp. 25; see also the cédula of Dec. 5, 1720, AGNM, Reales Cédulas (originales), vol. 41.

75. The regression, with t-statistics in parentheses, is:

$$ST = 235489 + 33.03S + 52523.1M + 180535W - 106.47P$$
$$ (2.58) \qquad (.77) \qquad (2.61) \qquad (-1.77)$$

With variables as in notes 59 and 72 above, and M added for annual median maize price. St = Stuffs.

$F(4,5) = 2.365$
$\bar{R}^2 = .38$
$D\text{-}W = 1.565$

76. [Adam Anderson], *Anderson's Historical and Chronological Deduction of the Origin of Commerce . . . of the British Empire . . .* , 6 vols. (Dublin, 1790), 3: 421-22; Fortune, *Merchants and Jews*, pp. 114, 125, and more generally, Part 3.

77. Allan Christelow, "Contraband Trade Between Jamaica and the Spanish Main, and the Free Port Act of 1766," *HAHR* 22 (1942): 313.

78. Consulta of Genaro Garza, Oct. 17, 1798, AGI, Indiferente General 2466.

79. Juan Antonio de Cobián et al. to the consulado of Mexico City, Aug. 24, 1815; and representation of the consulado of Mexico City to the viceroy, Aug. 21, 1815, AGNM, Alcabalas, vol. 364.

80. John Fisher, *Commercial Relations Between Spain and Spanish America in the Era of Free Trade, 1778-1796* (Liverpool, 1985), p. 45.

81. Carlos Martínez Shaw, *Cataluña en la carrera de Indias* (Barcelona, 1981), p. 236; Fisher, *Commercial Relations*, p. 49.

82. Diego de Agreda to the viceroy, México, Jul. 12, 1791, "Informe reservado del oidor . . . don Eusebio Ventura Beleña . . . sobre el estado del comercio libre," Biblioteca Nacional, México, Ms. 1334.

83. Angel Puyade to the viceroy, México, n.d., "Informe reservado . . . sobre el estado del comercio libre," Biblioteca Nacional, México, Ms. 1334.

84. López Cancelada, *Ruina de la Nueva España*, pp. 26-27.

85. Guía No. 3, Veracruz, Apr. 4, 1791, AGNM, Aduanas, vol. 133; *Reglamento y aranceles para el comercio de España a Indias de 12 de Octubre de 1778*

(facsimile ed., Seville, 1978), p. 57; "Balance y reconocimiento judicial . . . 19 de Julio de 1796 . . . del difunto don Diego Ignacio Sáenz de Escobosa," AJM, leg. 193; "Informe que dieron los señores . . . Ruíz de la Barcena . . . Echabe . . . y Sáenz de Sicilia" (México, 1818), in Chávez Orozco, *La libertad del comercio*, pp. 132-201, par. 47.

86. "Informe que dieron los señores . . . Ruíz de la Barcena . . . Echabe . . . y Sáenz de Sicilia," in Chávez Orozco, *La libertad del comercio*, par. 47.

87. AGNM, Infidencias, vol. 184, exp. 17, f. 62v.

88. Mar. 7, 1798, Daybook of Sáenz de Escobosa, AJM, leg. 192.

89. "Relación de los efectos y frutos sobre las cuales recae el derecho de alcabala," AGNM, Aduanas, vol. 7, f. 68.

90. Brading, "Notas sobre la economía de Querétaro," p. 281.

91. Clemente de Apresa to the joint directors of the Royal Excise, Acámbaro, Apr. 30, 1781, AGNM, Alcabalas, vol. 521.

92. Quirós, "Memoria de Estatuto," in Florescano and Gil Sánchez, eds., *Descripciones económicas generalaes*, p. 244.

93. AHINAH, Actas de Cabildo de Querétaro (typescript), session of Jul. 4, 1811.

94. AHINAH, Jul. 8, 1811; Miguel Domínguez to the viceroy, Querétaro, Dec. 4, 1811, AGNM, Subdelegados, vol. 5.

95. AHINAH, Oct. 17, 1811.

96. Cf. Doris M. Ladd, *The Mexican Nobility at Independence, 1780-1826* (Austin, 1976), p. 116.

97. For these and the following statistics, see the breakdown of obrajes, working looms, and inventories in Querétaro in 1812, AGNM, Indiferente de Guerra, vol. 281-A, exp. 1; Miguel Domínguez to the viceroy, Querétaro, Dec. 4, 1811, AGNM, Subdelegados, vol. 5.

98. AGNM, Indiferente de Guerra, vol. 281-A, exp. 1.

99. Petition dated Feb. 1, 1812, AGNM, Indiferente de Guerra, vol. 281-A, exp. 1; Hamnett, "Independence in Mexico," pp. 18-19.

100. Primo, *Querétaro en 1822*, p. 40.

101. *Registro Oficial*, May 21, 1831.

102. *Registro Oficial*, May 24, 1831.

103. Ibid.

104. Ladd, *Mexican Nobility*, pp. 135-40.

105. María Cristina Urrutia de Stebelski and Guadalupe Nava Oteo, "La minería (1821-1880)," in Cardoso, ed., *México en el siglo XIX*, pp. 119-21.

106. Harold Sims, *Descolonización en México. El conflicto entre mexicanos y españoles (1821-31)* (México, 1982), pp. 223-24, and *La expulsión de los españoles de México (1821-28)* (México, 1974), pp. 246-52; Luis Chávez Orozco, *La guerra de independencia y el crédito agrícola* (México, 1953), p. 43; Harris, *Mexican Family Empire*, pp. 116, 120, 122, 231-32, 255.

107. Landes, *Unbound Prometheus*, p. 233.

108. México, Congreso, Comisiones de hacienda y comercio unidas, *Dicta-*

men de las comisiones unidas de hacienda y comercio sobre prohibiciones de efectos (México, 1824), p. 4.

109. *Dictamen de la comisión de industria de la cámara de diputados sobre el nuevo arbitrio . . . para proporcionar . . . ocupación y medias de subsistir a la clase de gentes pobres de la república mexicana* (México, 1829), p. 5.

110. *Representación del exmo. ayuntamiento de la capital de Puebla al soberano congreso general* (Puebla, 1836), pp. 5, 7, 8.

111. "Nota estadística que . . . se remite por el gobernador del estado de Puebla," in *Gaceta del gobierno supremo de la federación mexicana*, Jun. 20, 1826.

112. *Libro de actas del honorable congreso del estado de Jalisco (1 de enero–31 de mayo de 1824)* (Guadalajara, 1975), p. 196; also Muriá, *Historia de Jalisco*, 2: 495.

113. *Memoria sobre el estado actual . . . del estado de Jalisco . . . 1o de febrero de 1826* (Guadalajara, 1974), p. 20.

114. Primo, *Querétaro en 1822*, pp. 29-30.

115. "Discurso dirigido al honorable congreso constituyente del estado libre de Querétaro . . . el día 17 de febrero de 1824," in *Gaceta del gobierno supremo de la federación mexicana*, Feb. 24, 1824.

116. For a good sampling, see Córdova, ed., *Protección y libre cambio*.

117. Potash, *Banco de Avío*, pp. 13-14; John E. Baur, "The Evolution of a Mexican Foreign Trade Policy, 1821-1828," *The Americas* 19 (1963): 239-40; Carlos J. Sierra and Rogelio Martínez Vera, *Historia y legislación aduanera de México* (México, 1973), pp. 13-39.

118. Potash, *Banco de Avío*, pp. 19-20; Baur, "Mexican Foreign Trade Policy," p. 241.

119. Taylor to the secretary of state, Veracruz, Jan. 10, 1827, National Archives, RG 59.

120. Potash, *Banco de Avío*, pp. 25, 30-32.

121. Luis Chávez Orozco, "La industria de transformación mexicana (1821-1910)," *Memorias de la Academia Mexicana de la Historia* 27 (1968): 103.

122. Testimony of Mr. William Graham, Jun. 28, 1833, "Report of the Select Committee on Manufacturing, Commerce, and Shipping" (1833), in the Irish University Press Series of British Parliamentary Papers. Report from the Select Committee on Manufactures, Commerce, and Shipping with Minutes of Evidence, Appendix and Index, *Industrial Revolution. Trade* (Shannon, 1968).

123. Bullock, *Six Months' Residence*, 1: 216.

124. Chávez Orozco, *Guerra de independencia*, p. 43, for an alternative estimate of textile output.

125. Richard J. Salvucci, "Aspects of United States–Mexico Trade, 1825-80: A Preliminary Survey" (unpub. ms., 1986). In 1825, about 85 percent of American exports to Mexico by value were reexports. The proportion did not fall below 50 percent until the 1840s. American trade with Mexico between 1825 and 1835 was essentially entrepot trade.

126. Mark Bils, "Tariff Protection and Production in the Early U.S. Cotton Industry," *JEH* 44 (1984): 1033, 1045.

127. Potash, *Banco de Avío*, pp. 31-32.

128. Computed from Marcello Carmagnani, "Finanze e stato in Messico, 1820-80," *Nova Americana* 5 (1982): 210.

129. Potash, *Banco de Avío*, p. 48.

130. *The Concise Oxford Dictionary of Quotations*, 2d ed. (Oxford, 1981), p. 102.

Epilogue

1. *The Wealth of Nations*, bk. 1, chap. 1.

2. Richard S. Eckaus, "The Factor Proportions Problem in Underdeveloped Areas," *American Economic Review* 45 (1955): 539-65.

3. H. G. Ward, *México en 1827* (México, 1981), bk. 5, sections 2 and 3.

4. Michael P. Costeloe, *La primera república federal de México (1824-35)* (Mexico, 1975), pp. 206-8, 216; Josefina Zoraida Vázquez, "Los primeros tropiezos," in *Historia general de México*, 4 vols. (México, 1976), 2: 22-23.

5. Platt, *Latin America and British Trade*, pp. 13-20.

6. Jan de Vries, *The Dutch Rural Economy in the Golden Age, 1500-1700* (New Haven, 1974), pp. 4-10.

7. Claude Bataillon, *Las regiones geográficas en México*, 7th ed. (México, 1985), pp. 180-82.

8. Carlos Sempat Assadourian, *El sistema de la economía colonial. Mercado interno. Regiones y espacios económicos* (Lima, 1982), p. 201; Javier Ortiz de la Tabla, "El obraje colonial ecuatoriano. Aproximación a su estudio," *Revista de Indias* 37 (1977): 506.

9. Sempat Assadourian, *El sistema*, pp. 22-25.

10. Miriam Salas de Coloma, *De los obrajes de Canaria y Chincheros a las comunidades indígenas de Vilcashuaman. Siglo XVI* (Lima, 1979), p. 121; Steve Stern, *Peru's Indian Peoples and the Challenge of Spanish Conquest. Huamanga to 1640* (Madison, 1982), pp. 84-85, 108-11.

11. Sempat Assadourian, *El sistema*, p. 206; Magnus Mörner, *Perfil de la sociedad rural de Cuzco a fines de la colonia* (Lima, 1978), p. 82; Ortiz de la Tabla, "El obraje colonial ecuatoriano," pp. 506-7.

12. Mörner, *Sociedad rural del Cuzco*, pp. 82-83.

13. Robson Brines Tyrer, "The Demographic and Economic History of the Audiencia of Quito: Indian Population and the Textile Industry, 1600-1800" (Ph.D. diss., Univ. of California, Berkeley, 1976), pp. 97, 161-62; Ortiz de la Tabla, "El obraje colonial ecuatoriano," pp. 506-7, 531; Sempat Assadourian, *El sistema*, pp. 201-2.

14. Sempat Assadourian, *El sistema*, p. 207.

15. Tulio Halperín-Donghi, *Politics, Economics, and Society in Argentina in the Revolutionary Period* (Cambridge, Eng., 1975), pp. 89-91.

16. Charles Milner Ricketts to George Canning, Lima, Dec. 27, 1826, FO 61/

8, in Heraclio Bonilla, comp., *Gran Bretaña y el Perú: informes de los cónsules Británicos, 1826-1919*, 5 vols. (Lima, 1975), 1: 19.

17. Ibid., p. 39.

18. Heraclio Bonilla, Lía del Río, and Pilar Ortiz de Zevallos, "Comercio libre y crisis de la economía andina: El caso del Cuzco," *Histórica* 2 (1978): 1-25, a major contribution to the debate.

19. Amiya Kumar Bagchi, "Deindustrialization in India in the Nineteenth Century: Some Theoretical Implications," *Journal of Development Studies* 12 (1976): 153.

20. For the "structuralist" view, see Gerald M. Meier, *Emerging from Poverty. The Economics that Really Matters* (New York, 1984), pp. 132, 135, 184-85.

21. *Report of the Secretary of Finance of the United States of Mexico of the 15th of January, 1879 on the Actual Condition of Mexico, and the Increase of Commerce with the United States* . . . (New York, 1880), pp. 184-85; Potash, *Banco de Avío*, p. 16, offers an alternate translation.

22. Antonio de María Campos, *Económica política en Mégico. Contestación a D. Carlos de Landa, sobre comercio libre* (Puebla, 1844).

23. Coatsworth, *Growth Against Development*, pp. 121-47.

24. Salvucci, "Aspects of United States–Mexico Trade, 1825-80."

25. Manuel Toussaint, *Arte colonial en México*, 4th ed. (México, 1983), pp. 147, 155-56.

26. Mathias, *First Industrial Nation*, pp. 56-57.

27. Shane Hunt, "The Economics of Haciendas and Plantations in Latin America" (unpub ms., 1972).

28. David A. Brading, *Prophecy and Myth in Mexican History* (Cambridge, Eng., 1984), p. 65.

29. Ross Hassig, *Trade, Tribute, and Transportation. The Sixteenth-Century Political Economy of the Valley of Mexico* (Norman, OK, 1985), p. 247.

30. Nigel Davies, *The Ancient Kingdoms of Mexico* (Middlesex, Eng., 1983), pp. 108-9, 117-18.

31. Hassig, *Trade, Tribute, and Transportation*, pp. 56-66, 274.

32. See, for example, the lengthy exchange between Jerome Offner and Pedro Carrasco in *American Antiquity* 46 (1981): 43-74.

33. Cf. Nancy M. Farriss, *Maya Society Under Colonial Rule. The Collective Enterprise of Survival* (Princeton, 1984), pp. 49-51.

Appendix

1. Manuel Carrera Stampa, "The Evolution of Weights and Measures in New Spain," *HAHR* 29 (1949): 2-24; Charles P. Kindleberger, "Standards as Public, Collective, and Private Goods," *Kyklos* 36 (1983): 377-96.

2. Statement of Bernardo Alcalde Romero, México, Oct. 4, 1740, AJM, leg. 92; José Pérez Becerra to the Directors of the Royal Excise, Querétaro, Aug. 25, 1780, AGNM, Aduanas, vol. 76, exp. 2, and the Directors' reply; see also "Obrajes o fábricas de paños burdos que hay . . . ," AGNM, Alcabalas, vol. 37.

3. Records of the composition of obrajes (1690), AGI, Contaduría 806, Ramo 3; "Relación de los obrajes que se hallaron en la ciudad de los Ángeles . . . ," and "Relación de los paños que de ordinario se hacen en México . . . ," both in AGI, México 23; for "Santa Ana Pacueco" see AGNM, Aduanas, vol. 44; and Luis Fernández Romero to the intendant of Guanajuato, Acámbaro, Sept. 23, 1800, AGNM, Civil, vol. 1682, exp. 3.

BIBLIOGRAPHY

ARCHIVAL SOURCES

Mexico

Archivo del Antiguo Ayuntamiento, México DF
  Real Audiencia, Fiel Ejecutoría, Inventario de Causas, vol. 3786
Archivo del Ayuntamiento de Querétaro
  Cabildo Sessions, bk. 3
Archivo General de la Nación, México, DF [all numbered by volume unless otherwise noted]
  Aduanas 7, 11, 13, 15, 23, 44, 67, 71, 76, 133, 134, 149
  Alcabalas 23, 37, 44, 98, 103, 105, 165, 177, 183, 205, 364, 382, 383, 401, 521
  Alcaldes Mayores 1
  Bandos 6, 11, 18, 20
  Civil 4, 76, 86, 87, 178, 188, 218, 220, 223, 234, 355, 477, 601, 820, 872, 880, 893, 918, 919, 987, 1359, 1418, 1435, 1519, 1526, 1531, 1628, 1674, 1682, 1689, 1712, 1735, 1742, 1795, 1813, 1871, 2046, 2085, 2296
  Consulado 2
  Correspondencia de Virreyes, 2d ser: 7, 12, 48
  Criminal 230, 880
  Historia 74, 122
  Hospital de Jesús [legajo] 302, 308, 319, 350
  Impresos Oficiales 5
  Indiferente de Guerra, 35-A, 281-A
  Indios 45, 63
  Industria 8
  Infidencias 184
  Inquisición 912
  Intendencias 48
  Media Anata 19
  Mercedes 81
  Padrones 6, 12, 39, 105, unnumbered volume with cuartel no. 30, 1811 census
  Reales Cédulas (Originales) 41
  Registro de Fianzas 4
  Subdelegados 5, 34
  Tierras 260, 261, 440, 578, 667, 676, 677, 680, 681, 686, 687, 697, 698, 813, 856, 932, 1034, 1181, 2009, 2015, 2016, 2738
Archivo Histórico de Hacienda, México, DF
  [leg.] 664-26

Archivo Histórico del Instituto Nacional de Antropología e Historia, México, DF
    Actas de Cabildo de Querétaro (typescript), 1811-13
    F.L. 97, 105, 116, 120, 122, 129, 150
Archivo Judicial de Jurisdicciones y Distritos Federales, México, DF
    [leg./sección "Civil"] 62, 71, 92, 99, 100, 101, 105, 106, 115, 124, 128, 146, 148, 167, 179, 192, 193
    [leg./sección "Concursos"] concurso de acreedores, Casa de Oteyza y Vértiz
Archivo Judicial, Puebla [Centro Regional Puebla-Tlaxcala, Instituto Nacional de Antropología e Historia]
    [leg./decade] 1730
Archivo Judicial, Querétaro
    [leg./"Civiles": decade] 1722, 1730
Archivo de Notarías, México, DF [by notary]
    Manuel Agustín López
    Manuel López de la Palma
    Ignacio José Montes de Oca
    José Pérez Cancio
    Eugenio Pozo
    Francisco Valdés
Archivo Parroquial del Sagrario, México, DF
    Libro de Difuntos Españoles, 24
Archivo de la Secretaría Municipal de Puebla
    [vol.] 221, 224
Biblioteca Nacional, México, DF
    Ms. 1334
Biblioteca Pública del Estado de Jalisco, Fondos Especiales
    Audiencia de Guadalajara: Ramo Judicial, Civil "Autos de la tropa que fue a México para obrajes el año pasado de 1722 . . ."

Spain

Archivo General de Indias, Seville
    Contaduría [leg./ramo] 806/3
    Cuba [leg.] 1506B
    Escribanía de Cámara [leg.] 196-A
    Indiferente General [leg.] 107, 2466
    México [leg.] 23, 25, 26, 71, 75, 132B, 209B, 412, 487, 644, 663A, 693B, 1047, 1130, 1257, 1275, 1283, 1328, 1366, 1387, 1416, 1809, 2098, 2372

United States

National Archives and Records Service, Washington, D.C.
    Record Group 59
New York Public Library, New York, NY
    Obadiah Rich Collection, item nos. 9, 45

Spanish Archives of New Mexico, Santa Fe, NM
  TW 559
Rosenbach Museum and Library, Philadelphia, PA
  Tlaxcala, Guild of Cotton Weavers
    462/25 pt. 15: #1, 3
    462/25 pt. 2: #6

PRINTED PRIMARY SOURCES

Actas Constitucionales Mexicanas (1821-1824). 10 vols. México, 1980.
Anderson, Adam. *Anderson's Historical and Chronological Deduction of the Origin of Commerce . . . of the British Empire. . . .* 6 vols. Dublin, 1790.
Beaufoy, Mark. *Mexican Illustrations*. London, 1828.
Bermúdez de Castro, Diego Antonio. *Theatro Anglopolitano*. Puebla, 1764.
Bonilla, Heraclio, comp. *Gran Bretaña y el Perú: informes de los cónsules Británicos, 1826-1919*. 5 vols. Lima, 1975.
Brading, David. "Notas sobre la economía de Querétaro y de su corregidor don Miguel Domínguez, 1802-1811," *Boletín del Archivo General de la Nación*, 2d ser., 11 (1970): 273-318.
Bullock, William. *Six Months' Residence and Travels in Mexico. . . .* 2 vols. London, 1825.
Cabrera y Quintero, Cayetano. *Escudo de armas de México*. México, 1746.
Campos, Antonio de María. *Económica política en México. Contestación a D. Carlos de Landa, sobre comercio libre*. Puebla, 1844.
Castañeda, Carmen. "Sobre una fábrica textil u obraje establecido en Guadalajara en el siglo XVIII," *Boletín del Archivo Histórico de Jalisco* 4 (1980): 13-16.
Cavo, Andrés. *Los tres siglos de México durante el gobierno español*. Edited by Carlos María Bustamente. México, 1836.
Chávez Orozco, Luis. *Cuadro de la situación económica novo-hispana en 1786*. México, 1934.
―――. *La guerra de independencia y el crédito agrícola*. México, 1953.
―――, ed. *La libertad del comercio en la Nueva España en la segunda década del siglo XIX*. México, 1943.
Chávez Orozco, Luis, and Enrique Florescano, eds. *Agricultura e industria textil de Veracruz. Siglo XIX*. Jalapa, 1965.
Córdova, Luis, ed. *Protección y libre cambio: el debate entre 1821 y 1836*. México, 1971.
Dictamen de la comisión de industria de la cámara de diputados sobre el nuevo arbitrio . . . para proporcionar . . . ocupación y medias de subsistir a la clase de gentes pobres de la república mexicana. México, 1829.
Dictamen de las comisiones unidas de hacienda y comercio sobre prohibiciones de efectos. México, 1824.
Donnan, Elizabeth, ed. *Documents Illustrative of the History of the Slave Trade to America*. 4 vols. Washington, D.C., 1930-35.

Fernández de Echeverría y Veytia, Mariano. *Historia de la fundación de la ciudad de Puebla de los Ángeles.* . . . 2 vols., 2d ed. Puebla, 1962.

Florescano, Enrique, and Isabel Gil Sánchez, eds. *Descripciones económicas generales de Nueva España, 1784-1817.* México, 1973.

—————. *Descripciones económicas regionales de Nueva España. Provincias del centro, surdeste, y sur, 1765-1827.* México, 1976.

Fonseca, Fabián de, and Carlos de Urrutia. *Historia general de real hacienda.* 5 vols. México, 1845.

Gaceta del gobierno supremo de la federación mexicana. 1824-26.

Hacienda y Crédito Público, Secretaría de, and Nacional Financiera, S.A. *Documentos para el estudio de la industrialización en México, 1837-45.* México, 1977.

Hardy, R. W., *Travels in the Interior of Mexico in 1825, 1826, 1827, and 1828.* London, 1829.

Herrera Canales, Inés. *Estadística del comercio exterior de México (1821-75).* México, 1980.

Humboldt, Alexander von. *Political Essay on the Kingdom of New Spain.* 4 vols. London, 1811-14.

Konetzke, Richard. *Colección de documentos para la historia de la formación social de Hispanoamérica, 1493-1810.* 3 vols. in 5 parts. Madrid, 1953-62.

Libro de actas del honorable congreso del estado de Jalisco (1 de enero–31 de mayo de 1824). Guadalajara, 1975.

López Cancelada, Juan. *Ruina de la Nueva España si se declara el comercio libre.* Cádiz, 1811.

Memoria de la Secretaría de Estado y del despacho de Relaciones Interiores e Exteriores. México, 1832.

Memoria sobre el estado actual . . . del estado de Jalisco . . . 1o de febrero de 1826. Guadalajara, 1974.

Morfi, Juan Agustín de. *Viaje de indios y diario de Nuevo México.* México, 1935.

Navarrete, Francisco Antonio. *Relación peregrina de la agua corriente . . . de Santiago de Querétaro.* México, 1739.

O'Gorman, Edmundo. "Visita de los obrajes y haciendas de la jurisdicción de la villa de Coyoacán (1660)," *Boletín del Archivo General de la Nación,* 1st ser., 11 (1940): 33-116.

Ortega y Pérez Gallardo, Ricardo. *Historia genealógica de las familias más antiguas de México.* México, 1910.

Pérez Velasco, Antonio. *Elogio histórico del señor don Juan Antonio del Castillo y Llata.* México, 1818.

Poinsett, J. R. *Notes on Mexico Made in the Autumn of 1822.* . . . London, 1822.

Primo, Pedro Telmo. *Querétaro en 1822. Informe.* México, 1944.

Registro Oficial. 1831.

Reglamento y aranceles para el comercio de España a Indias de 12 de Octubre de 1778. Facsimile ed. Seville, 1978.

BIBLIOGRAPHY

Report of the Secretary of Finance of the United States of Mexico of the 15th of January, 1879 on the Actual Condition of Mexico, and the Increase of Commerce with the United States. . . . New York, 1880.

Representación del exmo. Ayuntamiento de la capital de Puebla al soberano congreso general. Puebla, 1836.

Revillagigedo, Conde de. *Instrucción reservada al Marqués de Branciforte [1794].* México, 1966.

———. "Notable carta reservada," *Boletín del Archivo General de la Nación,* 1 (1930): 190-211, and 2 (1931): 196-211.

Reyes G. Cayetano. "Hilanderos y tejedores de Santa Ana Chiautempan, Tlaxcala, 1674" *Boletín del Archivo General de la Nación,* 3d ser., 1 (1977): 11-12.

Rubio Mañé, J. Ignacio. "Alcaldes ordinarios y procuradores de la villa de San Miguel el Grande, 1700-1785," *Boletín del Archivo General de la Nación,* 2d ser., 2 (1961): 375-92.

———. "Gente de España en la ciudad de México. Año de 1689," *Boletín del Archivo General de la Nación,* 2d ser., 7 (1966): 5-406.

———. "Informes del estado económico y social de la villa de San Miguel el Grande, año de 1754," *Boletín del Archivo General de la Nación,* 2d ser., 2 (1961): 355-74.

San Miguel el Grande [ca. 1777]. México, 1950.

United Kingdom, *Parliamentary Papers,* vol. 2.

Ventura Beleña, Eusebio. *Recopilación sumaria de todos los autos acordados de la Real Audiencia. . . .* 2 vols. México, 1787.

Villaroel, Hipólito. *México por dentro y fuera.* México, 1831.

Villa Sánchez, Juan. *Puebla sagrada y profana. Informe dado a su muy ilustre ayuntamiento en el año de 1746.* Puebla, 1835.

Villaseñor y Sánchez, Antonio. *Theatro Americano.* 2 vols. México, 1746-48.

Ward, H. G. *México en 1827.* México, 1981.

———. *Mexico.* 2d ed. 2 vols. London, 1829.

SECONDARY SOURCES

The items listed are essentially those cited in the text. Additional ones on the textile industry have been included for those wishing to read further.

Aguirre Beltrán, Gonzalo. "El trabajo del indio comparado con el del negro en Nueva España," *México Agrario* 4 (1942): 203-7.

Alatriste, Oscar. *Desarrollo de la industria y la comunidad minera de Hidalgo del Parral durante la segunda mitad del siglo XVIII.* México, 1983.

Alchian, Armen. *Economic Forces at Work. Selected Works by Armen A. Alchian.* Indianapolis, 1977.

Altman, Ida, and James Lockhart, eds. *Provinces of Early Mexico.* (Los Angeles, 1976.

Anawalt, Patricia. "Costume and Control: Aztec Sumptuary Laws," *Archaeology* 33 (1980): 33-43.

Anderson, Rodney D. *Guadalajara a la consumación de la Independencia: Estudio de su población según los padrones de 1821-1822.* Guadalajara, 1983.

"Apuntes estadísticos que escribió el Sr. D. J. Francisco Bustamante relativo al departamento de Querétaro," *Boletín de la sociedad mexicana de geografía y estadística* 7 (1859): 534-44.

Aracil, Rafael. "El treball tèxtil. Per una história de la societat pagesa tradicional: Les formes de treball (XI)," *L'Avenç* [Barcelona], 41 (1981): 45-51.

Archer, Christon. *The Army in Bourbon Mexico, 1760-1810.* Albuquerque, 1977.

Arcila Farías, Eduardo. *Comercio entre Venezuela y México en los siglos XVII y XVIII.* México, 1950.

————. *Reformas económicas del siglo XVIII en Nueva España.* 2 vols. México, 1974.

Báez Macías, Eduardo. "Planos y censos de la ciudad de México, 1753," *Boletín del Archivo General de la Nación,* 2d ser., 8 (1967): 487-1115.

Bagchi, Amiya Kumar. "Deindustrialization in India in the Nineteenth Century: Some Theoretical Implications," *Journal of Development Studies* 12 (1976): 135-64.

Bakewell, Peter J. *Silver Mining and Society in Colonial Mexico, Zacatecas 1546-1700.* Cambridge, Eng., 1971.

Bataillon, Claude. *Las regiones geográficas en México.* 7th ed. México, 1985.

Bauer, Arnold J. "The Church and the Economy of Spanish America: Censos and Depósitos in the Eighteenth and Nineteenth Centuries," *Hispanic American Historical Review* 63 (1983): 707-33.

————. "The Church and Spanish American Agrarian Structure, 1765-1865," *The Americas* 28 (1971): 78-98.

Baur, John E. "The Evolution of a Mexican Foreign Trade Policy, 1821-1828," *The Americas* 19 (1963): 225-61.

Bazant, Jan. "Evolution of the Textile Industry in Puebla, 1544-1845," *Comparative Studies in Society and History* 7 (1964/65): 55-69.

Benedict, Burton. "Family Firms in Economic Development," *Southwestern Journal of Anthropology* 24 (1968): 1-19.

Benedict, Philip. "Rouen's Foreign Trade During the Era of the Religious Wars (1560-1600)," *The Journal of European Economic History* 13 (1984): 29-74.

Bils, Mark. "Tariff Protection and Production in the Early U.S. Cotton Industry," *Journal of Economic History* 44 (1984): 1033-45.

Blaug, Mark. *Economic Theory in Retrospect.* 3d ed. Cambridge, Eng., 1978.

Blouet, Brian W., and Olwyn M. Blouet, eds. *Latin America. An Introductory Survey.* New York, 1982.

Bonilla, Heraclio, Lía del Río, and Pilar Ortiz de Zevallos. "Comercio libre y crisis de la economía andina: El caso de Cuzco," *Histórica* 2 (1978): 1-25.

Borah, Woodrow. *Early Colonial Trade and Navigation between Mexico and Peru.* Berkeley, 1954.

————. "El Status Jurídico de los Indios en Nueva España," *America Indígena* 45 (1985): 257-76.

————. *Justice by Insurance. The General Indian Court of Colonial Mexico and the Legal Aides of the Half-Real.* Berkeley, 1983.

————. "Race and Class in Mexico," *Pacific Historical Review* 23 (1954): 331-42.

Borcherding, Thomas E., and Eugene Silberberg. "Shipping the Good Apples Out: The Alchian and Allen Theorem Reconsidered," *Journal of Political Economy* 86 (1978): 131-38.

Brading, David A. *Haciendas and Ranchos in the Mexican Bajío: León, 1700-1860.* Cambridge, Eng., 1978.

————. "The Historical Demography of Eighteenth-Century Mexico: A Review," *Bulletin of the Society of Latin American Studies*, no. 25 (1976): 3-17.

————. "Los españoles en México hacia 1792," *Historia Mexicana* 23 (1973): 126-44.

————. *Miners and Merchants in Bourbon Mexico, 1763-1810.* Cambridge, Eng., 1971.

————. *Prophecy and Myth in Mexican History.* Cambridge, Eng., 1984.

————, and Harry E. Cross. "Colonial Silver Mining: Mexico and Peru," *Hispanic American Historical Review* 52 (1972): 545-79.

Braudel, Fernand. *Capitalism and Material Life, 1400-1800.* New York, 1973.

————. *The Mediterranean and the Mediterranean World in the Age of Philip II.* 2 vols. New York, 1972.

Bronson, J. *The Domestic Manufacturer's Assistant . . . in the Arts of Weaving and Dyeing . . . in the Manufacture of Cotton and Woolen Goods.* Utica, NY, 1817.

Burkholder, Mark A., and D. S. Chandler. *From Impotence to Authority. The Spanish Crown and the American Audiencias, 1687-1808.* Columbia, MO, 1977.

Burzio, Humberto F. *Diccionario de la moneda hispanoamericana.* 3 vols. Santiago de Chile, 1958.

Calderón Quijano, Antonio, ed. *Los virreyes de Nueva España en el reinado de Carlos III.* 2 vols. Seville, 1967-68.

Carabarín García, Alberto. *El trabajo y los trabajadores del obraje en la ciudad de Puebla, 1700-1710.* Puebla, 1984.

Cárdenas, Enrique. "Algunas cuestiones sobre la depresión mexicana del XIX," *Historia económica y social de America Latina* 3 (1984): 3-22.

Cardoso, Ciro, ed. *México en el siglo XIX (1821-1910). Historia económica y de la estructura social.* México, 1983.

Carmagnani, Marcello. "Finanze e stato in Messico, 1820-80," *Nova Americana* 5 (1982): 175-213.

Carrera Stampa, Manuel. "El obraje novo-hispano," *Memorias de la Academia Mexicana de la Historia* 20 (1961): 148-71.

————. "The Evolution of Weights and Measures in New Spain," *Hispanic American Historical Review* 29 (1949): 2-24.

Chandler, Alfred D., Jr. *The Visible Hand. The Managerial Revolution in American Business.* Cambridge, MA, 1977.

Chapman, S. D. *The Cotton Industry in the Industrial Revolution.* London, 1972.

Chaunu, Pierre. *La españa de Carlos v.* 2 vols. Barcelona, 1976.

————. *Sevilla y América. Siglos XVI y XVII.* Seville, 1983.

Chávez Orozco, Luis. *Historia económica y social de México.* México, 1938.

————. "La industria de transformación mexicana (1821-1910)," *Memorias de la Academia Mexicana de la Historia* 27 (1968): 102-6, 219-24.

Chevalier, François. *Land and Society in Colonial Mexico. The Great Hacienda.* Berkeley, 1963.

Christelow, Allan. "Contraband Trade Between Jamaica and the Spanish Main, and the Free Port Act of 1766," *Hispanic American Historical Review* 22 (1942): 309-43.

Cipolla, Carlo M. *Before the Industrial Revolution. European Society and Economy, 1000-1700.* New York, 1976.

Clarke, Richard N. "Scale Economies, Entry, and Welfare," *Journal of Economics and Business* 36 (1984): 161-76.

Cline, Howard F., ed. *Latin American History. Essays on Its Study and Teaching, 1898-1965.* 2 vols. Austin, 1967.

Coatsworth, John H. *Growth Against Development. The Economic Impact of Railroads in Porfirian Mexico.* DeKalb, IL, 1981.

Collier, George A., Renato I. Rosaldo, and John D. Wirth, eds. *The Inca and Aztec States, 1400-1800. Anthropology and History.* New York, 1982.

Colón Reyes, Linda Ivette. "La manufactura textil mexicana antes de la fundación del Banco de Avío (1830)," *Revista Mexicana de Ciencias Políticas y Sociales* 21 (1976): 9-70.

Cook, Alicia Skinner. "India's Working Children," *Horizons* [Agency for International Development] 3 (1984): 24-27.

Cook, Sherburne F., and Woodrow Borah. *Essays in Population History.* 3 vols. Berkeley, 1971-79.

Cooper, J. P., ed. *The Decline of Spain and the Thirty Years' War, 1609-48/59 (Volume 4 of The New Cambridge Modern History).*

Cordry, Donald, and Dorothy Cordry. *Mexican Indian Costumes.* Austin, 1968.

Costeloe, Michael P. *La primera república federal de México (1824-35).* México, 1975.

Crosby, Alfred W., Jr. *The Columbian Exchange. Biological and Cultural Consequences of 1492.* Westport, CT, 1972.

Curtin, Philip. *Cross-Cultural Trade in World History.* Cambridge, Eng., 1984.

Davies, Nigel. *The Ancient Kingdoms of Mexico.* Middlesex, Eng., 1983.

Detweiler, Robert, and Ramón Ruíz, eds. *Liberation in the Americas. Comparative Aspects of the Independence Movements in Mexico and the United States.* San Diego, 1978.

de Vries, Jan. *The Dutch Rural Economy in the Golden Age, 1500-1700*. New Haven, 1974.

Dusenberry, William H. *The Mexican Mesta. The Administration of Ranching in Colonial Mexico*. Urbana, IL, 1963.

Eckaus, Richard S. "The Factor Proportions Problem in Underdeveloped Areas," *American Economic Review* 45 (1955): 539-65.

Encyclopaedia of the Social Sciences. New York, 1937.

Engerman, Stanley L. "Some Considerations Relating to Property Rights in Man," *Journal of Economic History* 33 (1973): 43-65.

Evans, Robert. "Some Notes on Coerced Labor," *Journal of Economic History* 30 (1970): 861-66.

Farriss, Nancy M. *Maya Society Under Colonial Rule. The Collective Enterprise of Survival*. Princeton, 1984.

Fenolatea, Stefano. "Slavery and Supervision in Comparative Perspective: A Model," *The Journal of Economic History* 44 (1984): 635-68.

Fernández del Castillo, Francisco. *Apuntes para la historia de San Angel (San Jacinto Tenanitla) y sus alrededores*. México, 1913.

Fisher, John. *Commercial Relations Between Spain and Spanish America in the Era of Free Trade, 1778-1796*. Liverpool, 1985.

Fisher, Nora, ed. *Spanish Textile Tradition in New Mexico and Colorado*. Santa Fe, NM, 1979.

Florescano, Enrique. *Precios del maíz y crisis agrícolas en México (1708-1810)*. México, 1969.

––––––– et al. *La clase obrera en la historia de México de la colonia al imperio*. 2d ed. México, 1981.

Floud, Roderick, and Donald McCloskey, eds. *The Economic History of Britain Since 1760*. 2 vols. Cambridge, Eng., 1981.

Fortune, Stephen Alexander. *Merchants and Jews: The Struggle for British West Indian Commerce, 1650-1750*. Gainesville, 1984.

Freudenberger, Herman, and Fritz Redlich. "The Industrial Development of Europe: Reality, Symbols, Images," *Kyklos* 26 (1964): 372-403.

Friedman, Milton. *Price Theory*. Chicago, 1976.

García-Baquero González, Antonio. *Cádiz y el Atlántico (1717-1778)*. 2 vols. Seville, 1976.

García Fuentes, Lutgardo. *El comercio español con América, 1650-1700*. Seville, 1980.

Gerhard, Peter. *A Guide to the Historical Geography of New Spain*. Cambridge, Eng., 1971.

Gibson, Charles. *The Aztecs Under Spanish Rule. A History of the Indians of the Valley of Mexico, 1519-1810*. Stanford, 1964.

Greenleaf, Richard E. "The Obraje in the Late Mexican Colony," *The Americas* 3 (1967): 227-50.

––––––. "Viceregal Power and the Obrajes of the Cortés Estate, 1595-1708," *Hispanic American Historical Review* 48 (1968): 365-79.

Halperín-Donghi, Tulio. *Politics, Economics, and Society in Argentina in the Revolutionary Period*. Cambridge, Eng., 1975.

Hamnett, Brian. "The Economic and Social Dimensions of the Revolution of Independence in Mexico, 1800-1824," *Ibero-Amerikanisches Archiv*, new ser., 6 (1980): 1-27.

———. *Politics and Trade in Southern Mexico, 1750-1821*. Cambridge, Eng., 1971.

———. *Revolución y contrarevolución en México y el Perú. Liberalismo, realeza y separatismo (1800-1824)*. México, 1978.

Harris, Charles H., III. *A Mexican Family Empire. The Latifundio of the Sánchez Navarros, 1765-1867*. Austin, 1975.

Harte, N. B., and K. G. Ponting, eds. *Textile History and Economic History. Essays in Honor of Miss Julia de Lacey Mann*. Manchester, Eng., 1973.

Hassig, Ross. *Trade, Tribute, and Transportation. The Sixteenth-Century Political Economy of the Valley of Mexico*. Norman, OK, 1985.

Heaton, Herbert. *The Yorkshire Woolen and Worsted Industries*. 2d ed. Oxford, 1965.

Hicks, John. *A Theory of Economic History*. Oxford, 1969.

Hilton, George W. "The British Truck System in the Nineteenth Century," *Journal of Political Economy* 55 (1957): 237-56.

Hinojosa, Gilberto Miguel. *A Borderlands Town in Transition, Laredo, 1755-1870*. College Station, TX, 1983.

Hirschman, Albert O. "Rival Interpretations of Market Society: Civilizing, Destructive, or Feeble," *Journal of Economic Literature* 20 (1982): 1463-84.

Historia general de México. 4 vols. México, 1976.

Hunter, Louis C. *A History of Industrial Power in the United States*. Charlottesville, VA, 1979.

Hurtado López, Flor de María. *Dolores Hidalgo: Estudio económico, 1740-1790*. México, 1974.

Intriligator, Michael. *Econometric Models, Techniques, and Applications*. Englewood Cliffs, NJ, 1978.

Israel, Jonathan I. *The Dutch Republic and the Hispanic World, 1606-1661*. Oxford, 1982.

Jenkins, J. Geraint. *The Wool Textile Industry in Great Britain*. London, 1972.

Jevons, W. Stanley. *The Theory of Political Economy*. Edited by R. D. Collison Black. Middlesex, Eng., 1970.

Kamen, Henry. *Spain, 1469-1714. A Society of Conflict*. London, 1983.

———. *Spain in the Later Seventeenth Century*. London, 1980.

———. *The War of the Succession in Spain, 1700-15*. Bloomington, IN, 1969.

Kindleberger, Charles P. "Standards as Public, Collective, and Private Goods," *Kyklos* 36 (1983): 377-96.

———, and Peter H. Lindert. *International Economics*. 6th ed. Homewood, IL, 1978.

———, and Guido di Tella, eds. *Economics in the Long View*. 3 vols. London, 1982.

Konrad, Herman W. *A Jesuit Hacienda in Colonial Mexico. Santa Lucía, 1576-1767*. Stanford, 1980.

Kubler, George. *Mexican Architecture of the Sixteenth Century*. 2 vols. New Haven, 1948.

Ladd, Doris M. *The Mexican Nobility at Independence, 1780-1826*. Austin, 1976.

Landes, David S. *The Unbound Prometheus. Technological Change and Industrial Development in Western Europe from 1750 to the Present*. Cambridge, Eng., 1969.

Lebret, Iveline. *La vida en Otavalo en el siglo XVIII*. Otavalo, Ecuador, 1981.

Lechuga, Ruth D. *La indumentaria en el México indígena*. México, 1982.

Lerdo de Tejada, Miguel. *El comercio exterior de México*. México, 1853.

Liehr, Reinhard. *Ayuntamiento y oligarquía en Puebla, 1787-1810*. 2 vols. México, 1976.

Lindley, Richard B. *Haciendas and Economic Development. Guadalajara, Mexico, at Independence*. Austin, 1983.

Lohman Villena, Guillermo. *Los americanos en las órdenes nobiliarias (1529-1900)*. 2 vols. Madrid, 1947.

Lorenzo Sanz, Eufemio. *Comercio de España con América en la época de Felipe II*. 2 vols. Valladolid, 1979.

McAlister, Lyle N. *Spain and Portugal in the New World, 1492-1700*. Minneapolis, 1984.

McCusker, John J. *Money and Exchange in Europe and America, 1600-1775. A Handbook*. Chapel Hill, 1978.

MacLachlan, Colin. *Criminal Justice in Eighteenth-Century Mexico. A Study of the Tribunal of the Acordada*. Berkeley, 1974.

Marglin, Stephen. "What Do Bosses Do? The Origins and Function of Hierarchy in Capitalist Production," *The Review of Radical Political Economics* 6 (1974): 60-112.

Marshall, Alfred. *Principles of Economics*. 7th ed. London, 1916.

Martínez Pelayo, Severo. *La patria del criollo. Ensayo de interpretación de la realidad colonial guatemalteca*. 8th ed. San José, Costa Rica, 1981.

Martínez Shaw, Carlos. *Cataluña en la carrera de Indias*. Barcelona, 1981.

Mathias, Peter. *The First Industrial Nation. An Economic History of Britain, 1700-1914*. London, 1969.

―――. *Transformation of England. Essays in the Economic and Social History of England in the Eighteenth Century*. New York, 1979.

Maza, Francisco de la. *San Miguel Allende*. 2d ed. México, 1972.

Meier, Gerald M. *Emerging from Poverty. The Economics that Really Matters*. New York, 1984.

Middle American Research Institute. *Synoptic Studies of Mexican Culture*. New Orleans, 1957.

Miño Grijalva, Manuel. "Espacio económico e industria textil: los trabajadores de Nueva España, 1780-1810," *Historia Mexicana* 33 (1983): 524-52.

Moreno Toscano, Alejandra. *Geografía económica de México (siglo XVI)*. México, 1968.

Mörner, Magnus. *Perfil de la sociedad rural de Cuzco a fines de la colonia*. Lima, 1978.

Muriá, José María, ed. *Historia de Jalisco*. 4 vols. Guadalajara, 1983.

Murrugarren, Paulino Iradiel. *Evolución de la industria textil castellana en los siglos XIII-XVI*. Salamanca, 1974.

Nickel, Herbert. "Reclutamiento y peonaje de los gañanes indígenas de la época colonial en el altiplano de Puebla-Tlaxcala," *Ibero-Amerikanisches Archiv*, new ser., 5 (1979): 71-104.

Nunn, Charles F. *Foreign Immigrants in Early Bourbon Mexico, 1700-1760*. Cambridge, Eng., 1979.

Offner, Jerome. "On the Inapplicability of 'Oriental Despotism' and the 'Asiatic Mode of Production' to the Aztecs of Texcoco," *American Antiquity* 46 (1981): 43-59, and the subsequent "Comment" by Pedro Carrasco.

Ortiz de la Tabla, Javier. "El obraje colonial ecuatoriano. Aproximación a su estudio," *Revista de Indias* 37 (1977): 471-541.

Palmer, Colin. *Slaves of the White God. Blacks in Mexico, 1570-1650*. Cambridge, MA, 1976.

Palomo, José Jesús Hernández. *La renta del pulque en la Nueva España, 1663-1810*. Seville, 1979.

Parry, John H. *The Spanish Seaborne Empire*. New York, 1966.

Pendleton Woolen Mills. *The Wool Story*. 5th ed. Pendleton, OR, 1980.

Pérez-Rocha, Emma. *La tierra y el hombre en la villa de Tacuba durante la época colonial*. México, 1982.

Platt, D.C.M. *Latin America and British Trade, 1806-1914*. New York, 1972.

Pohl, Hans, Jutta Haenich, and Wolfgang Loske. "Aspectos sociales del desarrollo de los obrajes textiles en Puebla colonial," *Comunicaciones. Proyecto Puebla-Tlaxcala* 15 (1978): 41-45.

Polanyi, Karl. *The Great Transformation. The Political and Economic Origins of Our Time*. Boston, 1957.

Posner, Richard A. *The Economics of Justice*. Cambridge, MA, 1981.

Potash, Robert A. *Mexican Government and Industrial Development in the Early Republic: The Banco de Avío*. Amherst, MA, 1983.

Quintana, Miguel A. "Papel histórico de Puebla en el proceso industrial de la Nueva España y de México," *Revista de la Universidad de Puebla* 1 (1944): 35-61.

Ramsay, G. D. *The English Woollen Industry, 1500-1750*. London, 1982.

Richards, J. F., ed. *Precious Metals in the Later Medieval and Early Modern World*. Durham, NC, 1983.

Riley, G. Michael. *Fernando Cortés and the Marquesado in Morelos, 1522-1547. A Case Study in the Socioeconomic Development of Sixteenth-Century Mexico*. Albuquerque, 1973.

Rodríguez Vallejo, José. *Ixcatl, el algodón mexicano*. México, 1976.

Rosenzweig Hernández, Fernando. "La economía Nova-Hispana al comenzar el siglo XIX" *Ciencias políticas y sociales* 9 (1965): 455-93.

Rudolph, Richard L. "Agricultural Structure and Proto-Industrialization in Russia: Economic Development with Unfree Labor," *Journal of Economic History* 45 (1985): 47-70.

Salas de Coloma, Miriam. *De los obrajes de Canaria y Chincheros a las comunidades indígenas de Vilcashuaman. Siglos XVI.* Lima, 1979.

Salvucci, Richard J. "Aspectos de un conflicto empresarial: El obraje de Balthasar de Sauto y la historia social de San Miguel el Grande, 1756-1771," *Anuario de Estudios Americanos* 36 (1979): 405-43.

Sánchez Flores, Ramón. *Historia de la tecnología y la invención en México.* México, 1980.

Sánchez de Tagle, Esteban. *Por un regimento, el régimen.* México, 1982.

Sandoval Zaraus, Roberto. "Artesanos y capital comercial en Nueva España: el callejón sin salida del capitalismo embrionario," *Investigación Económica* 162 (1982): 101-28.

———. "Los obrajes de Querétaro y sus trabajadores (1790-1820)," *Anuario II* [Centro de Estudios Históricos. Universidad Veracruzana] (1980): 126-47.

Schaedel, Richard P., Jorge E. Hardoy, and Nora Scott Kinser, eds. *Urbanization in Latin America from its Beginnings to the Present.* The Hague, 1978.

Schumpeter, Elizabeth Boody. *English Overseas Trade Statistics, 1697-1808.* Oxford, 1960.

Scranton, Philip. *Proprietary Capitalism. The Textile Manufacture of Philadelphia, 1800-1885.* New York, 1983.

Sempat Assadourian, Carlos. *El sistema de la economía colonial. Mercado interno. Regiones y espacios económicos.* Lima, 1982.

Septién y Septién, Manuel. *Historia de Querétaro desde los tiempos prehistóricos hasta el año de 1800.* Querétaro, 1967.

Serrera, Ramón María. "La ciudad de Santiago de Querétaro a finales del siglo XVIII: Apuntes para su historia," *Anuario de Estudios Americanos* 30 (1973): 489-555.

———. *Guadalajara ganadera: estudio regional novohispano, 1760-1805.* Seville, 1977.

Sierra, Carlos J., and Rogelio Martínez Vera. *Historia y legislación aduanera de México.* México, 1973.

Sims, Harold. *Descolonización en México. El conflicto entre mexicanos y españoles (1821-31).* México, 1982.

———. *La expulsión de los españoles de México (1821-28).* México, 1974.

Smith, Adam. *The Wealth of Nations.* Cannan ed.

Soberanes Fernández, José Luis, coord. *Memoria del II Congreso de Historia del Derecho Mexicano.* México, 1981.

Soustelle, Jacques. *Daily Life of the Aztecs on the Eve of the Spanish Conquest.* Stanford, 1961.

Spalding, Karen, ed. *Essays in the Political, Economic, and Social History of Colonial Latin America*. Newark, DE, 1982.

Spores, Ronald. *The Mixtecs in Ancient and Colonial Times*. Norman, OK, 1984.

Stern, Steve. *Peru's Indian Peoples and the Challenge of Spanish Conquest. Huamanga to 1640*. Madison, 1982.

Stigler, George J., and Kenneth E. Boulding, eds. *Readings in Price Theory*. Chicago, 1952.

Super, John C. "Querétaro Obrajes: Industry and Society in Provincial Mexico, 1600-1810," *Hispanic American Historical Review* 56 (1976): 197-216.

———. *La vida en Querétaro durante la colonia, 1531-1810*. México, 1983.

Swann, Michael. *Tierra Adentro. Settlement and Society in Colonial Durango*. Boulder, 1982.

Temin, Peter. *Causal Factors in American Economic Growth in the Nineteenth Century*. London, 1975.

Tenorio, Blanca Lara. *Algunas mercancías que llegaron de España a Puebla en 1549*. México, 1978.

Toussaint, Manuel. *Arte colonial en México*. 4th ed. México, 1983.

Usher, Abbott Payson. *The Industrial History of England*. Boston and New York, 1920.

Vanderwood, Paul. *Disorder and Progress. Bandits, Police, and Mexican Development*. Lincoln, NE, 1981.

Van Young, Eric. *Hacienda and Market in Eighteenth-Century Mexico: The Rural Economy of the Guadalajara Region, 1675-1820*. Berkeley, 1981.

Vázquez de Prada, V. *Historia económica y social de España*. 3 vols. Madrid, 1978– .

Vicens Vives, Jaime, ed. *Historia de España y América social y económica*. 5 vols., 2d ed. Barcelona, 1971.

Viqueira Landa, Carmen. "Los orígenes de la industria textil en México," *Ingeniería* [Universidad Nacional Autónoma de México], new ser., 53 (1983): 91-105.

West, Robert C., and John P. Augelli. *Middle America: Its Lands and Peoples*. 2d ed. Englewood Cliffs, NJ, 1976.

Whitecotton, Joseph W. *The Zapotecs. Princes, Priests, and Peasants*. Norman, OK, 1977.

Wilson, Kax. *A History of Textiles*. Boulder, CO, 1982.

Wolfskill, George, and Stanley Palmer, eds. *Essays on Frontiers in World History*. Austin, 1981.

Yates, P. Lamartine. *Mexico's Agricultural Dilemma*. Tucson, AZ, 1981.

UNPUBLISHED PAPERS, MASTERS' THESES,
AND DOCTORAL DISSERTATIONS

Acuña-Ortega, Victor H. "Le commerce extérieur du Royaume de Guatemala au XVIII siècle, 1700-1821: Une étude structurelle." Thèse du doctorat, Université de Paris-Sorbonne, 1978.

Borah, Woodrow. "Inflation in Nueva Galicia, 1557-1598: Auctions of Tribute Maize." Unpub. ms., 1985.

Brazil, Blas. "A History of the Obrajes of New Spain, 1535-1630." M.A. thesis, Univ. of New Mexico, 1962.

Hunt, Shane. "The Economics of Haciendas and Plantations in Latin America." Unpub. ms., 1972.

Kagan, Samuel. "Penal Servitude in New Spain: The Colonial Textile Industry." Ph.D. diss., City University of New York, 1977.

Lampros, Peter James. "Merchant–Planter Cooperation and Conflict: The Havana Consulado, 1794-1832." Ph.D. diss., Tulane Univ., 1980.

Pratt, Francis Edward. "The Obraje in New Spain: A Case Study in the Failure of Royal Authority to Impose its Will." M.A. thesis, Univ. of the Americas, 1965.

Rabell Romero, Cecilia Andrea. "Los diezmos de San Luis de la Paz. Economía de una región del Bajío en el siglo XVIII." Unpub. ms., 1984.

Romero Frizzi, María de los Ángeles. "La industria textil novohispana." Thesis, Escuela Nacional de Antropología e Historia [México, DF], 1972.

Salvucci, Richard J. "Enterprise and Economic Development in Eighteenth-Century Mexico: The Case of the Obrajes." Ph.D. diss., Princeton University, 1982.

———. "United States Trade with Mexico, 1825-1880." Unpub. ms., 1986.

Scardaville, Michael. "Crime and the Urban Poor: Mexico City in the Late Colonial Period." Ph.D. diss., Univ. of Florida, 1977.

Taylor, James William. "Socio-economic instability and the Revolution for Mexican Independence in the Province of Guanajuato." Ph.D. diss., Univ. of New Mexico, 1976.

Thomson, G.P.C. "The Cotton Textile Industry in Puebla During the 18th and 19th Centuries." Unpub. paper, 1982.

———. "Economy and Society in Puebla de los Angeles, 1800-50." Ph.D. diss., Oxford Univ., 1978.

Tyrer, Robson Brines. "The Demographic and Economic History of the Audiencia of Quito: Indian Population and the Textile Industry, 1600-1800." Ph.D. diss., Univ. of California, Berkeley, 1976.

Valdés, Dennis Nodín. "The Decline of the *Sociedad de Castas* in Mexico City." Ph.D. diss., Univ. of Michigan, 1978.

INDEX

Super, John, 101
Szewczyk, David, 103, 110

Tacuba, 50, 55, 65, 66, 67, 69, 102, 137, 138
Talamantes, Melchor de, 158
tariff: effect of, 167-68; history after 1821, 163-64; Mexican versus American experience, 166; Mexican versus Peruvian experience, 172-73
technology. *See* obraje
telar suelto, 44-45, 159; debt in, 12, 14, 15, 17; definition of, 10, 11, 12; location, 12-14; *maps*, 22-23; productivity of, 14, 15, 42
Temascaltepec, 20-21
Texcoco, 25, 27, 55, 58, 138, 144, 149
Thomson, G.P.C., 29, 30
tienda de raya. *See* obraje
Tlaxcala, 13, 14, 21, 27, 55, 103-105 *passim*, 109-10, 121, 136, 149
transhumance. *See* wool (raw material)
trapiche, 15-18; definition, 11, 16; expansion in late colonial Querétaro, 141-42; miscellaneous statistics, 16, 17
Treaty of Paris, 155
Trinidad, 154

Unzaga family, 47, 87

Valdés, Dennis, 111
Valero, Marqués de, 97
Valiño, Joaquín, 90
Valladolid, 20, 25, 131
Van Young, Eric, 71
Varela, Bernarda, 71

Velasco the younger, Luis de, 10, 108, 112, 131
Velasco, Matías de, 60
Vértiz, Josefa de, 78
Vértiz, Juan Miguel de, 78, 79
Vértiz, María Teresa de, 78
Vértiz y Oteyza, Pedro, 78, 79
Vértiz y Vértiz, Pedro de, 78, 79
Victoria, Guadalupe, 164
Villamanrique, Marqués de, 109, 131
Villanueva y Oribay, Santiago, 105
Villaseñor y Sánchez, Antonio de, 10

War of American Independence, 152
War of the Austrian Succession, 152
War of the Spanish Succession, 153
Ward, Bernardo, 9
Ward, H. G., 135, 171
water: and production in obrajes, 53-54, 56
Wealth of Nations. See Adam Smith
weaving, 12, 41, 47, 99-100, 115, 125. *See also* carding; dyeing; spinning
wool (raw material), 28, 39-40, 45-47, 48, 56-57; consumption, 47, 136, 140-41, 160; fluctuations in supply, 53; measurement, 177; sorting, 48-49
wool (textile): measurement, 177; new draperies, 50; manufacturing process, 47-54; seasonality in supply, 54, 114, 118-19; use and distribution, 57-61. *See also* bays; friezes; palmilla; says; serges

Yáñez, María Rosa, 84

Zacatecas, 14, 26, 76, 96, 163

LIBRARY OF CONGRESS CATALOGING-IN-PUBLICATION DATA

Salvucci, Richard J., 1951-
Textiles and capitalism in Mexico.

Bibliography: p.   Includes index.
1. Textile industry—Mexico—History. 2. Weavers—
Mexico—History. I. Title. II. Title: Obrajes.
HD9864.M62S25 1987   338.4′767702824′0972   87-45535
ISBN 0-691-07749-5 (alk. paper)